MARSILIO FICINO AND
THE PHAEDRAN CHARIOTEER

Published under the auspices of the

CENTER FOR MEDIEVAL AND RENAISSANCE STUDIES

University of California, Los Angeles

Publications of the

CENTER FOR MEDIEVAL AND RENAISSANCE STUDIES, UCLA

Introduction, Texts, Translations

By MICHAEL J. B. ALLEN

Marsilio Ficino and
the Phaedran Charioteer

UNIVERSITY OF CALIFORNIA PRESS
BERKELEY   LOS ANGELES   LONDON

University of California Press
Berkeley and Los Angeles, California

University of California Press, Ltd.
London, England

Copyright © 1981 by The Regents of the University of California

Library of Congress Cataloging in Publication Data
Ficino, Marsilio, 1433-1499.
  Marsilio Ficino and the Phaedran charioteer

  English and Latin.
  Bibliography: p. 257.
  Includes index.
  1. Plato. Phaedrus. 2. Love. 3. Rhetoric,
Ancient. I. Allen, Michael J. B. II. Title.
B380.F52 1981   184   80-20439
ISBN 0-520-04222-0

Printed in the United States of America

1 2 3 4 5 6 7 8 9

To
My Parents and the Three Whiskies

Contents

Acknowledgments

Again I am deeply indebted to the immense, magnanimous scholarship and the personal kindness of Professor Paul Oskar Kristeller, and also to Professor Fredi Chiappelli, director of the Center for Medieval and Renaissance Studies at the University of California, Los Angeles, for his quick eye, his friendship, and his continual support. I would like to thank too Dr. Carol Lanham, Professor Charles Trinkaus, Ms. Susan Wing, and two anonymous University of California Press readers for a number of helpful comments, as well as the British, Laurentian, Vatican, Huntington, and Ghent's Rijksuniversiteit libraries for permission to use their manuscripts and incunabula.

The project was begun in the Suburra during a sabbatical partially funded by the generosity of UCLA's Academic Senate, but was substantially completed during a year's leave of absence made possible by the gift of a fellowship from the John Simon Guggenheim Memorial Foundation. This year began with Benjamin's arrival, but eventually took the four of us to Cangrande, to Gattamelata, to the great haunched horse in Mantua, and to a farmhouse with persimmons on a ridge across from Barga, hornet haunted and within sound of Pascoli's persuading bell, the source of some romantic memories and probably of my worst errors.

Sigla

E   = *Commentaria in Platonem,* Florence, 1496

P   = University of Prague, Lobkowitz Collection from Roudnice, MS RVI Ef11, probably circa 1493

G   = Rijksuniversiteit Library, Ghent, MS 354, between 1484 and 1490

H   = British Library, London, MS Harleian 3481, circa 1491

L   = Laurentian Library, Florence, MS Laur. 82. 6, a little before 1484?

F   = *Platonis Opera Omnia,* Florence, 1484?

V   = *Platonis Opera Omnia,* Venice, 1491

Introduction

τὸν μὲν ἀγάλλων θεὸς
ἔδωκεν δίφρον τε χρύσεον πτεροῖ-
σίν τ᾽ ἀκάμαντας ἵππους.

> The god honored Pelops and gave
> him a golden chariot and wing-swift,
> untiring steeds.
>
> Pindar, *Olympian* I. 86-87

Socrates's mythical hymn in the *Phaedrus* 243E-257A, with its charioteer struggling to master his stallions in flight with the gods, is, along with the flickering cave of the *Republic* and the *Phaedo*'s hemlock death, one of Plato's most dazzling and memorable pieces. It is also the most self-consciously poetic in terms of its diction, gorgeous rhythms and figures, dramatic juxtapositions, elaborate allegory, and symphonic structure.[1] Socrates himself emerges, though through veils of irony, not as the gadfly at the cabbage ears of Athenian youth or the lips of their favorite Sophists, the choplogician with his tradesman's analogies archly analyzing terms, but as the ecstatic seer, the poet-prophet, singing to Corybantian measures of man's agonistic ascent to heaven, of the fall, of true knowledge, of immortality; singing, moreover, in an unfamiliar setting, aureoled by cicadas beside a river at noon, in a grove hallowed by the local deities, and 400 yards upstream from an altar dedicated to the rape of Oreithyia by the North Wind; his companion, the radiant Phaedrus, the initiator of the night's debate in the *Symposium* and the champion there of Love's divinity.

This mythical hymn—which Socrates so describes at 265BC—is beguilingly distanced and qualified, however, by various literary devices. Inaugurated by the analysis of two syllogisms and ended by a prayer, it offsets two previous speeches, one by

Lysias and another by Socrates, and is itself presented as a palinode to the god of Love. It is also orbited by satellite myths and invocations—themselves calling for sensitive interpretation—which underscore its mythic nature and simultaneously reinforce its concern with the kinds and degrees of divine inspiration, *mania,* madness. Though formally bracketed in this way, the hymn nevertheless exercises dominion over the rest of the material and serves, in the opinion of both ancient and modern commentators, as the dialogue's prismatic centerpiece.

I have spoken of the hymn rather than of the dialogue as a whole, since it was this that also fascinated Marsilio Ficino, the fifteenth-century Florentine whose work was patronized by three generations of the Medici and who was one of the most interesting and exotic luminaries of the European Renaissance. Translator from the Greek and commentator; Christian apologist, theologian, teacher, exegete, priest; musical theorist and notable performer; mythologist, metaphysician, lapsed astrologer; belletrist, ethician, versifier, dialectician; medical theorist and practitioner and love theorist; psychiatrist, Thomist, demonologist; Hermetist, Orphic, Augustinian, Dantean, dietician; historian of poetry, religion, philosophy, and pleasure; quietist, mystic, mage, humanist, wit; devout son and timid sycophant; above all, Neoplatonist, Ficino was a highly derivative and original, conservative and bizarre, succinctly repetitive scholar-thinker, as difficult for us to assess in detail now as in entirety. Despite the research of several scholars this century, and preeminently that of Paul Oskar Kristeller,[2] much remains to be discovered and understood about him, for his enormous influence, contemporary and posthumous, has been better charted than many of his guiding conceptions and motifs, including that of the Phaedran chariot and its charioteer.

A symbol of the sun's disk for many of the ancient Semitic and Indo-European peoples, in the West the chariot has long been associated with the world of Homer, where it bears Achaian and Trojan princes alike to victory and defeat on the windy plains.[3] It was, of course, the ultimate war machine of antiquity as well as an image of royalty, the embodiment of

superhuman speed, awesome and ineluctable. In his career the charioteer united the strength and beauty of the stallion with the intelligence and courage of man and thereby became a being who transcended the limitations of both the human body and the brute mind. Within but not enslaved to the chariot—like his parodic counterpart, the lust-driven centaur—he was man at the height of terrible triumph, self-determining and free.[4] Sung by Pindar and later carved in the Arch of Titus, he thundered forward in an intensification of life towards a mastery of death; and he was the hero, in both ancient and Renaissance depictions and allegorizations of the triumph theme, who returned, bringing peace into his city with the spoils of conquest.[5] He was active man, that is, in his paradoxical struggle to achieve serenity through violence.

Just as the *Bhagavad Gita* has Arjuna turn to the charioteer, the god Krishna, on the very threshold of battle, however, to ascend the spiraling contradictions of being and nonbeing, so too many texts in the pre-Christian and the Christian West also recognized the value of the charioteer as a symbol of mystical ascent. Ficino knew the fragmentary *Poema* of Plato's most distinguished predecessor, Parmenides, the Eleatic monist, where the poet describes a visionary chariot ride up through the gates of Night and Day, accompanied by the daughters of the Sun, to be welcomed by an unnamed goddess whose instruction fails to inspire the rest of the plodding hexameters.[6] He was even more familiar, though, with the fiery chariot in the second book of Kings which caught Elijah (Elias) up to heaven in a whirlwind;[7] with the apocalyptic four-wheeled "chariot" of the cherubim which Ezekiel witnessed in a vision by the river of Chebar in the land of the Chaldees;[8] and with the four horses, the white one bearing a rider later called Faithful and True, which John sees at the opening of the seven seals in Revelation.[9] In addition, and perhaps with Dante's description of the triumph of Beatrice also in mind, he was drawn to the enigmatic verses in 2 Corinthians where Paul speaks of being caught up to the third heaven, to paradise, for he interpreted it as taking place in the chariot of "upright faith, and steadfast hope, and

burning charity."[10] Though none of these classical or biblical
chariots or charioteers is winged per se, they all translate the
horizontal warrior's onslaught into a vertical flight: endowed
with the power of wings, they might well have been endowed
with actual wings, the archetypal symbols of transcendence. As
precedents here Ficino could recall the god-given horses of
Pelops; Pegasus, the symbol, for the Romans, of immortality
itself; and Ezekiel's four-faced cherubim with the likeness of
the hands of a man under their wings.

While these several associations, along with others undoubtedly derived from contemporary carnivals and *trionfi,* all had
something to contribute, it was nevertheless the *Phaedrus'*s palinode that supplied Ficino, as it had supplied the ancient Neoplatonists commencing with Plotinus and Iamblichus,[11] with the
paradigmatic symbol of the soul's struggle to ascend as a uni-
fied being to the vision of immutable reality. And not only the
human soul: indebted perhaps to Orpheus and the Pythagoreans, Plato had ventured further than Homer or Parmenides
and depicted the souls of the gods themselves as charioteers too,
gazing upwards at the supracelestial place of the Ideas beyond
the bounds of their intellectual heaven. He had transformed the
Homeric charioteer into a symbol not only of the human soul in
divine ecstasy, but of Jove as the world-soul, the progenitor of
motion and of life, leading the cosmic cavalcade of all the souls
and gods back to their metaphysical source. The old symbol of
war and triumph, even of spiritual triumph, had thus become a
theological type prefiguring, for Ficino, the ascension of men
and angels under Christ as the first, last, and sovereign charioteer at the head of the hosts of the saved returning to God.

Also associated with the image of the charioteer, though less
obviously, were Plato's intriguing references in the *Phaedrus* to
a mysterious but supremely important entity, the soul's "aethereal vehicle," the spiritual body or envelope that had been the
concern of much ancient theosophical and theurgical speculation but was also the object of considerable fascination for
Ficino and his Renaissance contemporaries, philosophers,
mages, and astrologers alike.[12]

In short, the *Phaedrus* was fundamentally about the mysteries at the heart of theogony, incarnation, soteriology, eschatology, and purification, as Iamblichus had long ago insisted by defining its genre as theological, not logical, physical, or ethical.[13] Indeed, for the Florentine, as for the Neoplatonists, the *Phaedrus* seemed to be one of Plato's most explicit works of theology (second only to the *Parmenides* and, possibly, the *Timaeus*), and its charioteer, therefore, one of his premier myths for truly liberated man, man as a peer of the angelic orders, of the gods themselves.

I

With the major exceptions of the *Meno* and *Phaedo,* and parts of the *Parmenides* and *Timaeus,* Plato's dialogues were completely lost to the West during the Middle Ages[14]—the Byzantine East is a different matter—though Platonism continued to flourish under various guises, and particularly Augustinianism. Not until Ficino himself translated it did the entire canon become accessible again after the passing of a millennium and Plato move into his European own. The *Phaedrus,* however, was one of several dialogues that had already captured the notice of humanists. A year after Aurispa and Traversari had brought over a complete Plato manuscript from Byzantium in 1423, Leonardo Bruni finished a partial Latin translation of the *Phaedrus* (up to 257C), the only attempt to precede Ficino's.[15] Occasionally, the dialogue figured in Plethon's reconstruction of ancient pagan theology and in the uproar that swirled around him as a consequence even after his death in 1458.[16] By that year it was also at the storm center of bitter debate between other Byzantine Plato enthusiasts (and their Italian admirers) and a Cretan Aristotelian lecturing in Italy, the great polemicist and anti-Plethonian, George of Trebizond, who charged it with advocating the "Socratic vice" of pederasty.[17] In 1459, not long before Ficino enbarked on his own Plato translations, Cardinal Bessarion, George's distinguished antagonist, defended the dia-

logue on the grounds that it portrayed love as a cathartic, not as a sexual, force and should be interpreted in the light of Diotima's ladder in the *Symposium*. Controversy smouldered during the 1460s until, after a final flare with the publication of Bessarion's magnum opus in 1469, it died away with the deaths of both George and the cardinal in 1472.[18] Thus, unlike most of the other dialogues, the *Phaedrus* had made an impact before Ficino began to translate and elucidate its secrets. After him it became one of the age's most treasured texts, whether read in the Greek, in Ficino's Latin—which quickly superseded Bruni's —or in Felice Figliucci's sixteenth-century Italian translation of Ficino's Latin.[19]

Apart from the manifest appeal and difficulty of the work and his contemporaries' ambivalent attraction to it, three external reasons must have influenced Ficino's decision to single it out, with a handful of other dialogues, for extended analysis and commentary—the first since antiquity. First would be his understanding of the status of the *Phaedrus* in the eyes of the ancient Neoplatonists. Attacked on various grounds by critics prior to Plotinus, the *Phaedrus* was radically upgraded by those who followed him. Plotinus himself was partially responsible for this turnabout, for he frequently lauds the *Phaedrus*'s myth along with sundry of its arguments and at one point argues that the "heaven" of 246E must be deemed, not the celestial heaven, but intelligible reality.[20] According to Bielmeier and, more recently, Dillon and Larsen, however, the real revolution came with Iamblichus. He not only promulgated what came to be, at least for a while, definitive answers to the complicated questions of the dialogue's genre, principal theme (*skopos*), and structure, but also insisted, apparently for the first time, on interpreting the Phaedran Zeus, not as a cosmic deity, as the celestial world-soul, but as the supramundane, supracelestial demiurgic leader from the intelligible realm.[21] While Plotinus had argued for the intelligibility of the heaven at 246E, he had accepted Zeus as the world-soul;[22] and Ficino thought this the preferable interpretation, as he says in chapter 11. Nevertheless, it was Iamblichus's supramundanist, uncompromisingly the-

ological interpretation that prevailed in late antiquity, and was, in essence, the one expounded and elaborated by Syrianus and his two pupils, Hermias and the brilliant Proclus—at least insofar as we can ascertain from Hermias's *Phaedrus* commentary, our primary source of evidence on this matter and the only extant *Phaedrus* commentary of the several we have references to.[23] Even if he rejected Iamblichus's views on the *Phaedrus,* Ficino was certainly aware of them, having drafted a Latin translation of Hermias's entire commentary.[24] This mediated knowledge of Iamblichus together with long years of working firsthand with Plotinus's extensive but often rather elusive and enigmatic references to the *Phaedrus* would be quite sufficient to furnish him with a good understanding of the ancient significance of the dialogue. Additionally, from as early as the 1460s he seems to have known Proclus's long masterpiece, the *Platonic Theology,* for we have his autograph notes and glosses in a manuscript containing the full extant Greek text of this and two other Proclan works, the *Elements of Theology* and the *Elements of Physics.* H. D. Saffrey has discovered that these notes seem to have been jotted down at various times during Ficino's career, though most of them probably date from the 1490s.[25] They cover all six books of the *Platonic Theology,* and therefore books 1 and 4, where Proclus had most to say on the *Phaedrus* and particularly on its various categories of gods, their ascent, and their gazing upward at "the supracelestial place." Though Ficino disagreed with many points in Proclus's reading, still, the area of Proclus's explicit concentration, his conviction of the work's theological importance, and his emphasis throughout on the inspired nature of Socrates's vision, must have all reinforced Ficino's own sense of the dialogue's structure and meaning and alerted him to the kinds of problems it posed. Indeed, of the three ancient *Phaedrus* interpreters Ficino had access to, I suspect that it was Proclus who most influenced his general approach to the mythical hymn, even though he barely mentioned him and though he rejected his supramundanist interpretation of Zeus, preferring Plotinus as his guide.[26]

The second reason for Ficino's interest in the *Phaedrus* would

be its appearance as the fourth member of the third tetralogy in Thrasyllus's arrangement of the dialogues as reported by Diogenes Laertius (to whom we often give little credence, but whom Ficino constantly used as an authority).[27] The other members of this tetralogy are the *Parmenides,* the *Philebus,* and the *Symposium.* Each we now assign to Plato's middle or late middle periods, when he was at the height of his powers, but the ancient Neoplatonists also acknowledged these works as the cornerstones of Plato's philosophy, even though they differed among themselves on the correct chronology. For Ficino the members of the tetralogy had as their themes the One, the Good, Love, and Beauty, respectively; that is, Ideas that transcended other Ideas in Plato's general theory and had thus become meta-Ideas, the ultimate abstract realities. Though Ficino subsequently paired off the members, the *Symposium* and the *Phaedrus* constituting the subordinate pair,[28] the four taken together formed a very special group—as the numerologically significant position of being the third tetralogy in a series of nine would also seem to testify. Ficino managed to write three long commentaries on the tetralogy's first three members, though one he never finished,[29] and clearly he intended an equivalent for the *Phaedrus,* in part, I surmise, to do justice to the Thrasyllean arrangement and its putative logic.

The third reason would be the outcome of one of those scholarly errors that very occasionally, as in the case of the Areopagite, give rise to speculation with its own enduring worth and fascination. Now usually placed between the *Republic* and the *Symposium* on the one hand and the *Theaetetus* and the *Parmenides* on the other,[30] the *Phaedrus,* so both Bruni and Ficino believed, was composed in Plato's youth along with the *Meno* and the *Phaedo.*[31] Indeed, but for the epigrams, elegies, and incinerated tragedies, it was the very first of Plato's writings and the product therefore of *poetic* inspiration (Plato's inspiration being, by Diogenes's influential account, initially poetic).[32] The original introduction Ficino wrote for his Latin translation of the *Phaedrus,* an introduction that afterwards also did duty as the opening three chapters of the *Phaedrus* commentary,

orients us as follows: "Our Plato was pregnant with the madness of the poetic Muse, whom he followed from a tender age or rather from his Apollonian generation. In his radiance, Plato gave birth to his first child, and it was itself almost entirely poetical and radiant." The themes of youth, beauty, love, and poetry are, as they are for the company in the *Symposium,* intertwined for Ficino, and they seem to be those he initially selected for mention, before the theological aspects came to dominate his attention. Their presence in the dialogue surely reinforced his conviction of its youthfulness.

This conviction was not uniquely his and Bruni's. Both were adhering to ancient doxographical tradition as transmitted by Diogenes Laertius, Olympiodorus, and others,[33] and which in turn they helped to transmit through to the first half of the nineteenth century. The *Phaedrus,* Diogenes claimed on anonymously reported testimony, had a youthful theme (*echein meirakiōdes ti to problēma*);[34] but the nature of this theme had always been a matter of debate, and particularly after Iamblichus had declared, on the basis of the *Phaedrus's* own argument at 264C that a speech should be put together organically, that "everything in the dialogue [indeed in any dialogue] must relate to some one end, that the dialogue may be, so to speak, one living being."[35] While Thrasyllus had simply assigned a dominant theme to each dialogue, the *Symposium* being on the Good, the *Phaedrus* on Love, and so forth, the post-Iamblichean Neoplatonists insisted that each dialogue had a unique, all-embracing theme, called the skopos, which other subordinate themes had as their end and goal and to which absolutely everything else, however minor or incidental, was tied.[36] Thus the *Parmenides* was on the One, the *Philebus* on the Highest Good, the *Symposium* on Love, the *Lysis* on Friendship. Since this was too rigid a schema for the multifariousness of what Plato had actually written, disagreement continued, even among orthodox Neoplatonists, over the skopoi of many dialogues: Was the *Philebus* on pleasure, the good for man, the highest good, and so on?[37] Still, to look for the skopos was to look for a dialogue's inner unity and, at the same time, for its special contribution to

the edifice of Platonic doctrine, its role in the greater whole of the canon. To rest content with the variegated play of ideas and their dramatic juxtapositions, with the experimental, experiential, paradoxical testing of theories and definitions, would have seemed to them, as to Ficino, rather the overingenious appreciation of a dramatist than the genuine understanding of a philosopher and theologian. The *Phaedrus,* though, presented peculiar problems.

Hermias spends a number of his opening pages reviewing—twice, in fact—the various skopological possibilities that had already been proposed—love, rhetoric, the soul, the good, prime beauty, each of these but none with absolute primacy.[38] Eventually he justifies Iamblichus's view that the skopos was beauty in all its forms (*peri tou pantodapou kalou*) on the grounds that it includes the other possibilities: we pass from the physical beauty inspiring love to the beauty of rhetoric, to the beauty of soul, to the beauty of the cosmic gods, to the beauty of intellect, to the Beautiful itself. Subsequently, in a corresponding descent, we pass, via the art of division (*diairesis*), to the beauty of soul, to the beauty of rhetoric, to the physical beauty inspiring love, and thus arrive at our point of departure.[39] Consideration of the skopos therefore provided an insight into the structure of the *Phaedrus* and reinforced Iamblichus's view of its genre as theological; for Plato's concern with other kinds of beauty was clearly subordinated here to that of the beauty of the soul, of the gods, and of the Beautiful itself.

While evincing some hesitation and without committing himself to the structural extension of Hermias's argument, Ficino accepted this "beauty in all its forms" as the dialogue's theme. Simultaneously, when penning the introduction if not later, he felt the *Phaedrus* naturally complemented the *Symposium.* Not only did Phaedrus figure prominently in both dialogues, but both treated the same inspirational themes, with the possible exception of rhetoric, and in both the ascent motif predominated. We must reverse our sense of the mutual relationship, however: for Ficino, Phaedrus's conversation with Socrates by the murmuring Ilissus preceded his passionate defense

of Love's antiquity at Agathon's celebration banquet; that is, Plato's consideration of love grew naturally out of a consideration of beauty. This is logical when we recall that beauty is traditionally both the most accessible of divine attributes and the mark of youth. By being beautiful, youth inspires in others the desire for beauty, which is love. In reciprocating love, youth then takes its first step on the road to wisdom, which is inner beauty (*Phaedrus* 279B).[40]

Phaedrus, to whom Plato had addressed a lovesick epigram,[41] whom Socrates and Lysias had also loved, and whose very name means youthful and radiant and inspiring love,[42] is therefore Plato's archetypal youth at the foot of the Diotiman ladder of ascent to ideal Beauty, waiting to become the godlike charioteer. By the same token he is the archetypal pupil inspiring the teacher to his heuristic task. Hence, Ficino observes, though devoted to beauty in all its forms, the dialogue is especially concerned with beauty as we perceive it via our three cognitive powers: intelligence, sight, and hearing.[43] Appropriately, therefore, the theme of Plato's first dialogue is beauty, since it is the trigger theme for all others. Appropriate, too, is the personal dimension, since Phaedrus had inspired both Socrates and Plato to their subsequent work: from him, his beauty, and his dialogue had come their desire to teach the mysteries. This unexpected angle was dramatically reinforced by Ficino's decision to entrust Phaedrus's *Symposium* speech to the aristocratic Cavalcanti, his own Platonic friend, the etymology of whose name, I believe, signified for Ficino in this context a mastery of the unruly Phaedran steeds.[44]

Whereas Diogenes Laertius referred in the first instance to the youthfulness of the *Phaedrus's* theme, others, such as Dicaearchus, had censured its youthful style, characterizing it as "turgid" and "overwrought" (*phortikos*), or, more positively, with Olympiodorus, as "dithyrambic"[45] (following Socrates himself at 238D!). According to Hermias, these stylistic strictures were widespread in antiquity, though he himself defended Plato on the grounds that he had utilized a variety of styles in the *Phaedrus* in order to deal with its variety of subject

matter.[46] While Ficino accepted the style as further proof of the dialogue's youthfulness, he was struck by its "radiance" and "loveliness", by its being demon endowed even with a "poetic" vision,[47] a vision that, as he forcefully points out on a number of occasions, reveals itself in virtually all the dialogues but is absolutely primary here. In the proem accompanying the 1484 edition, Ficino draws Lorenzo's attention to Plato's amphibian style:

Plato's style does not so much resemble human speech as a divine oracle, often thundering from on high, often dripping with the sweetness of nectar, but always comprehending heavenly secrets.... The Platonic style, in containing all things, has three principal gifts in abundance: the philosophic usefulness of its opinions, the oratorical order of its arrangement and expression, and the ornament of its poetical flowers.[48]

Again, in a letter of 1476-1477 to the humanist Bartolomeo della Fonte, Ficino writes:

If you hear the celestial Plato you immediately recognize that his style, as Aristotle says, flows midway between prose and poetry. You recognize that Plato's language, as Quintilian says, rises far above the pedestrian and prosaic, so that our Plato seems inspired not by human genius but by a Delphic oracle. Indeed the mixing or tempering of prose and poetry in Plato so delighted Cicero that he declared: "If Jupiter wished to speak in human language, he would speak only in the language of Plato."[49]

If this is true of Plato's style in general, it is eminently so for that of the *Phaedrus,* where Ficino sees Socrates inspired by a number of deities and subject to an ascending series of divine madnesses, beginning with the poetic. Thus as the first great poem by Plato—whom Ficino believed to be the last and greatest of the *prisci theologi,* the tradition of ancient poets, prophets, priests, and philosophers[50]—the *Phaedrus* establishes poetry as the philosophic mode par excellence and the poetical style as the authentically Platonic style.

Whatever the nature of the thematic and stylistic evidence from Diogenes, Olympiodorus, Hermias, and others, the fact of the priority of the *Phaedrus* was especially meaningful to Ficino, despite his lack of interest otherwise in chronological or developmental questions.[51] Given a syncretistic approach to the canon and a commitment to the notion of its internal consistency and unity, each dialogue will necessarily reflect in varying degrees, if not monadically contain, the whole; but none to a greater degree than the first. It will be the seminal work from which later works take their origin and in which they are potentially contained—the protodialogue. If the tradition had fastened upon apprentice work, juvenilia in the pejorative sense, then Ficino might have decided to ignore it, despite its priority. But since tradition had assigned priority to a piece so consummately conceived and executed, it became inevitable and even logical, given a Neoplatonic perspective and values, that Ficino approach the *Phaedrus* as a cipher to Plato's subsequent mysteries. Ironically, this line of argument supplied the grounds for Schleiermacher's acceptance of the tradition of the priority of the *Phaedrus* as late as the nineteenth century,[52] and the manifest quality of the piece merely served to reinforce the tradition. In other words, the priority amounted to a kind of primacy,[53] at least with regard to those matters touched upon in the mythical hymn.

I say "a kind of primacy" advisedly, however, for some aspects of the piece had to be interpreted with extreme delicacy and circumspection, since they dealt with notions that Socrates was conveying to Phaedrus from his predecessors, notably the Pythagoreans, rather than those that he and Plato wholly espoused themselves. Hence, for Ficino, the particular prominence of the pastoral setting and of Socrates' "divine sign," the apotropaic voice warning us that Socrates is consistently speaking, not in propria persona, but as the medium of an earlier wisdom. The *Phaedrus,* being first, was more closely tied to the pre-Platonic past than were later dialogues; hence Ficino's comment on the description of the soul's loss of flight and its de-

scent through nine degrees: "Throughout [Socrates/Plato] uses poetic license and describes Pythagorean notions rather than his own."[54] Briefly, these Pythagorean notions were centered around the doctrines of reincarnation and transmigration, but the point to be stressed is that Ficino saw Plato resorting to "poetic license" in order to articulate the wisdom he had inherited (and he treasured the legend that had Plato wandering the length of the Mediterranean world in search of youthful enlightenment until he chose the Pythagorean way as closest to the truth;[55] Aristotle had claimed, by contrast, and with number ontology principally in mind, that the Pythagoreans had influenced Plato only in later life).[56] Not that Ficino ever rejected Pythagorean theories and dicta outright; he saw the need, rather, to allegorize them with the range and flexibility of interpretation developed by Christian theologians to deal with figurative passages in the Bible.[57] Poetic license extended beyond metaphor, of course, to questions of tone, and notably the jocularity, facetiousness, and Silenian irony of Socrates, which was as evident to Ficino as it is to us, though considerably more integral to his conception of philosophizing Platonically: "At the very beginning, amidst his joking." Ficino observes, "Socrates gives us some exceedingly important injunctions."[58] As the youthful priority went along with poeticality and a certain indebtedness to Plato's predecessors, the *Phaedrus* demanded perhaps more sensitive treatment than other dialogues: it posed a similar problem, Ficino notes, to that posed by the Song of Solomon, the mythical hymn of the Old Testament, which it resembled in so many ways, both thematically and stylistically.[59]

For these three extrinsic reasons—its Neoplatonic fame, its membership in the third tetralogy, and its canonical priority, the first, I suspect, acquiring more prominence as the years wore on—as well as for innumerable intrinsic reasons, interpreting the *Phaedrus* confronted Ficino with a supreme test of his Platonic skills. It, not the *Symposium,* might have moved him to write the great Florentine meditation on human ecstasy; or, at the very least, to compose a worthy companion piece for the *De Amore.*[60]

II

The history of his attempt, however, is one of procrastination. In neophytic zeal, Ficino had planned, after translating Plato's dialogues into Latin, to supply them with comprehensive commentaries. During the 1460s, the most productive decade in an exceptionally productive life, he succeeded not only in producing near-final drafts of his translations of the canonical and a few of the apocryphal works,[61] but also in translating the *Pimander* of Hermes Trismegistus, in composing a substantial body of letters, and in preparing the material for his major work of philosophy and apology, the *Platonic Theology*. In addition, he finished the long commentary on the *Symposium,* the *De Amore,* which he later translated into the vernacular and which soon became and remained his most popular work; and he was also well into what would have been a vast commentary on the *Philebus* had he not laid it aside to write the *Platonic Theology*. The Plato translations were eventually published in 1484 and far surpassed the various medieval and early-fifteenth-century versions of individual dialogues.[62] Their publication, as Kristeller has emphasized, was an intellectual event of the first magnitude, since they established Plato as a newly discovered authority for the Renaissance who could now take precedence over Aristotle and whose work—alone from antiquity—was of sufficient profundity to be set above his rival's.[63]

In the 1484 edition, the *Phaedrus* translation was placed between translations of the *Symposium* and the *Apology;* and the position of the *Phaedrus* commentary in Ficino's own 1561 and subsequent *Opera Omnia* reflects this placement. Since no other plan for the order adopted in the 1484 edition has ever come to light, either in Ficino's letters or in those of his correspondents and associates, and since it fails to correspond to any ancient order, Thrasyllean, Iamblichean, or otherwise, Kristeller has hypothesized that it merely repeats the order in which Ficino translated the dialogues, itself the result of whim (with the exception, possibly, of the ten dialogues he hurriedly prepared for the dying Cosimo).[64] There must be more here than

meets the eye, but currently Kristeller's is the only plausible
hypothesis, and it would date the *Phaedrus* translation between
April 1466 and November 1468.[65]

However arbitrary or idiosyncratic its cause, the collocation
with the *Symposium* and the *Apology* is suggestive. With the
former, it points, as I have noted, to an enduring sense of kin-
ship, though one that gradually faded from prominence. With
the latter, as the first of the triad of dialogues depicting Socrates's last hours and culminating in the *Phaedo* (a triad Ficino
kept intact), it points to Socrates's special status as a spiritual
guide to the afterlife, a psychopomp in charge of the soul's
journey away from earth, whether in visionary ecstasy or liberated by corporeal death. Though Ficino never wrote extended
commentaries on the triad, he did write three introductions that
discuss many of the same themes that absorbed him in the *Phaedrus,* and notably the nature of Socrates's inspiration.[66] Whereas the *Symposium's* concern with love and beauty may have
automatically propelled him towards translating the *Phaedrus,*
the latter's own eschatological features may have propelled him
in turn towards the *Apology* and its triad. At all events, having
the *Apology* follow gives an ironic poignancy to the *Phaedrus's*
portrayal of the soul's ascent: it makes Socrates bear an
intensely personal witness to the truth of his myth of the
charioteer.

With a few exceptions, all the translations in the 1484 and
subsequent Plato editions also had introductions, or *argumenta.*
These vary in length from a quarter page to several pages but are
written in one continuous block of unparagraphed, unchap-
tered prose, the argumentum of the *Phaedrus* being in every way
typical. Never mere summaries—though summary is one of
their functions—they provide orientations that sometimes seem
strange to us and often betray assumptions, distortions, and
emphases we no longer share. They also, by the same token,
supply evidence for an understanding of Ficino himself, and en
bloc they constitute the most penetrating, detailed, and original
study of Plato in the West since late antiquity. Ficino's succes-
sors were well aware of the value of these argumenta, for they

either extracted, abbreviated, or copied them out in full in their commonplace books, often as a substitute for actually reading Plato. Indeed, references to Plato throughout the sixteenth and seventeenth centuries are more likely to be to Ficino's argumenta than to the dialogues themselves.[67]

Kristeller has argued that the argumenta were composed concurrently with the Latinizing of their respective dialogues rather than collectively in 1475-1476, as della Torre once supposed and Raymond Marcel has resupposed.[68] If so, then the *Phaedrus* argumentum would also date from the period April 1466 to November 1468 and reflect, as I have already suggested on other grounds, Ficino's initial reaction to the work.

Two factors, however, give us momentary pause and have led Kristeller himself, erroneously I believe, to exclude the *Phaedrus* argumentum (at least as it has come down to us) from his general argumentum theory and to argue for a later date of composition.

First, the argumentum contains two references to the *Platonic Theology* and one to the *De Amore,* completed in 1474 and 1469, respectively.[69] Had they been included in the original draft, then, as Kristeller correctly observes, around 1474 or somewhere between 1469 and 1474 would be the *terminus a quo*.[70] I suggest, though, that all three references were inserted later, probably in the 1480s when Ficino was putting the final touches to his 1484 edition.[71] The last sentence of what became the very first paragraph has general references to the *Platonic Theology* and the *De Amore* and could easily have been tacked on. The third reference, now in the middle of the opening paragraph of chapter 2, is part of an insertion that runs, I believe, from *Quid vero in anima currus* through to *Pythagorici putant,* and is none too well integrated,[72] its aim being to enlarge on the meaning of the word *wings* (a feature of the allegory which had come sharply into focus during his work on the *Philebus* commentary in 1469).[73] Thus, the three references suggest their own date of insertion, not the date of the completion of the argumentum, which is unlikely anyway to have been in the 1469-1474 luster.[74]

Second, from the onset of his work on Plato, Ficino had
something greater than an argumentum in mind for the *Phaedrus.* In the codices (but not the printed versions) of the so-
called first catalogue of his works—a letter written to Poliziano
in 1474-1476—Ficino refers to a *commentariolum,* a small commentary, on the *Phaedrus,* along with a *commentarium* on the
Philebus.[75] Elsewhere Ficino occasionally uses the term *com-
mentariolus/um* to designate works whose lengths ranged from
that of the huge *Timaeus* commentary, or the first part or some
draft thereof,[76] to that of his comments on the *Apology* (which
is nothing but a long argumentum, as he himself notes, and
which he otherwise calls an epitome).[77] It is difficult to assess
the force of the term *commentariolum,*[78] since, when Ficino
intended to furnish a full-scale commentary for a dialogue, he
composed either no argumentum, as with the *Symposium* and
the *Timaeus,* or else a very brief one, as with the *Parmenides*
and the *Philebus.*[79] *Commentariolum,* however, is descriptive
here, not of what he had actually written, but of what he hoped
to write, using the argumentum as a springboard for a future
commentary on the scale of those already attempted by 1474 on
the *Symposium,* the *Philebus,* and possibly the *Timaeus.* Kristeller is misled then by a rhetorical deployment of the term and
postulates a *Phaedrus* commentariolum but no argumentum,[80]
even though he recognizes that it is the same block of material
which the editions and preparatory manuscripts of the Plato
translation all call an argumentum.[81] Significantly, neither the
second[82] nor third[83] catalogues of 1489 and early 1493 mention
a *Phaedrus* commentariolum, though both mention the *Symposium* and the *Philebus* commentaria and also the translation
of Hermias: Ficino merely says that he has written argumenta
for the Plato dialogues. The first catalogue's entry has become
a ghost.

In sum, neither the references to the *Platonic Theology* and
the *De Amore* nor the variations in Ficino's nomenclature
should persuade us that the first catalogue's entry refers to anything but the argumentum of the *Phaedrus.* Since we have no
draft of an earlier argumentum and since the history of other

argumenta suggests nothing to the contrary,[84] we must suppose that the present argumentum remains substantially the same as it was first composed and that Ficino did not revise it when he made it into the opening three chapters of the commentary. It therefore dates from the period when Ficino translated the *Phaedrus* and thus fits into Kristeller's general argumentum theory, despite his own reservations.

Apart from retouching the argumentum for the 1484 edition, Ficino did not return to comment on the *Phaedrus* till a few years before his death in 1499. By then he had translated the whole of Plotinus into Latin and had written commentaries on him, the Areopagite, and Saint Paul, in addition to having prepared a number of other translations, extracts, commentaries, and notes on various ancient and Byzantine Platonists. The year was probably 1493, for, having failed to get into the third catalogue, the present commentary nevertheless contains fully integrated references to the *Parmenides* commentary,[85] begun after November 7, 1492, and finished before August 1494 (and also missing from the third catalogue).[86] It also refers to a treatise, *On the Sun,* which does appear in the third catalogue[87] and a draft of which is mentioned in a letter to Uranius dated January 18, 1493.[88]

The stimulus for this renewed concern with commenting the *Phaedrus* was the hope, born in 1490-1491, that Lorenzo de' Medici was prepared to finance a completely revised and augmented luxury edition of the 1484 *Platonis Opera Omnia,*[89] which would contain full-scale commentaries on the major dialogues (on the model of those completed or on the way to completion) and also such study aids as chapter breakdowns, summaries, and varying amounts of notes and comments to accompany the existing argumenta. This sumptuous edition, however, never saw the light, because by 1494 the Medici had been expelled and Ficino's own life was drawing to a close. The project was also too ambitious, and Ficino soon must have realized this, for in 1496 he published an interim volume entitled *Commentaria in Platonem* and dedicated it to the rising political star Niccolò Valori.[90] It comprised *commentaria, distinctiones capi-*

tum, summae (including revisions to the 1484 edition), and
commenta or *collectanea* in differing proportions for the *Parmenides,* the *Sophist,* the *Timaeus,* the *Phaedrus,* the *Philebus,*
and the section on numbers in the *Republic,* book 8.[91] Prefacing
the volume was a proem to Valori, and concluding it, a letter to
Paolo Orlandini.[92] Also included were the argumenta for the
Parmenides, the *Sophist,* and the *Phaedrus,* but not, curiously,
that for the *Philebus.* The *De Amore* was omitted, since it was
already available in the 1484 edition,[93] but the *Timaeus* commentary was included along with new "distinctiones et summae
capitum." Bar two, these six commentaries and protocommen-
taries were incomplete, and Ficino intended to supplement them
with another volume containing the introductory material and
paraphernalia he had prepared for other dialogues;[94] but it too
never saw the light. Ficino's *Opera Omnia* editions of 1561,
1576, and 1641 incorporate all this material from the 1496 volume in substantially unaltered form (though rearranged[95] and
wretchedly repunctuated and proofed), together with the argumenta from the 1484 edition (some of the longer ones now
redesignated epitomes). The order adopted is also that of the
1484 edition.

Thus, as it appears in the 1496 edition, between the chapter
breakdown and summaries of the *Timaeus* commentary and
chapter 1 of the *Philebus* commentary, the *Phaedrus* commentary consists of: (1) a general title, *Argumentum et commentaria Marsilii Ficini in Phedrum;* (2) the argumentum, now
divided into three chapters, each with a heading but, except for
paragraphing and a handful of variants, otherwise identical
with the argumentum of the 1484 edition; (3) a postscript for
these three chapters, *Hec fuerit hactenus totius dialogi summa;*
(4) eight new chapters, numbered four to eleven, titled, and
paragraphed; (5) a postscript, *Finis argumenti in Phedrum;* (6)
a new title on the same line, *Sequitur commentum cum summis
capitulorum;* and (7) fifty-three summae of varying length.

At first glance it seems a muddle. The initial three chapters
have been set off as a summa, though they are the old argumentum and are so designated in the opening paragraph of chapter 1
and also, presumably, by the general title. The eight chapters of

true commentary are subscribed an argumentum. The general title makes no mention of the summae; and the summae's specific title makes no mention of what other works call distinctiones capitum. However, since 1496 the assemblage has been known as the *Phaedrus* commentary, despite the succession of terms upon which Ficino had drawn to describe it or parts of it: commentarium, commentariolus/um, argumentum, summae, summa. A pigmy beside the giant *Parmenides* and *Philebus* commentaries, it is still a signal achievement. Some preliminary observations may give a sense of its scope, pending the completion of my full-length study.

III

Though the argumentum embodies Ficino's assessment of the *Phaedrus* during the 1460s, the fact that he neither ever reneged on nor revised it, but instead let it stand both at the head of his *Phaedrus* translation and as the prefatory chapters of his commentary, must mean he was confident it provided an adequate bird's-eye view and correct orientation. One might argue that the later division into three chapters was not just a convenient adaptation to a changed format (though the subscript still sets them off), but rather a novel attempt, inspired perhaps by half-memories of Iamblichus's and Hermias's comments on the structure,[96] to define the *Phaedrus* as a triptych, Lysias's speech and Socrates's first speech being panel one, Socrates's second speech panel two, and the oratorical debate panel three. Each panel would then be linked by the overriding concern with beauty and the whole make up a complex unity with the palinode as the centerpiece. Despite Neoplatonic precedents, however, this argument cannot be sustained, for in practice Ficino dismantles the triptych and treats panel two as a freestanding work of art. His choice of phrase even suggests misgivings about the need to consider it along with panels one and three at all: "Nor is it totally irrelevant that Plato inserts Lysias' speech and the argument over oratory."[97]

The eight chapters of commentary proper, by contrast, treat

the initial section of Socrates's second speech, 245A to 248B or 248E (the terminus is vague), a mere—albeit climactic—twenty-fifth of the whole dialogue that runs in the Stephanus pagination from 227A to 279C. These were clearly intended to be part, not even the start, of a long commentary, for they differ in kind from the argumentum. Conceived in paragraphs and far removed from summary, they reflect the ongoing speculative energy that characterizes comparable chapters in the *Parmenides* and the *Philebus* commentaries. One can conveniently divide them into three groups and subdivide the last. Chapter 4 takes off abruptly at 245A and deals exclusively with the divine madnesses, primarily the poetic. Chapters 5 and 6 deal with the rigorously syllogistic section from 245C to 246A, which concerns the soul's immortality. And chapters 7 through 11 deal with the ramifications of the charioteer myth, 246A to 248 and following: 7, 8, and 9 with the soul's nature and power, 10 and 11 with the Jovian cavalcade and its cosmological flight.

In treating the opening of the palinode, Ficino was not faced with a straightforward line of argument and could not proceed, as he had in his *Platonic Theology* or in a more limited way in his exposition on numbers, by building proposition upon proposition. Indeed, the transitions in the dialogue are sometimes so superficially abrupt that one can imagine him choosing to work on the three groups of commentary material separately without cross-referring. I say superficially, for the divisions that both Ficino and modern editors impose upon the *Phaedrus,* though useful in a way, often obscure the fact that we are riding a wave of continuous thought, an organically structured sequence of ideas, as Iamblichus had long ago emphasized.[98] Socrates's discourse on the divine madnesses runs straight into the soul syllogisms, which in turn run straight into the account of the charioteer, his circuit, and the gods. Though the transitions may be startling, they are definite stages in a coherent drama, awareness of which soon overrides any impression of discontinuity. Whether Ficino consciously planned them as such, the eight chapters do recognize this drama, for all are concerned, fundamentally, with the soul's ascent: first with the individual soul's

ascent through the four divine inspirations, then with the ascent
to immortality of Soul, generically conceived, and finally with
the ascent of Soul and all souls, as a company of gods led by
Jove, the world-soul, beyond the arch of the intellectual heaven
to gaze upon the supracelestial place, the portals of the transcendent One. This drama of cosmic ascent is inadvertently
heightened by Ficino's failure to deal with the crippling of the
wings, the rebellion of the dark steed, and the soul's—and Iamblichus would argue the dialogue's—descent again to earthly
beauty and desire, material that, I suspect, he found philosophically uncongenial.

Apparently self-contained, the three groups of commentary
chapters thus reflect Ficino's perception of the dramatic unity
of the opening sections of the palinode and are themselves
bonded by the optimistic theme of man's destiny to rise through
ecstasy to a knowledge of immortality and beyond, to apothe-
osis and to God himself. From what is in several respects one of
Plato's more tragic dialogues, certainly one attuned to an
awareness of the unrelenting nature of man's struggle with
destructive passion, Ficino carved out an epic fragment to the
glory of his passion-mastering intelligence, concentrating, as it
were, on the shape of the head rather than the musculature of
the torso. In doing so, he vindicated the ancient Neoplatonists'
decision to classify the *Phaedrus* as a theological work. He
ends, not on any note of fatigue or dissatisfaction, but on the
flood tide of commentary; several sections of ascent material
were still ahead of him before he needed to tackle the chariot's
descent, the toils of homosexual love, Trebizond's calumny,
and Cardinal Bessarion's noble vindication.

Of the fifty-three summae, the first twelve cover 227A to
243E, and the last twenty, 257A to 279C. Those in between,
numbers 13 to 33, concentrate on the palinode, including the
section treated by the commentary proper; they constitute nearly
two-thirds of the total bulk of summae, as many of the earlier
and later ones are only a few lines long. It is worth noting that,
though they were designed to function independently, this two-
thirds of the summae and all of the commentary proper embrace

just a third of the dialogue. Ficino heads the summae with the double title *Sequitur commentum cum summis capitulorum* (and he might well have added, as he did with summae of other dialogues, *et distinctiones capitum*). The idea of breaking down a dialogue into smaller units called chapters is of ancient origin, but the actual breakdown into fifty-three chapters seems to be entirely his own. It certainly does not correspond to that of the one commentator we might have expected to influence him, Hermias, though there are certain transitions that they agree upon and that other commentators have habitually recognized. Since Ficino had no standard system for referring to the Plato text—no Stephanus pagination—he keys the summae to his 1484 edition by way of incipits: summa 1, for instance, is prefaced by *O amice etce.* (227A), and summa 15 by *Anima omnis immortalis etce.* (245C). Where pertinent the incipits indicate the speaker either in full or by abbreviation.[99] Concluding each summa in the 1496 volume are revisions for the 1484 edition, sometimes half a dozen or more, each signaled by a paragraph; for instance, summa 29 concludes with two such: ¶*Et serere filios nititur/corrige/et concumbere nititur.* ¶*Volandi necessitatem/corrige/necessitatem natura volatilem.* I say "revisions" rather than "corrections" because the changes throughout go beyond the rectification of authorial slips or typesetting errors (the 1484 edition has its own corrigenda for these). Rather, they suggest a level of revision we might anticipate if Ficino were preparing for the augmented Plato edition promised by Lorenzo, and would date, therefore, from the early 1490s.[100]

Apart from the incipits and revisions, each summa is a self-contained unit. About a third merely summarize their sections, sometimes overly briefly: for instance, summa 1 reads *Phedrus a Lysia profecturus rogatur a Socrate ut sermonem et orationem Lysie referat. Dissimulat nolle; tandem concedit.* This hardly conveys an adequate idea of the substance—let alone the details —of several pages of text, 227A-229A, pages that one might have thought, on the evidence of Hermias, Thompson, Robin, and even de Vries, would have appealed to Ficino.[101] Other summae, however, are good accounts of their respective sec-

tions, and still others introduce allegorization and interpretation, sometimes so extensively as to render them eligible for inclusion in the commentary proper.[102] The length of each individual summa is not necessarily proportionate to the number of lines being glossed, since the lemmas Ficino finds especially interesting are often clustered together. Though not systematically expounding his views, they give us a vivid sense of his day-to-day reactions as a commentator, his habitual Platonic responses, and his general cast of mind. Moreover, since they chart the rise and fall of specific enthusiasms as he proceeds sequentially through the text, sparking off some things and ignoring others, they point to the passages he would either have selected to comment on at length had he continued, or else have largely ignored. Finally, they reinforce our understanding of Ficino's overall interpretation and once again highlight the centrality of the "doctrines" transmitted in the palinode. By comparison, say, with the summae of the *Philebus,* they are sufficiently full that I doubt there is any area where we would find no clue to his reactions. Thus we cannot dismiss them merely as notes, as Marcel suggests;[103] for their omissions, their mode of summarizing, and their speculative excursus alike are based on principles of interpretation which are not just vaguely Neoplatonic but distinctively Ficinian. Had he been granted magical access to modern *Phaedrus* scholarship, with its red-herring chases after Plato's attitude towards Isocrates, the authenticity of Lysias's speech,[104] the dramatic date, the age of Phaedrus, and the historical circumstances attending the debate on oratory, I doubt his summae would have given them more than passing mention or his orientation rotated more than a few degrees.

Even if we stay within the gravitational field of the *Phaedrus* commentary, we should be aware of its penumbra, other passages where he explored the interpretive possibilities of the dialogue and worked out various avenues of response. Aside from the many incidental references to the *Phaedrus,* a number of passages composed across the span of his career variously make use of the immortality proofs, the theory of the divine mad-

nesses, the Theuth legend, the myth of the cicadas, and the like, as well as the charioteer myth. To have included all these would have fleshed out our understanding of the power the *Phaedrus* exercised over the Florentine's imagination, but the additional hundreds of pages would have lost the wood in the trees without generating many critical modifications. My final section of texts does, however, select seven such passages that deal with the charioteer myth in some detail: those in the *De Voluptate* of 1457, in the *Symposium* and *Philebus* commentaries of 1468-1469 and 1469, and in the seventeenth and eighteenth books of the *Platonic Theology* of 1473-1474.[105] The *Phaedrus* argumentum has closer affinities with these, incidentally, than with the eight chapters of commentary proper which eventually succeeded it. Even at first glance, one can see that the myth was subject to radical changes in interpretation as Ficino groped towards the range of solutions he would not fully deploy until twenty years later. Only gradually did he come to realize, for instance, that the horses could be, and had to be, interpreted on several different ontological planes: at the lowest level as the irascible and concupiscible appetites, at another as the reason and the fantasy, at another as the intellect's pursuit and the will's ardor, at another, possibly, as intelligible powers. The palinode became, in other words, a plurisignifying myth, true for each and every realm in the Neoplatonic model of reality; and Ficino could draw upon the martial image coursing the banks of the Scamander as well as the mystical chariot of Ezekiel's cherubim.

Nevertheless, something is wanting in his reaction. Though he might sincerely have felt that the assemblage of material printed in the 1496 volume could stand on its own as a valid introduction to and partial exposition of the salient features of the *Phaedrus,* the variations in nomenclature alone suggest that even in 1496 he still thought he had made only a beginning: hence the postscript to chapter 11, *Finis argumenti in Phedrum*. With the exceptions of the *Parmenides* commentary and of the *De Amore* with its clear-cut episodes (though even here Ficino chose to anticipate and rework the contribution of Alcibiades

and the narrative coda),[106] Ficino seems to have been consistently incapable of finishing, or better, perhaps, defining the limits of, a commentary on Plato or any Platonic author. His reaction to the *Sophist,* another cornerstone in the Neoplatonic edifice,[107] was even more skeletal. This incapacity does not extend to works cast in forms other than commentary: the *Platonic Theology, De Christiana Religione,* and *De Vita* are complete, at least in the conventional sense that Ficino wound them up. Since he did not return to the *Phaedrus* commentary till the 1490s, under the impact possibly of a rereading of book 4 of Proclus's *Platonic Theology,* the bare logistics of time and waning energy can account for his failure to live up to earlier expectations. After all, he had only six more years to live in politically and personally unhappy times (and this is assuming that he stopped working on the dialogue in 1493). He was engaged too on several other equally demanding commentaries, some of them still in preliminary form and all projects to which he had long been committed.[108]

Conversely, what took him so long to start the commentary? From the beginning the dialogue had supplied him with some of his most haunting concepts and images, and he recognized that it would require his analysis as much as or more than its peers, given its theological complexities and Neoplatonic past. Moreover, even compared to such Platonists as Cusanus, Bessarion, and Pico, he was probably the best equipped by training and by temperament to rise to the challenge of its speculative richness. Having cited it continually and embarked on exploratory analyses, by the 1470s he must have felt that he could deal with its difficulties and manifold possibilities. Ironically, perhaps these very analyses had siphoned off some of the urgency from the task and left him with a false sense of confidence that he could take it up again at any time. Perhaps, alternatively, they had made him apprehensive of reaching authoritative conclusions about this youthful masterpiece until he had studied all the dialogues and their commentators and not just the other members of the tetralogy, uniquely demanding though they were. In this case he would have deliberately postponed his commentary in

order to gain experience and expertise with Plato's Pythagorean elements. Whatever the reasons—and no one explanation seems wholly satisfactory—the work remained in cartoon. Even so, it served to articulate the response of an entire epoch; for the Ficinian-Phaedran charioteer was soon to become, along with Vitruvian man, one of the Renaissance's most potent and expressive self-images.

Notes to the Introduction

N.B. Cross-references are made both to other Notes to the Introduction and to the separate section of References in the Texts.

[1] An analogy cited by Léon Robin in his Budé edition of the *Phaedrus* (Paris, 1947), p. lviii.

[2] In his *Supplementum Ficinianum,* 2 vols. (Florence, 1937)—hereafter cited as *Sup. Fic.;* in the English edition of *The Philosophy of Marsilio Ficino* (New York, 1943)—the Italian edition, *Il pensiero filosofico di Marsilio Ficino* (Florence, 1953), is superior; in *Studies in Renaissance Thought and Letters* (Rome, 1956)—hereafter cited as *Studies;* and in a large number of essays over the last forty years (see the Select Bibliography below).

[3] *Iliad* 5. 837; 6. 41; 16. 148-154, 467. The *Iliad* also speaks of the chariots of Zeus and Poseidon in 8. 41-50, 438-440; 13. 23-38. By contrast there are the admonitory myths of Phaethon and Bellerophon (see Ficino's *Opera Omnia* [Basel, 1576], pp. 29. 2, 1439. 2; hereafter cited as *Op.*).

[4] As R. Hackforth notes in his translation of and commentary on the *Phaedrus* (Cambridge, 1972), p. 77, *hēniocheuein* ("to act as a charioteer") and its cognates are commonly used metaphorically to mean "to guide, govern, or direct."

[5] See Jacob Burckhardt's famous pages on triumphal chariots at the close of Part 5 of *The Civilisation of the Renaissance in Italy* (in Irene Gordon's revision of S. G. C. Middlemore's English translation [New York, 1961], pp. 294-301).

[6] See Diels-Kranz, *Die Fragmente der Vorsokratiker,* 3 vols., 6th ed. (Zurich and Berlin, 1964), 1, 28B 1 (pp. 227-230). Ficino specifically refers to the *Poema* in *Op.,* pp. 1138. 3; 1169. 1, 2; 1176. 2; 1177. 2; 1180. 1; 1199r; 1199v; 1269. 1, etc.

The chariot of Empedocles was almost certainly unknown to him, since it is alluded to in an obscure line by Sextus (Diels-Kranz, 1, 31B 3, line 5 [p. 310]), which he never mentions.

Leonardo Tarán notes in his commentary on the *Poema* that by late antiquity it had become the fashion to read Parmenides's proem with the myth of the *Phaedrus* in mind (*Parmenides: A Text with Translation, Commentary, and Critical Essays* [Princeton, 1965], p. 18). He cites Hermias's gloss on 246A as evidence (*In Plat. Phaedr.,* ed. Couvreur, p. 122. 19 ff.):

οὐ πρῶτος δὲ ὁ Πλάτων ἡνίοχον καὶ ἵππους παρέλαβεν, ἀλλὰ
πρὸ αὐτοῦ οἱ ἔνθεοι τῶν ποιητῶν, Ὅμηρος, Ὀρφεὺς, Παρμενίδης

Since Ficino had read Hermias, this would suggest that he supposed Plato indebted in part to Orpheus and Parmenides, as well as to Homer's allusion to the chariots of Zeus and Poseidon (see n. 3 above). Hermias's Orpheus reference here was as obscure to Ficino, however, as it is to us.

⁷2 Kings 2:11-12. Ficino alludes to this in *Op.,* p. 698. 1 (see n. 10 below).

⁸Ezek. 1:15-25; 10:8-22. Cf. Ficino's *Theologia Platonica* 13. 2 (ed. and trans. Raymond Marcel under the title *Marsile Ficin: Théologie Platonicienne de L'Immortalité des Âmes,* 3 vols. [Paris, 1964 and 1970], 2:222), which refers to Ezekiel's vision of the valley of dry bones in 37:1-14. Talmudic speculation had centered on what was identified as Ezekiel's divine chariot (the *Maaseh Merkabah*), and the Merkabah mystics had sought admission to the seven heavenly halls (the *Hekaloth*) in order to receive a vision of it. I know of no evidence that Ficino was familiar with this Jewish current, though by the 1490s Pico della Mirandola might possibly have served as an informant. See Umberto Cassuto, *Gli Ebrei a Firenze nell'età del rinascimento* (Florence, 1918), pp. 277-281.

⁹Rev. 6:2-8; 19:11.

¹⁰2 Cor. 12:2-4. Ficino wrote a commentary on these verses in the form of a 1476 letter (*libellus*) to Giovanni Cavalcanti which he refers to as the *De raptu Pauli ad tertium coelum* (*Op.,* pp. 697. 2-706. 3). He begins the second chapter thus: "Trino autem hoc coelo, quasi vehiculo quodam [curru *in the title*], id est, fide recta, spe firma, ardentissima charitate, septies percurres triplex coelum, ubi dulcem patrem patriamque revises, unde ter quaterque, id est septies, foelix evades" (*Op.,* p. 698. 2).

The description of Beatrice's triumph in the *Purgatorio* canto 29 also draws upon imagery from Ezekiel and from Revelation (see Burckhardt, p. 295), as does Lorenzo Valla's depiction of the soul's ascent as a "triumph" (*De Vero Falsoque Bono,* 3:xxv [ed. Maristella de Panizza Lorch (Bari, 1970), pp. 130-136]).

¹¹P. A. Bielmeier, *Die neuplatonische Phaidrosinterpretation* (Paderborn, 1930); see nn. 23 and 24 below.

¹²See Texts IV, extract VI, and Texts, ref. 113 below.

¹³Bent Dalsgaard Larsen, *Jamblique de Chalcis: Exégète et Philosophe* (Aarhus, 1972), pp. 366-367.

¹⁴Raymond Klibansky, *The Continuity of the Platonic Tradition during the Middle Ages* (London, 1939 and 1950), and "Plato's Parmenides in the Middle Ages and the Renaissance," *Medieval and Renaissance Studies* 1 (1943): 281-330. The translations made before the fifteenth century are now available in *Corpus Platonicum Medii Aevi,* ed. Klibansky et al., 4 vols. (London, 1940-1962).

¹⁵There are copies of this in the Vatican Library (Vat. lat. 3348 and Urbinas lat. 1314), in the Laurentian Library (Plut. 76. 43), in Siena's Biblioteca Comunale (J IX 2), and in Berlin (Lat. fol. 582). See Hans Baron, *Leonardo Bruni Aretino: Humanistisch-philosophische Schriften* (Leipzig-Berlin, 1928),

pp. 125-128 (the text of Bruni's preface to his *Phaedrus* translation) and 172. See also Kristeller, *Sup. Fic.* 1:clii, clvi, and *Iter Italicum*, 2 vols. (London, vol. 1, 1963; vol. 2, 1967), 2:167, 360. Bruni also translated the triad of the *Apology*, the *Crito*, and the *Phaedo*, as well as the *Gorgias*, the *Letters*, and part of the *Symposium*. For these and other humanist versions of Plato, see Kristeller, *Sup. Fic.* 1:clv-vii; Marcel, *Marsile Ficin* (Paris, 1958), p. 381; and especially Eugenio Garin, "Ricerche sulle traduzioni di Platone nella prima metà del sec. XV," in *Medioevo e Rinascimento: Studi in onore di Bruno Nardi* (Florence, 1955), 1:339-374.

No one has yet attempted to compare Ficino's Plato translations with those of Bruni or of other humanists, though Kristeller has called for such a study and outlined a methodology in "L'état présent des études sur Marsile Ficin," *XVIe Colloque International de Tours: Platon et Aristote à la Renaissance* (Paris, 1976), 59-77 at pp. 65-66.

[16]F. Masai, *Pléthon et le Platonisme de Mistra* (Paris, 1956). This should be supplemented by details in John Monfasani's *George of Trebizond: A Biography and a Study of His Rhetoric and Logic* (Leiden, 1976), pp. 201-229. See also Milton Anastos, *Pletho's Calendar and Liturgy*, Dumbarton Oaks Papers, 4 (1948): 183-305; and A. Keller, "Two Byzantine Scholars and Their Reception in Italy," *Journal of the Warburg and Courtauld Institutes* 20, 3-4 (1957): 363-370.

[17]In his *Comparationes phylosophorum Aristotelis et Platonis*, written and published in 1458 but not printed until 1523 (Venice; repr. Frankfurt-Am-Main, 1965), and particularly in bk. 3, 2-4 (sigs. N5r-03v), George of Trebizond, a perfervid Aristotelian, assailed those like Bessarion who defended the cultural value of Plato's dialogues. See Monfasani, pp. 166-170 and 201-229, for the dating and further details; also Eugenio Garin, *L'età nuova* (Naples, 1969), pp. 287 ff. ("La distruzione di Platone del Trapezuntio"), and André Chastel, *Arte e umanesimo a Firenze al tempo di Lorenzo il Magnifico*, trans. Renzo Federici (Turin, 1964), p. 298.

[18]Bessarion's *In Calumniatorem Platonis* was written in at least four drafts, the first three in Greek, the fourth in Latin; while the first draft was completed in early 1459, the final draft was not published until 1469. See both Monfasani, pp. 166-170 and 220, for these and other dates, and the earlier magisterial study by Ludwig Mohler, *Kardinal Bessarion als Theologe, Humanist, und Staatsmann*, 3 vols. (Paderborn, 1923-1942). Vol. 1, pp. 346-398, contains an accounts of the controversy (to be read in the light of Monfasani's later study of George); and vols. 2 and 3 contain various texts, vol. 2 the complete Latin and Greek texts of the *ICP*. Of especial interest is Bessarion's bk. 4, chap. 2, "De amore et eius differentia," where the *Phaedrus* is repeatedly referred to in answer to George's charges (Mohler, 2:442-493).

[19]For Figliucci's Italian translation published in Rome, 1544, see Kristeller, *Sup. Fic.* 1:clv. No comprehensive study of the *Phaedrus*'s *fortuna* in the Renaissance exists, but we have only to think of Pico and Sadoleto, Ronsard

and Chapman to glimpse the possibilities. Perhaps the most suggestive comments so far have been Richard Cody's in *The Landscape of the Mind* (Oxford, 1969): "By virtue of being read as Orphic revelation [by Ficino], the mythology of the *Phaedrus* becomes a model for the pastoral eclogue, as in Pico's commentary on a love poem by Benivieni" (p. 4); and again, "[Ficino] reads the landscape or locus amoenus in the *Phaedrus* as an allegory of the Academic life" (p. 11).

See also Eugenio Garin, *G. Pico della Mirandola: vita e dottrina* (Florence, 1937), p. 125 and note; E. R. Curtius, *European Literature and the Latin Middle Ages,* trans. W. R. Trask, Harper ed. (New York, 1963), pp. 187, 474-475; and Edgar Wind, *Pagan Mysteries in the Renaissance,* rev. ed. (New York, 1968), pp. 58, 61, 69, 162, 183; "The *Phaedrus* [is] the classical text on divine madness" (p. 61), and again, "For combining a Bacchic with a Socratic spirit, the *Symposium* of Plato and the Bacchic passages in the *Phaedrus* were the venerated ancient models" (p. 183).

Note that Ficino's Latin translation of the *Phaedrus* (see Texts I below) differs in its interpretation of many difficult or ambiguous passages from such modern translators and commentators as Hackforth, G. J. de Vries (*A Commentary on the* Phaedrus *of Plato* [Amsterdam, 1969]), and C. Moreschini (*Platonis Parmenides Phaedrus recogn. etc.* [Rome, 1966]), who can often, of course, disagree among themselves. This is inevitable given Ficino's Renaissance context and individual orientation.

[20]*Enneads* 5. 8. 10. See Ficino's *Phaedrus* commentary, chap. 11, passim, and Texts, ref. 59 below (also n. 47 below for Ficino's caveats on Plotinus).

[21]Bielmeier, pp. 19 ff.; Larsen, pp. 361-372 (also the supplement, *Testimonia et fragmenta exegetica,* pp. 87-89); and John M. Dillon, *Iamblichi Chalcidensis: In Platonis Dialogos Commentariorum Fragmenta* (Leiden, 1973), pp. 92-99, 248-256. Iamblichus and his school had put the *Phaedrus* eighth in the decade of their first teaching cycle, which concluded with the *Symposium* and the *Philebus* (Larsen, pp. 333-334, 363; Dillon, pp. 15, 258, 264-265; and L. G. Westerink, *Anonymous Prolegomena to Platonic Philosophy* [Amsterdam, 1962], pp. xxxvii-xxxviii). Students then went on to study the *Timaeus* and the *Parmenides,* the climactic texts for the ancient Neoplatonists. See Texts, refs. 56 and 58 below.

[22]*Enneads* 5. 8. 9, 10, 12, and 13. See Texts, refs. 58 and 59 below.

[23]P. Couvreur, ed., *Hermiae Alexandrini in Platonis Phaedrum Scholia* (Paris, 1901; repr. Hildesheim, 1971, with an *index verborum* by C. Zintzen). From comments in Hermias and Proclus, we can assume that Iamblichus, Syrianus, Proclus himself, Harpocration, and Olympiodorus all wrote *Phaedrus* commentaries; but none of them has survived (see Couvreur's *index scriptorum,* pp. 267-270, and also the testimonies collected by Dillon and Larsen). Bielmeier's, Larsen's, and Dillon's accounts of the Neoplatonic *Phaedrus* are all based primarily on Hermias, not on Proclus. See nn. 25 and 26 below.

[24]MS Vat. lat. 5953, fols. 134-316v. See Kristeller, *Sup. Fic.* 1:cxlvi; Michael J. B. Allen, "Two Commentaries on the *Phaedrus:* Ficino's Indebtedness to Hermias," *Journal of the Warburg and Courtauld Institutes* 43 (1980): 110-129; and Allen and Roger A. White, "Ficino's Hermias Translation and a New Apologue," *Scriptorium* (in press).

[25]H. D. Saffrey, "Notes platoniciennes de Marsile Ficin dans un manuscrit de Proclus (Cod. Riccardianus 70)," *Bibliothèque D'Humanisme et Renaissance* 21, 1 (1959): 161-184 (Saffrey acknowledges that the link between this manuscript and Ficino was first noticed by Raymond Klibansky, *Proceedings of the British Academy* 34 [London, 1948]: 7-9). Saffrey presents us for the first time with a text of these notes and glosses, which he has transcribed and edited. While supplementing our knowledge of Ficino as a reader and note taker, they are especially interesting in that they provide us with detailed evidence that Ficino knew Proclus's work in Greek (that is, he need never have known, or even known about, the Latin translation completed in 1462 by Pietro Balbi for Cusanus). Saffrey draws our attention to the "attentiveness" and "seriousness" of Ficino's reading and to his "profound understanding of an extremely difficult text" (p. 181); and also admires Ficino's insights into Proclus's methodology (p. 180). He repeats this laudatory evaluation in his and L. G. Westerink's *Proclus: Théologie Platonicienne,* 6 vols. (Paris, 1968-), 1:lxxiii-lxxiv (three volumes of this superb edition have now appeared and are hereafter cited as Saffrey and Westerink 1, 2, and 3).

Until Saffrey's discovery, Ficino's debts to Proclus generally, and not just to the *Platonic Theology,* had hardly been suspected, let alone explored, even by Kristeller, Marcel, or Michele Schiavone (*Problemi filosofici in Marsilio Ficino* [Milan, 1957]—see, for example, the paucity of references in the index). It is appropriate, therefore, that we briefly take stock of the situation.

Apart from Ficino's notes on the *Platonic Theology* and the tacit acknowledgment of its importance for him in the choice of title for his own great work on the immortality of the soul (though the two have little else in common), we have his Latin translation of excerpts from Proclus's commentary on the first *Alcibiades* (*Op.,* pp. 1908-1928; *Sup. Fic.* 1:cxxxiv-cxxxv). The second and third so-called catalogues of his works refer to them respectively as *quaedam* and as *multa* (*Sup. Fic.* 1:cxiii-cxiv and 2-4), but they are in fact brief extracts entitled *De Anima et daemone,* the title reflecting the reasons underlying their selection. Ficino also translated a theurgical fragment, which was called *De Sacrificio et Magia* (*Op.,* pp. 1928-1929; *Sup. Fic.* 1:cxxxiv-cxxxv); and two manuscripts may contain his Latin versions of the Proclan hymns, for a letter says he translated them in his youth (*Op.* p. 933. 2; *Sup. Fic.* 1:cxlv).

Ficino's first catalogue refers to his having translated *The Elements of Physics* and *The Elements of Theology* (*Sup. Fic.* 1:clxiv-clxv and 1), but these have been lost. He might have known the latter initially through William of Moerbeke's translation of 1268, particularly given its importance for Aquinas. The third catalogue, on the other hand, speaks of his having trans-

lated [*multa*] *in Rempublicam et de sacerdotio.* Some of this material from Proclus's commentary on the *Republic* may have worked its way into Ficino's own collection of notes, epitomes, and commentary on the *Republic* (*Op.*, pp. 1396-1438; *Sup. Fic.* 1:cxxiii), but is otherwise also lost, as is the *De sacerdotio* (unless this is the *De Sacrificio et Magia*).

Though he never translated them, Ficino probably had access to the three shorter Proclan treatises translated by Moerbeke and entitled *De decem dubitationibus circa providentiam, De providentia et fato,* and *De malorum subsistentia* (see Saffrey and Westerink 1:xci). I am becoming increasingly convinced that he knew Proclus's commentaries on the *Timaeus* and the *Parmenides* too; especially the latter, for again Moerbeke had translated it (his translation including by lucky chance a portion from the end of the work now lost in the Greek; see Klibansky and C. Labowsky, *Plato Latinus III: Parmenides...necnon Procli Commentarium in Parmenidem* [London, 1953]). Ficino was quite capable, however, of turning directly to the Greek, more particularly since he was much concerned with Proclus's views on the *Parmenides.* He dealt with some of them at length in his own *Parmenides* commentary (see nn. 29 and 86 below), though he might, admittedly, have been working solely from the copious *Parmenides* material in Proclus's *Platonic Theology* (see Saffrey and Westerink 1:lxxv-lxxxix).

We should recall, finally, that the pseudo-Dionysius, whom Ficino and his contemporaries believed was not only the true Areopagite but the master of Proclus, rather than vice versa, had a profound influence on Ficino and was the medium whereby many Proclan ideas entered into his work.

In sum, we have an entire Proclan dimension to the Florentine's thought and spirituality which has not yet been sufficiently recognized or explored (Klibansky's illuminating remarks on Proclus and Cusanus, for instance, are succeeded by others on Ficino and Pico which are both disappointing and unduly dismissive of Ficino—"Plato's Parmenides," pp. 304-325). Even so, we should bear in mind that Ficino never became a committed Proclan and that he frequently turns away from Proclus to invoke the greater authorities of Plato and Plotinus on the one hand and of Christian Platonists such as Augustine and Origen on the other: see nn. 26 and 47 below.

[26]The major passages on the *Phaedrus* in Proclus's *Platonic Theology* are 1. 4, 5, 6, 20, 24, 26 (Saffrey and Westerink 1: 17-18, 22, 24-25, 27, 30, 96, 106-108, 115) and 4. 4-27, 5. 8-9, and 6. 18-22 (all, alas, available at the moment only in the faulty Renaissance edition by Aemilius Portus [Hamburg, 1618; facs. 1960], pp. 186-220, 261-264, and 394-404. Cf. Texts, ref. 59 below, and Dillon, pp. 251-253. See also Proclus's comments on the four divine madnesses in his commentary on the *Republic,* diss. 6 (ed. Kroll, 1:180-182).

The notes affixed to MS Ricc. 70 supply us with the only definite evidence that Ficino was familiar with Proclus's analysis of material in the *Phaedrus.* Two paragraphs are pertinent, and both come from a section on Proclus's theology entitled *Ordo divinorum apud Platonem secundum Proculum* (in

Saffrey, "Notes platoniciennes," pp. 171-172, ll. 112-120 and 155-167); I quote them in full:

Post sequitur vita per essentiam et imparticipabilis; vita cum tamen sit participatum ens, discreta in tres similiter trinitates, que omnes sunt vite imparticipabiles, participantes ens et habentes novem unitates, sicut ipse sunt novem vite, et sunt dii intelligibiles simul intellectualesque. Quorum prima trinitas dicitur locus supercelestis vel prima alteritas vel sursum ducens, secunda locus celestis vel primus numerus, primus motus, vel continuativum, tertia locus su[b]celestis, vel perfectivum. (ll. 112-120)

Ficino is here describing the nine intelligible-intellectual gods who constitute the middle group of Proclus's twenty-five totally transcendent deities. Divided into three trinities, they occupy, respectively, "the supercelestial place," the "celestial" place, and the "subcelestial" place of the *Phaedrus* 246E-248C (see Texts II, headnote, for an analysis of this terminology). This group of gods is the preoccupation of book 4 of Proclus's *Platonic Theology* (see Saffrey and Westerink 1:lx-lxvii). Note that in his own analysis in chap. 11, Ficino has twelve, not twenty-five, transcendent—or what he calls intellectual—gods.

The second quotation also concerns a middle group of three groups of gods, but this time of immanent or cosmic gods. Referred to as the hypercosmic-encosmic twelve, it follows on the twelve hypercosmic gods and is itself followed by an undetermined number of encosmic gods (whom Proclus was going to describe in book 7, a book that was either never written or has not survived). It consists of twelve Olympians, except that Pluto has been dropped to make room for Vesta and his actual position supplanted by Vulcan:

Sequitur ordo deorum qui supermundani mundanique simul. Et sunt similiter duodecim, illi scilicet quos ponit Plato in Phedro, et Ennius, et Apuleius, et Manilius. Qui dividuntur in quattuor trinitates. Prima est opificativa in qua est Iuppiter, Neptunnus; Vulcanus; ille agit in intellectus, animas, corpora, iste in animas, hic in corpora. Secunda trinitas est custoditiva; prima eius deitas est Vesta, secunda Minerva, tertia Mars, illa custodit essentias, ista fluxus, ista corpora. Tertia trinitas est vitalis in qua est Ceres, Iuno, Diana; prima vivificat intellectus, animas, corpora, secunda animas, tertia corpora. Quarta trinitas est conversiva, in qua est Mercurius, Venus, Appollo; ille trahit ad supera per phylosophiam, iste per amorem, hic per musicam. (ll. 155-167)

Proclus's source is again the *Phaedrus* 246E-247A, along with, of course, the *Parmenides*. Leaving aside the internal problems posed by Proclus's scheme, the paragraph raises several questions about Ficino's analysis. Why did he insert the references to Ennius (the *Euhemerus?*), Apuleius (the lost *Astronomica?*), and Manilius (the *Astronomica*)? Had they been suggested to him by another, perhaps patristic, source? More importantly still, is he making the connection with the *Phaedrus* or noting that Proclus himself was making it (as

indeed he was)? The identification of the names of the hypercosmic-encosmic gods does not imply in itself that the Jovian cavalcade in the *Phaedrus* consisted of such gods or that the Jove there was the hypercosmic-encosmic Jove. Ironically, in fact, this particular set of names coincides with those Iamblichus had given to the encosmic gods, and both Iamblichus and Proclus had insisted, of course, that the *Phaedrus*'s "great Jove" (246E) was higher than the encosmic gods (see Texts, refs. 58 and 59 below).

Though interesting from the viewpoint of Ficino's appreciation of Proclus's *Platonic Theology,* these questions need not detain us here. Even a casual reading of chapters 10 and 11 of his *Phaedrus* commentary will immediately indicate the degree of his essential independence from Proclus. This is true in matters not only of detail, such as the definitions of Vesta, of Adrasteia, of the ambrosia and nectar, but also of his basic analysis of the myth. For instance, Ficino identifies the twelve members of the Jovian cavalcade differently and then parallels them, unlike Proclus, to the twelve (not, note, the twenty-five) gods of the transcendent or intellectual realm. His denotations for mundane and celestial and for supermundane and supercelestial are different from Proclus's and, in the case of mundane and supermundane, much simpler (see Texts II, headnote, below, and cf. *Op.,* p. 1194r). He also seems to have dismissed the notion of dividing the higher cosmic gods into hypercosmic and hypercosmic-encosmic; and so on. More generally, he does not regard the *Parmenides* as the cipher for absolutely every theological problem in Plato, as Proclus had done (see Saffrey and Westerink 1:lxvii-lxxv), though glad to accept the traditional Neoplatonic view that it was the greatest and most profound of the "theological" dialogues. In his own *Parmenides* commentary, notably, he specifically objects to Proclus's oversubtlety in linking together the negations and affirmations of the dialogue's first two hypotheses and to the resulting unnecessary multiplication of the divine orders (*Op.,* pp. 1137-1203 passim but especially pp. 1194r-v). Similarly, in his own *Platonic Theology,* he draws attention to Proclus's overliteralness and overcomplicatedness as a Plato commentator (see n. 47 below).

In sum, we should bear in mind that however arcane and difficult it might appear to us now, Ficino's response to the *Phaedrus*'s mythical hymn was relatively straightforward compared to Proclus's interpretation. Though Proclan in a way in inspiration, as I have suggested, it gave a schematically simpler interpretation of the great myth, one that was wholly compatible not only with Ficino's understanding of Plato and Plotinus but also with his own Christian Platonism, as Proclus's, palpably, was not. Further detailed study of the relationship between Ficino and Proclus, particularly with regard to the *Phaedrus,* would do well to wait upon the appearance of Saffrey and Westerink's last three volumes, promised within the next few years.

[27]Diogenes Laertius, *Lives of the Philosophers* 3. 56-61 (ed. and trans. R. D. Hicks, 2 vols. [Cambridge, Mass., and London, 1959]). Diogenes claimed Thrasyllus had maintained that "Plato published his dialogues in tetralogies, *like those of the tragic poets"* (56; my italics).

²⁸They form a pair not only because Phaedrus himself appears prominently in both dialogues but because they have major themes in common. At the very beginning of the second paragraph of his *Phaedrus* commentary, Ficino observes, "The *Symposium* treats of love principally and of beauty as a consequence; but the *Phaedrus* talks about love for beauty's sake."

²⁹Complete are the commentaries on the *Parmenides* (*Op.*, pp. 1136-1206) and the *Symposium* (*Op.*, pp. 1320-1363); incomplete is the commentary on the *Philebus* (*Op.*, pp. 1206-1269). Cf. n. 91 below.

³⁰De Vries examines the various dating solutions proposed from antiquity to 1969 in his *Commentary*, pp. 7-11.

³¹See Bruni's preface to his partial *Phaedrus* translation, last paragraph—the dedicatee is Antonius Luscus: "Nunc autem librum Platonis, qui inscribitur *Phaedrus*, admirabilem profecto atque divinum, quadam ex parte in Latinum converti tuoque illum nomine dedicavi, cum propter alia multa divinitus in eo perscripta, quibus te gavisurum esse putabam, tum maxime, quia poeticae vis naturaque in illo describitur, quod ad te unicum ac summum nostri temporis poetam vel peculiari quodam iure pertinere videbatur. Est autem Graecorum assertio, non temeraria illa quidem, sed ab optimis vetustissimisque auctoribus profecta: hunc esse primum omnium librum a Platone compositum" (ed. Baron, pp. 127-128).

Ficino's acceptance of this tradition was first made explicit in his *In Convivium Platonis sive de amore* 1. 1, and 6. 13 (ed. and trans. Raymond Marcel as *Marsile Ficin: Commentaire sur le Banquet de Platon* [Paris, 1956], pp. 137, 228); see n. 51 below. The reasons why Ficino grouped the *Phaedrus*, the *Meno*, and the *Phaedo* together as early works is the stuff of a future article. All three are concerned to some degree with anamnesis, the soul's immortality, and the liminal ordeals of birth and death.

³²Diogenes, *Lives* 3. 5; see nn. 27 above and 42 below.

³³Diogenes, *Lives* 3. 38 (and 5); Olympiodorus, *Vita Platonis* 3. See de Vries, pp. 7-8.

³⁴Diogenes, *Lives* 3. 38. De Vries's translation of *meirakiōdes* as "juvenile" (p. 7) seems less preferable than Hicks's "something of the freshness of youth about it" (p. 311). W. H. Thompson, *The Phaedrus of Plato* (London, 1868), p. xxiv, anticipates de Vries, however.

³⁵Bielmeier, pp. 22-23; Larsen, pp. 367-368; Dillon, pp. 92-93 (frag. 1a, 1b) and 248-249. I am quoting from Dillon's translation of 1b on p. 93.

³⁶Larsen, pp. 363-366; Dillon, pp. 92-93, 248. Cf. n. 27 above.

³⁷Michael J. B. Allen, ed. and trans., *Marsilio Ficino: The Philebus Commentary* (Berkeley and Los Angeles, 1975), pp. 5-6, 126-127—hereafter cited as *Philebus Commentary*.

³⁸Hermias, pp. 8-11; the second time, Hermias alters the order of skopoi (see de Vries, p. 22, and Larsen, p. 363n).

³⁹Bielmeier, pp. 22-23; Larsen, pp. 366, 367-368; Dillon, p. 248-249.

⁴⁰See *Phaedrus* Commentary chap. 3, par. 3, "the souls' beauty . . . that is . . . wisdom"; and summa 53, "the inner beauty which he declares exists in

wisdom." Surprisingly, Alicja Kuczyńska makes only one mention of the *Phaedrus* commentary in her study of Ficino's aesthetics, *Filozofia i teoria piękna Marsilia Ficina* (Warsaw, 1970), p. 182n.

⁴¹The (spurious?) epigram where "Plato" complains about the loss of "Phaedrus" is now preserved in the *Palatine Anthology* 7. 100, though Ficino almost certainly knew it from Diogenes, *Lives* 3. 31 (at 3. 29 Diogenes had maintained that "some aver" Plato had loved Phaedrus). Ficino believed this and similar epigrams and elegies to be authentic (see his "Life" of Plato, which eventually prefaced the 1484 Florence edition of the Plato translations but had first appeared as a proem to his *Philebus* commentary and had then reappeared in the fourth book of *Letters* [specifically at p. 764. 1, misnumbered as p. 774]).

⁴²For homophonic and etymological punning on Phaedrus, compare *pais* ("child") and its cognates, *paideia* and so forth, *phaidros* ("bright, beaming") and its cognates, *phaidrotēs,* and so forth, and possibly *erōs* ("love"); see Hermias, pp. 14. 27 ff., 81. 7. For a sense of Phaedrus's beauty and youth, Ficino could also, of course, turn to the *Symposium:* see Allen, "Cosmogony and Love: The Role of Phaedrus in the *Symposium* Commentary," *Journal of Medieval and Renaissance Studies* 10. 2 (1980):131-153. L. Parmentier has shown that in actuality Phaedrus could not have been young (*Bull. Ass. G. Budé* 1926, pp. 8 ff., cited in de Vries, p. 6).

⁴³The three cognitive powers are so defined in Ficino's *De Amore* 2. 2 (ed. Marcel, p. 147); cf. his *Philebus* commentary 1. 5 (ed. Allen, pp. 110-111, and p. 539, ref. 26). They are the intelligence, sight, and hearing.

⁴⁴From *caballus* came a number of medieval Latin derivatives, *cabalcata, caballaria, caballarius, caballicaria,* and so on, most of whose stems appear orthographically as *caval-*. From these in turn came the Italian *cavallo* and its cognates, *cavalcare, cavalcatura, cavaliere,* and so forth. Thus Ficino can pun on the name Cavalcanti in both Latin and Italian, and in particular on the participial form of the verb *caballicare/cavalcare,* meaning "riding" or "the rider." Cavalcanti's name is therefore magically appropriate for the spokesman for Phaedrus in the *De Amore:* as "the charioteer" he is the living embodiment of the Phaedran myth and its ideal, the beautiful youth who has mastered his twin steeds. For a note on Cavalcanti see Kristeller, *Sup. Fic.* 1:118.

Though this onomastic pun cannot be substantiated from the *Phaedrus* commentary itself or from extant letters to Cavalcanti, it would be typical of Ficino's witty practice elsewhere: for instance, the etymological puns on Bernardus Canisianus and Johannes Canacius (*canis,* "dog"), on Amerigus Cursinus (*cursor,* "hunter"), on Braccio Martelli (*bracchium,* "arm"), and—the old chestnut—on Cosimo (*cosmos, pan,* "universe, all things"); see *Op.,* pp. 574. 2; 918. 3; 608. 2 (and these are just four typical examples). The most memorable instance, however, is provided by Michelangelo, who was indebted to Ficino in so many ways. In a sonnet to his beloved young friend Tommaso

de' Cavalieri, written in the 1530s, "A che più debb'io mai l'intensa voglia," he puns in the last climactic line on the name's embodiment of a condition, "Resto prigion d'un Cavalier armato." Cavalieri is the cavalier, the Renaissance counterpart to the charioteer who rides over physical desire in unquestioned mastery of the chariot of the poet's soul; see Erwin Panofsky, *Studies in Iconology,* Harper ed. (New York, 1962), pp. 171-230, especially p. 218.

For the depth of Ficino's commitment to both verbal and situational punning, see my remarks in "Ficino's Lecture on the Good?" *Renaissance Quarterly* 30, 2 (1977): 160-171, and especially pp. 162-164 and 170. Etymological punning was vindicated not only by the *Cratylus* but by the *Phaedrus* itself at 244B ff.

⁴⁵Dicaearchus's view is cited by Diogenes, *Lives* 3. 38; and Olympiodorus gives his own in his *Vita Platonis* 3. Cf. n. 33 above. Interestingly, Diogenes asserted that Plato's first literary products were "dithyrambs" and that he then moved on to lyrics and tragedies (3. 5).

⁴⁶Hermias, p. 9. See Bielmeier, p. 7, and Larsen, pp. 361-362. The criticism of the *Phaedrus* did not stop, incidentally, with Iamblichus; see Themistius's objections in H. Kesters, *Plaidoyer d'un Socratique contre le Phèdre de Platon: XXVIᵉ discours de Thémiste* (Louvain, 1959), a text, however, which Ficino gives no indication of knowing.

⁴⁷See his opening paragraph. Again, in chap. 1, par. 3, Ficino talks of the "splendor" that Socrates seeks from the Muses for his delivery and of his playing here "not a philosophical so much as a poetical role": indeed, he has been seized by a demon, Ficino says, "so that he may divide love poetically rather than dialectically" (cf. chap. 2, par. 4: "Like a poet Socrates then depicts the passions...). Proclus consistently refers to the divine inspiration that has seized Socrates in the *Phaedrus*, e.g., *Theologia Platonica* 1. 4, and 3. 22 (ed. Saffrey and Westerink 1:17-18, 3:78-79), *ibid.* 4. 4, and 6. 18 (ed. Portus, pp. 186, 394), and *In Rempublicam* (ed. Kroll, 1:180-182).

In referring to the mythical hymn, Ficino chooses the word *fabula* (see Texts I, chap. 31, below), a choice that should alert us to the need for allegorization and for not proceeding overliterally. See the *Platonic Theology* 17. 1 and 4 (ed. Marcel, 3:148-149, 165-166 ff.) for Ficino's decision to align himself both with the oldest of the Platonic Academies under Xenocrates and with the Egyptian Academy under Ammonius. In 17. 1 he sees them adopting a position midway between the Roman and Lycian Academies under Plotinus and Proclus on the one hand, who understood all that Plato wrote on the soul's journey (*de animarum circuitu*) too literally (*ipsam verborum faciem curiosius observarunt*), and the two Greek Academies under Arcesilas and Carneades on the other, who interpreted it as wholly fictional (even if in Arcesilas's view it bore some resemblance to the truth). In 17. 4 he restates his position thus: "Following in the steps of Xenocrates and Ammonius, I do not deny that Plato actually affirmed certain facts about the soul; but many things he wrote about the soul's journey [and Ficino has the *Phaedrus* particularly in

mind] are poetic and we should not understand them overliterally (*aliter intelligimus quam verba videantur significare*), especially since Plato did not come upon (*haud ipse invenerit*) this journey himself, but reported (*narraverit*) the journeys of others: first those imagined (*confictos*) by the Egyptian priests under the figure of the purifying of souls, then those which Orpheus, Empedocles and Heraclitus sang about only in poetical texts (*poeticis dumtaxat carminibus decantatos*). And I leave aside the transmigrations of souls which Pythagoras always introduced into his daily discussions and into his symbols [i.e., the *Symbola*)" (p. 166). See nn. 54, 57, and 59 below, and also Texts, ref. 59 below. The stumbling block was, of course, Plotinus's reading of the Phaedran myth (and particularly 249B) as if it depicted the transmigration of some souls into brute beasts; in nearly all other respects Plotinus was Plato's sublime interpreter. The dialogue's poetry, in short, had to be read very carefully if one as great as Plotinus had gone astray. See E. N. Tigerstedt, *The Decline and Fall of the Neoplatonic Interpretation of Plato,* Commentationes Humanarum Litterarum: Societas Scientiarum Fennica 52 (Helsinki, 1974): 19-20.

⁴⁸"Stylum inquam non tam humano eloquio quam divino oraculo similem, saepe quidem tonantem altius, saepe vero nectarea suavitate manantem, semper autem arcana coelestia complectentem.... Ita Platonicus stylus continens universum tribus potissimum abundat muneribus: philosophica sententiarum utilitate, oratorio dispositionis elocutionisque ordine, florum ornamento poeticorum" (reprinted in *Op.,* p. 1129).

⁴⁹"Sive coelestem Platonem audis, agnoscis protinus eius stylum, ut Aristoteles inquit, inter solutam orationem et carmen medium fluere. Agnoscis orationem Platonicam, ut Quintilianus ait, multum supra prosam pedestremque orationem surgere, ut non humano ingenio Plato noster, sed Delphico quodam oraculo videatur instinctus. Mixtio vero eiusmodi vel temperatio adeo in Platone placuit Ciceroni ut dixerit, Si Iupiter humana lingua loqui velit, illum non alia lingua quam Platonica locuturum" (*Op.,* p. 724; it is rehashed in a letter to Francesco Bandini, *Op.,* p. 766. 3). The Quintilian reference is to *Institutio Oratoria* 10. 1. 81, and the Cicero to *Brutus* 31. 121. While the Aristotle reference is to Diogenes' *Lives* 3. 37, Diogenes is in fact misrepresenting *Rhetoric* 3. 7. 11, where Aristotle, in talking specifically of the *Phaedrus,* says that Plato adopted the mixed style for the dialogue ironically (*met' eirōneias*); see Thompson, p. xxiiin.

I quote from the translation made by members of the Language Department of the School of Economic Science in London (*The Letters of Marsilio Ficino: Volume 2* [London, 1978], p. 9). For further information on della Fonte, see C. Marchesi, *Bartolomeo della Fonte* (Catania, 1900), and M. E. Cosenza, *Biographical Dictionary of Humanism and Classical Scholarship,* 5 vols. (Boston, 1962), pp. 1448-1453.

⁵⁰See D. P. Walker, *The Ancient Theology* (London, 1972), and in particular the two seminal articles that first appeared in the *Journal of the Warburg*

and Courtauld Institutes in 1953 and 1954, "Orpheus the Theologian and Renaissance Platonists" (16:100-120), and "The *Prisca Theologia* in France" (17:204-259). See also Charles Trinkaus, *In Our Image and Likeness,* 2 vols. (London, 1970), Pt. 4, sec. 15 ("From *Theologia Poetica* to *Theologia Platonica*").

[51]He believed that the *Meno* and *Phaedo* were also early works (as mentioned in n. 31 above), but that the *Laws* and *Letters* 2 and 7 were Plato's last works and the only ones written, along with the *Epinomis,* in propria persona (preface to his 1484 *Plat. Op.,* and again in *Op.,* pp. 766. 2 and 1488. 2 [= epitome to *Laws* 1] and in the *Platonic Theology* 17. 4 [ed. Marcel, 3:168-169, 174]). Having divided the dialogues into three groups—those that confute Sophists, those that exhort the young, and those that instruct the mature—the preface emphasizes that "what Plato discussed in his *Letters,* in the [twelve] books of the *Laws,* and in the *Epinomis,* using himself as speaker (*ipse suo disserit ore*), he means us to take as certainties (*certissima*); but what he says in the rest of the dialogues, when he uses Socrates or Timaeus or Parmenides or Zeno as speakers, he wants us to understand as only resembling the truth (*verisimilia*)." The *Phaedrus* falls into the latter category. The epitome to *Laws* 1 develops this further by underscoring Plato's reconciliation of Pythagorean contemplation with Socratic action, the former's speculative with the latter's ethical wisdom. With this reconciliation, Ficino says, Plato made them both more humanly accessible: "Platonis [disciplinam] vero doctrinam speculativam pariter et moralem ubique ita divinum cum humano contemplare ut et communi hominum consuetudini facile possit accommodari et simul homines ad divina aeternaque convertere" (1488.1) Ficino's sense of both Pythagoras and Socrates, however, has not yet been explored in any detail.

[52]See Thompson, p. xix: "[Schleiermacher] regards the *Phaedrus* as a preface to the entire series of Dialogues" and the mythical hymn as "a mythical proem to a course of philosophy hereafter to be developed in a graver and more didactic manner by means of dialogues as yet unwritten." He also maintained that a work that discussed whether one ought to write must derive from the beginning of a writer's career, an argument that de Vries is correct to doubt (p. 8) but that might well have appealed to Ficino in light of both the Theuth fable and Socrates's remarks at 277E-278E, and the Pythagoreans' rejection of writing as the proper way to transmit wisdom (see Texts, ref. 12 below).

[53]Ficino was not, on the other hand, Wordsworthian enough to believe that the earliest (ontogenetically or phylogenetically) was ipso facto the best. The *Meno,* after all, argues for the need to educate memories, and this takes time and experience. And Plato always leaves one with the distinct impression that the wisest professors are emeriti.

[54]Chap. 2, par. 1. E. N. Tigerstedt writes, "It cannot be a mere chance that Socrates so often stresses the abnormal, 'inspired' mental state in which he is during the first part of the dialogue [228B, 234D, 238C-D, 241D, 262D, 263D,

278B]. Clearly, he does not want to be wholly responsible for what he is saying" (*Plato's Idea of Poetical Inspiration,* Commentationes Humanarum Litterarum: Societas Scientiarum Fennica 44, 2 [Helsinki, 1969]: 51). But what
Tigerstedt sees as "provocative paradoxality" (p. 56) Ficino saw as the complex reaction of Plato to Socrates's (and to his own) indebtedness to Pythagoras; that is, what the modern commentator tends to see as artistic/ironic dis-
tancing Ficino saw as Plato's way of orienting himself to his own intellectual
past (see n. 55 below).

⁵⁵*Platonic Theology* 17. 4 (Marcel, 3:168): "We should recall that Plato
learned the Pythagorean wisdom (which emanated from Zoroaster) from
Archytas, Eurytos and Philolaus. After he had wandered around the world
and examined all the other opinions of philosophers, he chose the Pythagorean path or school (*sectam*) before all the rest as the one nearest to the truth
(*verisimiliorem*) and as one he might explain (*illustraret*) in his writings. This
is why he introduces Pythagoreans as the protagonists in his principal dialogues: Timaeus of Locris, Parmenides of Elea, and Zeno. It is from their
mouths that Socrates, in Plato's account, learns what he then transmits to
others in the rest of Plato's dialogues." Note that Plato learns not from Socrates, but rather from Archytas, Eurytos, and Philolaus; and that Socrates
"in Plato's account" if not in reality learns from Timaeus, Parmenides, and
Zeno. See nn. 51 and 54 above.

⁵⁶*Metaphysics* 1. 6. 987b; Gilbert Ryle, *Plato's Progress* (Cambridge, 1966),
pp. 2 and 256, suggests that this developed as a result of Plato's second visit to
Italy and found literary expression in the *Philebus* and the lost *Lecture on the
Good.*

⁵⁷Ficino's remarks on fourfold allegoresis are suggestive rather than fully
thought through. He seems to have toyed with the notion that the ancient theologians had adumbrated the fourfold method prior to Christianity in order
to "explain" the gods. The poets had made three mistakes about the gods'
nature: "First they sang that the gods burst forth from confusion (which they
call chaos). Second, they asserted that some of the gods were begotten from
others without right reason as if from human intercourse. And third, in their
criminal impiety, they attributed to the gods all the vexations, errors and vices
of men" (*Op.,* p. 1516—Ficino is glossing *Laws* 10. 886C, 890A). In order to
avoid such mistakes the Platonist must utilize the four ways of "enumerating
or multiplying" the gods outlined in chap. 10 of Ficino's commentary: that is,
via the Plotinian hypostases, the Platonic Ideas, the divine powers, and Neoplatonic demonology. In practice Ficino rarely refers to any of the four traditional methods except the anagogical, which means, essentially, that, in order
to explain classical polytheism monotheistically, we must draw upon the
"Orphic" principle that all the gods can be conceived of in any one god.

⁵⁸Chap. 1, par. 2, cf. summa 5's reference to an *ironic* Socrates. The 1484
preface had already warned Lorenzo that "Plato often seemed to joke and
play while he deployed secret ways (*occultis modis*) of discussing mankind's
fundamental duties; even so Platonic games and jokes are much more porten-

tous (*admodum graviores*) than the serious statements of the Stoics" (it appears again in *Op.*, p. 1129). The role of laughter in Ficino's conception of Plato and Platonizing still awaits exploration, despite suggestions by Edgar Wind and by André Chastel in two important works, *Marsile Ficin et l'art* (Geneva and Lille, 1954) and *Art et humanisme à Florence au temps de Laurent le Magnifique* (Paris, 1961). We should bear in mind that a picture of Democritus decorated Ficino's study, along with a tearful Heraclitus (A. della Torre, *Storia dell'accademia platonica di Firenze* [Florence, 1902], pp. 639 ff.; Kristeller, *Philosophy*, p. 294; Wind, "The Christian Democritus," *Journal of the Warburg Institute* 1 [1937]:180-182; also his *Pagan Mysteries*, pp. 48-49). The *Phaedrus* itself alerts us at 265C to the fact that Socrates is, or says he is, playing: "For the most part I think our festal hymn has really been just a festive entertainment" (Hackforth; in Jowett, "mostly playful"). See particularly Ficino's excursus on the exclusiveness of play to gods and men in *Op.*, p. 1508 (= epitome for *Laws* 7 and in particular glossing 803C, "for man is made to be the plaything of God"). Johan Huizinga, unfortunately, does not mention Ficino, but his remarks in *Homo Ludens*, Beacon Press ed. (Boston, 1962), pp. 108-182 and 211-212, are extremely pertinent, and stimulated both Chastel's and Wind's later observations.

⁵⁹*Phaedrus* commentary, end of chap. 2. For Ficino, the parallels between the *Phaedrus* and Canticles would be manifest. Both treat of love, beauty, and ecstasy; both depict the soul's ascent; both are uncompromisingly metaphorical and poetical; both demand careful allegorizing (to read Canticles as an unabashed love poem Ficino would have considered naive rather than blasphemous); both he considered the youthful outpourings of men later renowned for their wisdom and gravity; and both partake above all else of the nature of hymns, the supreme activity of Christian and Platonist alike.

⁶⁰In fact, the actual companion for the *De Amore*, at least in terms of length and theme if not of completion, turned out to be the *Philebus* commentary, as I suggested in my edition (p. 3): the love of beauty became, as Socrates claimed Diotima said it necessarily must, the love of goodness and of the highest good (*Symposium* 204E-206A).

⁶¹Of the apocrypha, he translated the Speusippean *Definitiones*, Xenocrates's *Axiochus*, the *Clitophon* (which he recognized as apocryphal), all the *Letters* (which he considered authentic), and the early dialogues (about which there is still some controversy), the *Theages, Amatores, Hipparchus, Hippias Major, Alcibiades* 1 and 2, *Minos* (all of which he thought authentic). See Kristeller, "Marsilio Ficino as a Beginning Student of Plato," *Scriptorium* 20 (1966): 44.

⁶²See n. 15 above. For a complete vindication of the 1484 date for the publication of the first Plato edition, see Kristeller, "The First Printed Edition of Plato's Works and the Date of Its Publication (1484)," in *Studia Copernicana XVI: Science and History*, Studies in Honor of Edward Rosen (Wroclaw, 1978), pp. 25-35.

⁶³"Renaissance Platonism," in *Facets of the Renaissance*, ed. William H.

Werkmeister, rev. ed. (New York, Evanston, and London, 1963), p. 109. This is despite the fact, Kristeller observes, that "the understanding of these Platonist sources continued to be affected by Neoplatonic and medieval ideas" (p. 109). We might word this more strongly and say that without the presence of these Neoplatonic and medieval ideas, the impact of the rediscovery of Plato's works would have been less profound and probably considerably delayed, for they served as necessary catalysts. Aristotle's primacy, on the other hand, was not only de facto because of the bulk of his works available to the West for several centuries (including, confusingly for us, both genuine and apocryphal Neoplatonic items), but de iure too because of Aquinas's and other eminent scholastics' assimilation of his thought into their own. Hence the first task for Plato enthusiasts such as Ficino was apologetics; cf. Kristeller's remark in "The First Printed Edition," p. 27, that the 1484 appearance of the Plato volume "would seem to be a major event in the history of Platonism, and of Western thought."

⁶⁴Kristeller, *Sup. Fic.,* 1:cxlvii ff.; also "Beginning Student," pp. 44-46.

⁶⁵Kristeller, *Sup. Fic.,* 1:cil, cli; and 2:88-89; Marcel, *De Amore,* introduction, pp. 26, 36, 41; James A. Devereux, "The Textual History of Ficino's *De Amore,*" *Renaissance Quarterly* 28, 2 (1975):173. Kristeller notes that we know from a letter to Michele Mercati that Ficino had finished twenty-three dialogues by April 1, 1466; and Marcel and Devereux accept November 7 (Plato's feast day), 1468, as the date of the Careggian banquet.

⁶⁶*Op.,* pp. 1386-1389 (*Apology* epitome: on p. 1389 Ficino says he must make an end to his argumentum or rather to his little commentary [commentariolus]); 1390 (*Crito* epitome); 1390-1395 (*Phaedo* epitome).

⁶⁷For instance, the British Library's MS Burney cod. 126 contains abstracts of Plato's dialogues lifted virtually verbatim by Thomas Traherne, the poet, from Ficino's argumenta (Kristeller, *Studies,* p. 160).

⁶⁸*Sup. Fic.* 1:cxvi-cxvii; della Torre, pp. 606-607; Marcel, *Marsile Ficin,* pp. 457-458.

⁶⁹Chap. 1, par. 1, and chap. 2, par. 1. See Texts, refs. 3 and 5 below.

⁷⁰*Sup. Fic.* 1:cxxii (around 1474 or certainly after 1469), clii (between 1469 and 1474).

⁷¹After all, as Kristeller himself observes, citing examples (*Sup. Fic.* 1:cxvi-cxvii), several argumenta have bits corrected or added to them, and particularly references to the *Platonic Theology,* to the *De Christiana Religione,* to the *De Vita,* to later letters, and to other argumenta (i.e. those composed subsequently). There is nothing odd, that is, about the notion that the *Phaedrus* argumentum had its references to other Ficino works added later. Incidentally, Ficino seems to have revised the material for his 1484 volume in at least two separate stints, probably "around 1477" to 1482, and again in 1483 before sending it off to the press (Kristeller, "Beginning Student," p. 43).

⁷²Jupiter had already been defined just a few lines previously as the *anima mundi,* and thus there is no need to turn to the *Platonic Theology* for an

explanation (the allusion, incidentally, is vague; cf. Texts, ref. 34 below); similarly for *currus,* also defined just beforehand as "celestial, sempiternal bodies" (see pp. 230 ff. below). The *casus in corpus,* on the other hand, for which Ficino again refers to the *Platonic Theology,* is defined immediately after the insertion as the distribution "into nine degrees."

[73]See Texts IV, extract III, below, for the equation of the wings with the intellect and will, man's two supreme faculties.

[74]Because Ficino turned away altogether from his work on Plato to compose the *Platonic Theology.* Immediately beforehand he was hard at work on the *De Amore* and the *Philebus* commentary; immediately afterward, on the *De Christiana Religione.*

[75]*Sup. Fic.* 1:1 and n. 1 (cf. *Op.,* p. 619. 3). See also della Torre, p. 68.

[76]*Op.,* pp. 1438-1484. It is so designated, not in the editions (where it is also called a commentarium), but in a letter to Filippo Valori, November 7, 1492, now printed in *Op.,* p. 948. 2 (Kristeller, *Sup. Fic.* 1:cxxi). While Kristeller argues that the *Timaeus* commentary is complete, Marcel claims that after 49D Ficino is summarizing rather than commenting (*Marsile Ficin,* pp. 456, 530-533). Since for Ficino the line between the two modes of response is nonexistent, Marcel's distinction is purely academic.

[77]*Op.,* p. 1389.

[78]Other instances of Ficino speaking of a *commentariolus* (or *-um*) are *Op.,* pp. 933. 2 (on Lucretius—Ficino set fire to this), and 948. 2 (see n. 76 above).

[79]For the *Parmenides* argumentum (*Op.,* p. 1136. 3) see Kristeller, *Sup. Fic.* 1:cxvii; for the *Philebus* argumentum, see Kristeller, "Beginning Student," pp. 47-48, and Allen, *Philebus Commentary,* pp. 480, 484-487.

[80]Kristeller, "Beginning Student," p. 47, "introductions [i.e., argumenta] are lacking... for the *Symposium, Phaedrus* and *Timaeus,* dialogues for which he composed lengthy commentaries at an early date." He continues, "The commentary on the *Symposium* and substantial parts of the commentaries on the *Phaedrus* and *Timaeus* are included in the Plato edition of 1484" (p. 48); cf. *Sup. Fic.* 1:cxvi, cxviii. All that the 1484 edition includes (or any of Ficino's Plato editions include), however, are the first three chapters of the *Phaedrus* commentary without the chapter divisions or headings, and these constitute an argumentum in no respects comparable to either the *Symposium* or the *Timaeus* commentaries. Surprisingly, Kristeller has ignored his own more cautious description in the *Sup. Fic.* 1:cxxi-cxxii, where he likened the *Phaedrus* commentariolus cited in the first catalogue (and as we find it in the codices and first edition of the Plato translations) to an argumentum (*argumenti instar*). See also n. 81 below.

[81]That is, in noting the contents of the manuscripts that he designates L 12, Ga, and Lo 1, Kristeller implies that the *Phaedrus* has an argumentum like those, say, for the *Apology,* the *Menexenus,* or the *Cratylus* (*Sup. Fic.* 1:xi, xxix, xxxii. Page xi, however, still fails to distinguish between Ficino's use of the term *argumentum* to describe all eleven chapters as well as the first three).

Marcel also does not distinguish between the *Phaedrus* argumentum and the larger commentary and fails, in addition, to establish a correct dating for this and companion argumenta (*Marsile Ficin,* p. 458).

[82]Kristeller, *Sup. Fic.* 1:2, and *Op.,* p. 899. 2. It is part of a letter to Uranius, dated June 11 or 12, 1489 (Klibansky, *The Continuity of the Platonic Tradition,* p. 47, opts in his edition of the letter for June 12; Kristeller for June 11).

[83]Kristeller, *Sup. Fic.* 1:2-4 and cxiii-cxiv (item viiib); even though the itemizing is cast in the third person, Kristeller argues that Ficino was the author.

[84]Apart from odd corrections and minor additions, particularly of references (see n. 71 above), the argumenta were eventually printed much as they were composed. Even the *Philebus* argumentum, which Kristeller uses as an instance of the "few" argumenta that underwent "more substantial" change ("Beginning Student," p. 47), acquires in fact only a short passage that serves as a bridge to the opening of the dialogue (see Allen, *Philebus Commentary,* p. 480). Otherwise the *Philebus* argumentum even as it appears in the 1576 edition is basically unchanged from its appearance in the earliest manuscript, an autograph draft probably written in 1464 and now in the Bibliothèque Nationale in Paris (as Nouvelles acquisitions latines 1633, f. 5-7; this is fully discussed by Kristeller in "Beginning Student," pp. 48-54).

[85]Texts, refs. 20, 21, and 52 below; Kristeller, *Sup. Fic.* 1:cxxii, omits mention of the last.

[86]For the dating of the *Parmenides* commentary, see Kristeller, *Sup. Fic.* 1:cxx; he uses the evidence of Ficino's letters to Filippo Valori (*Op.,* p. 948. 2) and Germanus Ganaiensis (*Op.,* p. 957. 2).

[87]Texts, ref. 47 below; Kristeller, *Sup. Fic.* 1:cxxii. The *De Sole* appears in Ficino's *Opera* on pp. 965. 2-975 (see *Sup. Fic.* 1:cxi-cxiii).

[88]*Op.,* p. 949. 3. Kristeller notes that the dating uses the common rather than the Florentine style: the year is therefore 1493, not 1492 (*Sup. Fic.* 1:cxii).

[89]*Op.,* pp. 918. 3 (a letter to Braccio Martelli, dated January 20, 1491), 929. 3 (a letter to Uranius, dated November 24, 1491). See Kristeller, *Sup. Fic.* 1:cxviii and clv.

[90]Kristeller, *Sup. Fic.* 1:lxviii, cxvii-cxxiii.

[91]For the major commentaries on the *Parmenides,* the *Timaeus,* and the *Philebus,* see nn. 29 and 76 above. In Ficino's *Opera* the minor commentaries are on pp. 1284-1294 (on the *Sophist*), 1363-1386 (on the *Phaedrus*), and 1413-1425 (on bk. 8 of the *Republic,* entitled an *expositio*).

[92]*Op.,* pp. 1136. 2 (the dedicatory letter to Valori; cf. n. 108 below), 1425. 2 (the letter to Orlandini; again cf. n. 108 below).

[93]As the twenty-fifth item. The *Symposium* was probably the twenty-fourth dialogue to be translated, and the *Phaedrus* twenty-fifth, since the *Clitophon,* the twenty-second item, apparently does not count, as Ficino doubted its authenticity (Kristeller, *Sup. Fic.* 1:cli; and n. 61 above).

[94]See the postscript to the 1496 volume: "Superioribus Commentariis hec adiungenda sunt: Catalogus, distinctiones capitum, summe, commentariola in ceteros Platonis libros, que Florentie mox imprimentur. Nunc autem seorsum hic imprimitur Dionysius de mystica theologia divinisque hominibus. Finis." Cf. Kristeller, *Sup. Fic.* 1:lxviii.

[95]They are rearranged so that the order of all the argumenta, epitomes, and commentaries should coincide with that in which the dialogues themselves appear in the 1484 and subsequent Plato editions; cf. nn. 29, 76, and 91 above.

[96]See Bielmeier, pp. 22-24 and 26 ff., and Dillon, pp. 92-95 and 248-249, for the importance for Iamblichus (and the evidence here is from Hermias) of viewing Plato's ascending and descending vision in the *Phaedrus* systematically; see Larsen, pp. 366-370, for reservations.

[97]Chap. 1, par. 2, "Neque ab re omnino inserta est oratio Lysie atque oratoria disputatio"; cf. n. 104 below.

[98]Bielmeier, pp. 22-23; Larsen, pp. 367-368; Dillon, pp. 92-93 (a and b), 248-249. Cf. n. 35 above.

[99]See the Appendix in this volume for the curious problem of what seems to be Phaedrus's alternative name, Pausanias, a designation that occurs frequently in both the 1484 and the 1491 Plato editions of the *Phaedrus* translation and occasionally in the Prague manuscript and in the 1496 edition of the *Phaedrus* commentary.

[100]The situation is not peculiar to the *Phaedrus:* the 1496 volume contains revisions for its five other dialogues too, though these were not included in the various *Opera Omnia* editions of Ficino's works. See Texts I, headnote, and the Appendix below. The second (Basel) edition of 1576, incidentally, included some substantial additions for the *Parmenides* and *Timaeus* commentaries not in the first or third editions.

[101]Because of the onomastic punning. Other examples of Ficino's ability to ride roughshod over material that did not catch his fancy are summae 34, 40, 42, 43, 46, and 47.

[102]For instance, summae 24, 25, 30, and 35. Ironically, these fail to function as good epitomes because they are too detailed.

[103]Marcel, *Marsile Ficin,* p. 533. Only a third could be so described, and even then they are condensed summaries rather than incidental jottings; they can still serve as study guides.

[104]In the *De Amore* 1. 2 (ed. Marcel, p. 137), Cavalcanti begins by remarking that "Lysias of Thebes, the famous orator, thought so highly of Phaedrus's friendship that he composed a speech full of lover's complaints to endear Phaedrus to him." This must refer to the first speech discussed in the *Phaedrus.* Lysian authorship was assumed by Diogenes Laertius (*Lives* 3. 25) and by Hermias (ed. Couvreur, p. 35. 20); and Ficino's summa 3 does not debate the issue. For Lysias see also Marcel, *De Amore,* pp. 248-249, 252, and 256.

[105]See Texts IV below.

[106]See Mario Corradi, "Alle origini della lettura neoplatonica del 'Convito': Marsilio Ficino e il 'De Amore,'" *Rivista di Filosofia neo-scolastica,* 69 (1977): 406-422. Of the Alcibiades episode he writes, "Di tutto questo nel Commento del Ficino non è rimasto niente. La settima Orazione, che dovrebbe essere una ripresa della narrazione di Alcibiade, è invece un lungo *excursus* sull'amore volgare e sulla 'mania' erotica" (p. 422). Corradi draws some negative conclusions from this "omission," however, which I cannot entirely share.

[107]Marcel, *Marsile Ficin,* pp. 533 and 685.

[108]Both the Valori preface and the Orlandini postscript (see n. 92 above) try, in a preliminary way, to "place" the *Phaedrus* in the context of some of Plato's other work.

The Valori letter concludes with a *dispositio* for the 1496 volume that follows, Ficino says, the order of the universe. To paraphrase: the *Parmenides* comes first since it treats of the universal principle itself, the *Sophist* second since it discusses being and nonbeing, the *Timaeus* third since it treats of science, the *Phaedrus* fourth since it blends divine matters with scientific and humane matters (*divina cum physicis humanisque permiscet*), and the *Philebus* fifth since, although it blends all these in a way, it should yield to the *Phaedrus* because the latter has a longer discussion of divine matters and possesses the great gift of divine madness more divinely (*praecipuumque divini furoris munus Philebo divinior*). This is to a certain extent an ad hoc thesis that ignores the preeminent position Ficino himself had accorded the *Philebus* in the 1460s and ignores too the *Symposium,* the *Republic,* the *Laws,* and the *Letters* as well as other dialogues, or parts of them, about which he had waxed equally eloquent on other occasions (see, for instance, n. 51 above). It does, however, underscore his sense of the multifaceted nature of the *Phaedrus* and of the thematic range it necessarily encompassed as the first dialogue.

The Orlandini postscript once again subordinates the *Philebus* to the *Phaedrus,* which is now linked with the *Symposium* as treating of the intelligence's ecstasy (*excessus*) as opposed to its natural process as discussed in the *Philebus* (*naturalis mentis incessus*); cf. Texts IV, extract III below. Both ecstatic dialogues are then subordinated to Dionysius the Areopagite and to his examination of divine love.

Both letters and postscript are especially interesting in that they were written just a few years before Ficino's death in 1499 and thus present us with his final assessment of the nature and function of the *Phaedrus,* not only in the Plato canon but in his own work as apologist, commentator, and philosopher-mage.

Texts I The Phaedrus's Mythical Hymn in Ficino's 1484 Latin Translation An Edition with Critical Apparatus

Headnote

The whole of Ficino's *Phaedrus* commentary and two-thirds of the bulk of its summae were based on the *Phaedrus*'s so-called mythical hymn (243E-257A). Ficino's Latin translation of the *Phaedrus* was first printed in the Florence edition of his *Platonis Opera Omnia* (F), recently definitively dated to 1484 by Kristeller ("The First Printed Edition of Plato's Works and the Date of its Publication (1484)," in *Studia Copernicana XVI: Science and History,* Studies in Honor of Edward Rosen [Wroclaw, 1978], pp. 25-35). In the Huntington copy (No. 104150 = Hain 3696) the hymn occupies quire signature g ii verso, column 1, to g vi recto, column 2, that is, folio ccl, column 3, to folio ccliv, column 2. (Kristeller has drawn our attention to the fact that the quire gatherings differ for various copies of the 1484 edition [pp. 29 ff.].)

A long corrigenda list was appended to this edition, and it included some two dozen corrections for the *Phaedrus,* entitled *Errores in Phedrum* (Fc). All these were incorporated into the second edition of the *Platonis Opera Omnia* (which also included the *Theologia Platonica*) printed in Venice in 1491 (V), the hymn occupying folio 161r, column 2, to folio 163v, column 1. This Venice edition was excellently proofed and had no corrigenda of its own. Apart, however, from a few orthographical variants (e.g., *pp* versus *p* or *tt* versus *ct*), a handful of unremarkable substantive variants, which I have noted, and of course the incorporation of F's corrigenda, its text for the hymn was identical with that of F. Though Ficino did not see V through the press, we learn from a letter to a friend, Martinus

Uranius, dated July 20, 1491, that he was aware of its progress: "Venetiis quotidie Platonis Theologiaeque libri iterum ut aiunt diligentius imprimuntur" (Ficino, *Opera Omnia* [Basel, 1576], p. 928. 2; Kristeller, *Supplementum Ficinianum,* 2 vols. [Florence, 1937], 1:clv).

Finally, in the years immediately preceding publication of his *Commentaria in Platonem* in 1496 (E), Ficino appended to each of the *Phaedrus* summae a number of revisions for the *Phaedrus* translation, incorporating into them all the Fc without comment. (This 1496 volume also had corrigenda, including corrigenda for the Fc, but none, it so happens, for those Fc pertaining to the mythical hymn.) That these 1496 revisions, apart from the Fc, had not appeared in the 1491 Venice volume would suggest they were composed after 1491; for Ficino would have had no reason not to make them available to the Venice printers had he had them ready at the time.

Since Ficino turned to his *Phaedrus* translation on a number of occasions during his career prior to his attempt to compose a formal commentary (see the Introduction above), I have thought it best to present the text for the mythical hymn as it first appeared. Scholars can then reconstruct the subsequent layers of correction and revision from the critical apparatus. Accordingly, the text is F's *unemended* except for the silent expansion of abbreviations and diacritics, the correction of purely typographical errors, and the introduction of the u/v distinction and of modern punctuation. The apparatus includes F's own corrections (the Fc), V's variants, and E's revisions; and also the readings from the Laurentian Library's MS Plu. 82. 6 (L), since Kristeller has dated it to just before 1484 (*Sup. Fic.* 1:clv), though the collation here suggests it dates from just afterward (the hymn itself occupies fols. 319r-323v).

My italicization observes Ficino's own method for keying the E revisions to F (why he failed to key them to V is odd, unless he had no copy to hand at the time or had already begun compiling them before 1491). E's own corrigenda have been incorporated without comment into the E readings in the apparatus, however. In brackets I indicate Ficino's summae numbering—for

the hymn this goes from 13 to 33—and also the Stephanus pagination to which it corresponds (cf. Texts III below).

[xiii = 243E] Sic ergo, o egregie puer, cogita priorem sermonem Phedri Pythocle geniti Myrrinusii fuisse, sequentem vero Stesicori Eufemi filii viri amabilis fore; huius hoc erit exordium. Non verus sermo ille est qui presente amatore non amanti magis iubet gratificari, quia amans furit, non amans vero sanus est. Si enim simpliciter verum esset furorem esse malum, recte a nobis dictum fuisset. Nunc autem maxima bonorum nobis fiunt per furorem divino quodam munere concessum. Nam et que in Delphis futura predicit vates et que in Dodona sacerdotes furentes quidem multa ac magna conmoda privatim et publice Grecis hominibus attulerunt, sane vero dum sunt exigua aut nulla. Quod si referamus Sybyllam et alios, quicunque divino usi sunt vaticinio quam multa predicentes in futurum profuerint, prolixum nimis extenderemus sermonem, et rem manifestam omnibus proferremus. Illud tamen dignum est testificari, quod veteres qui nomina rebus imposuerunt, non turpe quiddam neque ignominiosum putaverunt furorem. Non enim preclarissime arti qua futurum discernitur, hoc nomen annectentes, eam **manicem** idest furorem nominassent, sed tamquam bonum quiddam sit furor, quando divina sorte provenit, honeste arti nomen huiusmodi indiderunt. At nunc iuniores isti interiecta **T** littera inperite nimium **manticem** dixerunt. Sane investigationes futuri sanorum hominum per aves et alia ostenta utpote a coniectura humane intelligentie procedentes mentem historiamque auguralem cognominarunt. Quam deinde posteriores **o** parvum in magnum vertentes honestiori vocabulo exornant. Quanto igitur perfectius prestantiusque vaticinium augurali coniectione et nomen nomine, opusque opere, tanto testificantur antiqui furorem ex deo profectum quam humanam prudentiam preclarius esse. Atqui adversus morbos et labores maximos ob antiqua delicta quandoque divina indignatione mortalibus inminentes gentibus quibusdam alicunde furor adveniens ac predicens quibus opus erat remedia adinvenit, confugiens ad vota cultusque deorum; unde expiationes propitiationesque consecu-

tus, incolumem reddidit possidentem et in presens tempus et in futurum, absolutionem presentium malorum recte furenti occupatoque adeptus. [xiv = 245A] Tertia vero a Musis occupatio et furor, suscipiens teneram intactamque animam, *suscitat illam atque afflat*.[1] Unde per cantus aliamque poesim, infinita antiquorum gesta exornans, posteros instruit. Qui autem absque furore Musarum poeticas ad fores accedit, confidens arte quadam poetam se bonum evasurum, inanis ipse quidem atque eius poesis pre illa, que ex furore procedit, qua quidem hec que ex prudentia sit evanescit. Tot equidem, ac etiam plura divini furoris preclara opera referre possum. Quare hoc ipsum ne formidemus, neve ulla nos ratio absterreat, ostendens prudentem et sanum potius quam concitatum amicum esse deligendum.[2] At illi insuper ostendat si potest, ac victoriam reportet, non pro utilitate amantis et amati amorem a diis esse concessum. Nobis vero nunc ostendendum est contra pro felicitate maxima huiusmodi furorem a diis hominibus esse datum. Demonstratio autem erit contentiosis quidem incredibilis, sapientibus vero contra. Oportet autem nos prius de natura anime divine et humane, affectus et opera intuentes, vera novisse. Hoc vero demonstrationis huius principium sit. [xv = 245C] Anima omnis inmortalis, quod enim semper movetur inmortale est, quod vero aliud movet ab alioque movetur, cum terminum habeat motus, terminum habet et vite. Solum ergo quod seipsum movet, quia nunquam se deserit, nunquam cessat moveri. Immo vero et aliis quecumque moventur id fons et principium est movendi. Principium autem sine ortu est. Ex principio enim necesse est quicquid generatur oriri. Ipsum autem ex nullo. Nam si principium oriretur ex aliquo, ex principio utique non oriretur. Cum vero sit absque ortu, et absque interitu sit necesse est. Nam si principium interiret, neque ipsum ex alio, neque ex ipso aliud nasceretur, siquidem ex principio omnia oriantur oportet. Sic ergo principium motus est quod seipsum movet, hoc autem neque mori neque nasci potest. Alioquin omne celum omnisque generatio concidat desinatque necesse est; neque rur-

---

[1]suscitat illam atque concitat E   [2]diligendum L

sus unquam constare possit, unde hec motum nacta oriantur.
Cum igitur appareat inmortale esse quod seipsum movet, anime
substantiam et rationem hanc ipsam qui dixerit, non erubescet.
Omne enim corpus, cui motus extrinsecus incidit, inanime[1] est.
Cui vero intus ex seipso id inest, animatum; tanquam hec anime
natura sit. Quod si ita est, ut non sit aliud quicquam *quo in seip-*
sum[2] moveat preter animam, necessario ingenita et inmortalis
est anima. De inmortalitate anime satis est dictum. [xvi = 246A]
De idea vero ipsius in hunc modum est dicendum. *Quale id*
omnino sit, divine penitus prolixeque[3] narrationis foret, similitudinem vero eius quandam describere, humane et brevioris.
Hoc igitur modo dicamus. Similis esto cognate potentie *subalati*
currus[4] et aurige. Deorum equi et aurige omnes boni sunt atque
ex bonis, aliorum vero permixti. Principio quidem nostri princeps[5] bigas habenis moderatur, deinde equorum alter bonus et
pulcher et ex talibus, alter contrarius et ex contrariis. Quo fit ut
dura et difficilis necessario sit aurigatio nostra. [xvii = 246B]
Qua vero ratione mortale et inmortale animal apellatum est
conandum est dicere. *Omnis anima*[6] totius inanimati curam
habet, *totumque percurrit*[7] celum, alias videlicet alias sortita
species. Perfecta quidem dum est et alata sublimis incedit, ac
totum gubernat mundum. Cui vero ale defluxerint fertur quoad
solidum aliquid apprehenderit, ubi habitaculum sortita cor-
pusve terrenum suscipit, sese movere apparens propter illius potentiam, animalque totum vocatur; anima simul corpusque
compactum, et mortale animal cognominatur. Inmortale autem
ex nulla ratione *discursu percepta, sed que fingitur, quippe cum*
neque viderimus neque satis intellexerimus, deum[8] inmortale
quoddam animal, habens quidem animam, habens etiam corpus
naturaliter omne tempus *coniuncta.*[9] Sed hec iam uti deo placet,
ita se habeant et dicantur. [xviii = 246D] Per quam vero causam
ale abiciantur decidantque ab anima nunc dicamus. Est autem
talis quedam. Naturalis alarum vis est grave in sublime attol-

[1]inane L   [2]quod in seipsum E   [3]quale id omnifariam omnino sit divine prolixeque E
[4]sub alti [sic] coniugii E   [5]principes LV   [6]anima omnis E   [7]totumque circum
percurrit E   [8]recto discursu percepta; sed cum neque noverimus, neque satis intellexerimus,
fingimus deum etc. E   [9]congenita E

lere, ubi deorum inhabitat genus. Omnium vero que sunt circa corpus maxime particeps divini est animus. Divinum autem pulchrum, sapiens, bonum, et quicquid tale dici potest. His utique alitur maxime augeturque ipsa alatio animi, turpi autem et malo contrariisque huiusmodi deficit atque interit. [xix = 246E] Magnus utique dux in celo Iupiter citans alatum currum primus incedit, exornans cuncta provideque disponens; hunc sequitur deorum demonumque exercitus per undecim partes ordinatus, *permanet autem*[1] Vesta in deorum ede sola. *Aliorum vero deorum*[2] quicunque in duodecim *numero censentur,*[3] ducunt per ordinem quilibet quisque [4] est ordinatus. Permulta igitur beataque *ut qui*[4] spectacula discursusque intra celum existunt, quibus deorum genus beatorum intendit suum quisque officium peragens. Sequitur autem semper volens et potens; livor enim a divino choro procul abest. [xx = 247A] *Cum vero ad convivium ac dapes vadunt sublimes,*[5] in celestem circunferentiam proficiscuntur iam ascendentes. Deorum quidem vehicula apta habenis equaliterque librata facile gradiuntur, alia vero vix. Gravatur enim pravitatis particeps equs, ad terram vergens *atque trahens,*[6] cuicumque aurigarum equs *non bonus nutritus*[7] fuerit. Ubi iam labor et certamen extremum anime proponitur. Que enim inmortales vocantur, cum ad summum pervenerint, extra progresse in celi dorso consistunt. Ibi constitutas circunferentia ipsa circunfert atque ille intuentur que sunt extra celum. [xxi = 247C] Locum vero supercelestem neque quisquam nostrorum laudavit adhuc poetarum, neque unquam pro dignitate laudabit; habet se vero in hunc modum. Audendum est enim verum dicere, presertim de veritate loquenti. *Sine colore,*[8] sine figura, sine tactu, *essentia vere existens*[9] anime gubernatore solo intellectu *contemplante utitur;*[10] circa quam vere scientie genus hunc habet locum. Utpote igitur dei cogitatio intellectu et scientia *inmaculata se vertens,*[11] cogitatio quoque omnis anime quecumque convenientem sibi conditionem susceptura est, intuita per

---

[1]permanet enim E   [2]alii vero dii E   [3]numero ordinati sunt ut principes E
[4]ut quisque E (*incorrectly keyed as a result of eye skip*); NB. V *repeats F's mistake*
[5]Cum vero ad mensam epulumque supremum vadunt E   [6]atque gravans E
[7]non bene nutritus E   [8]essentia sine colore E   [9]vere existens E
[10]contemplatore utitur E   [11]inviolabili nutrita E

tempus *id quod est, contenta veritatis*[1] contemplatione nutritur et gaudet, donec circulo in idem circunferentia referat. [xxii = 247D] In hoc autem *circuitu conspicit*[2] ipsam iustitiam, *conspicit temperantiam,*[3] *conspicit scientiam, non qua adsit generatio, nec qua alia alicubi sit in alio,*[4] *quales videlicet sunt eorum*[5] que nos entia nunc apellamus, sed illam que in eo quod est ens vere scientia est; et alia eodem modo *que vere sunt*[6] speculata atque his enutrita, subiens rursus intra celum, domum revertitur. Cum autem redierit, auriga ad presepe sistens equos obicit illis ambrosiam, *et post ipsam*[7] nectar potandum. Atque hec deorum est vita. [xxiii = 248A] Ceterarum vero animarum, alia optime deum secuta similisque effecta extulit in supercelestem locum aurige caput, et cum ipsa circunferentia simul delata est, sed perturbata ab equis, et vix ea que vere sunt intuita; alia vero modo caput extulit, modo submisit, *at violantibus*[8] equis, partim vidit quidem, partim vero non vidit. Alie autem[9] anime affectantes quidem omnes superiorem locum secuntur, cum vero nequeant, *submerse circunferuntur,*[10] calcantes sese invicem atque incumbentes, alia aliam preire contendens. Tumultus igitur et certamen et sudor fit extremus. Ubi quidem aurigarum vitio multe claudicant, multe multas pennas confringunt. Omnes vero magno implicate labore, expertes eius quod vere est intuendi, discedunt; post discessum vero alimento utuntur opinabili. Cuius quidem gratia multus inest conatus veritatis campus ubinam sit intueri. Nam ex huiusmodi prato optima vis anime convenientem accipit alimoniam, et alarum natura, qua anima elevatur, hoc alitur. [xxiv = 248C] Regulaque Adrastie dee, id est, inevitabilis numinis hec est, ut quecumque anima deum comitata aliquid verorum inspexerit, ea usque ad circuitum alium sit indennis; et si semper hoc facere queat, sit semper illesa. Si vero impotens assequendi non inspexerit, et casu aliquo usa, repletaque oblivione et pravitate gravetur, gravata autem pennas confregerit in terramque ceciderit[11] tunc prohibet lex hanc in prima generatione in aliquam brutalem ire naturam;

---

[1]ipsum ens amat et eorum que vera sunt E   [2]circuitu perspicit E   [3]perspicit temperantiam E   [4]animo L   [5]perspicit scientiam, non eam cui adsit generatio, nec que alicubi alia sit in alio, nec eam que sit eorum E   [6]que vere entia sunt E   [7]subinde E   [8]at compellentibus E   [9]vero L   [10]submerse simul circunferuntur E   [11]deciderit L

sed iubet eam que plurima viderit in genituram viri futuri philosophi aut pulchritudinis cupidi aut musici atque amatorii. Eam
vero que secundo loco in regem legitimum ut[1] bellicosum virum
et imperatorium descendere. *Tertio in gubernatorem rei publice,*
ut[2] *rei familiaris dispensatorem*[3] vel questuarium. Quarto in
laboriosum gymnasticum, aut circa *medelam curamque*[4] corporis versaturum. Quinto in eos qui *vates futuri*[5] sunt, *et circa*
mysteria[6] quedam. *Sexto in poetam*[7] vel alium quemvis eorum
qui apte in imitatione versantur. Septimo in artificem vel agrico-
lam. Octavo *in sophistam et popularem.*[8] Nono in tyrannicum.
In his autem omnibus quicumque iuste vitam egerit, *sortem pos-*
tea nanciscitur[9] meliorem; qui vero iniuste, deteriorem. [xxv =
248E] In idem enim unde profecta est cuiusque anima *annis de-*
cem milibus[10] non revertitur. Nam alas ante hoc spatium non
recuperat, preter illius animam[11] qui philosophatus est sine
dolo, vel una cum sapientie studio pulchritudinem amavit. He
quidem tertio ambitu mille annorum, si ter hanc ipsam deinceps
elegerint vitam, sic recuperatis alis, post ter millesimum annum
evolant abeuntes. *Alio vero anime*[12] prime vite finem *consecute*
iudicantur.[13] Iudicate autem alie sub terra *in iudicii locum eun-*
tes[14] meritas illic penas substinent, alie in celi quemdam locum
per iudicium elevate ita degunt ut dignum est ea vita qua in
hominis figura vixerunt. Millesimo anno ambe redeuntes sortem
et electionem secunde vite suscipiunt; deligit unaqueque eam
vitam quam velit, hic et in bestie vitam humana anima transit, et
ex bestia rursus in hominem, si modo ea anima quandoque prius
fuerit hominis. Nam que numquam veritatem inspexerit, in hanc
figuram venire non poterit. Oportet vero hominem intelligere
secundum speciem ex multis procedentem sensibus in unum
ratiocinatione conceptum.[15] Hoc autem est recordatio illorum,
que olim vidit anima nostra cum deo perfecta, et illa despiciens
que nunc esse dicimus, et ad id quod vere *est sursum reflexa.*[16]
Quapropter sola philosophi cogitatio merito recuperat alas.
Nam illis semper quantum fieri potest memoria inheret, quibus

---

[1]aut L   [2]aut L   [3]Tertio in civilem aut rei familiaris curatorem E   [4]medelam
aliquam E   [5]vaticinatores futuri E   [6]et circa sacrificia E   [7]Sexto in poeticum E
[8]in sophisticum vel popularem declamatorem E   [9]sortem nanciscitur E   [10]decem annorum
milibus E   [11]anima L   [12]Alie vero anime L E   [13]consecute iudicium subeunt E
[14]in locum iudicio destinatum euntes E   [15]ratiocinatione collectum E   [16]est suspiciens E

deus inherens divinus est. [xxvi = 249C] Talibus autem conmentationibus qui recte utitur, perfectisque mysteriis semper imbuitur, perfectus revera solus evadit. Ab humanis autem studiis segregatus divinoque inherens carpitur a multitudine *quasi extra se positus,*[1] sed ipse deo plenus multitudinem latet. Tendit igitur huc totus sermo qui est circa quartum furorem. Quo quando quis visa hic pulchritudine aliqua, vere illius reminiscens, alas recipit, receptisque evolare nititur. Cum vero id facere nequeat, tanquam avis superna suspiciens et inferiora contemnens crimen reportat quasi furore correptus. Hec itaque divina alienatio omnium alienationum optima atque ex optimis fit et habenti et participanti, et qui hoc tenetur furore, cum amet pulchra, amator vocatur. [xxvii = 249E] Ut enim dictum est, omnis anima hominis ea que vere sunt intuita est, alioquin in hoc animal non venisset. Recordari vero ex his que hic sunt illorum non facile est omnibus, nec quot ex illis *breve tempus*[2] illic inspexerunt, neque quot huc descendentes infortunate fuerunt, ita ut quibusdam consuetudinibus depravate sacrorum que aliquando inspexerant oblivionem susceperint. Quamobrem pauce restant, quibus satis memorie supersit. He vero, quando hic similitudinem aliquam eorum que illic[3] inspexerant intuentur, obstupescunt, et quasi extra se ponuntur; que tamen sit hec affectio ignorant, quia non satis omnino persentiunt. Iustitie quidem et temperantie et aliorum quot animis venerabilia sunt splendorem nullum in his imaginibus cernimus, sed per obscura quedam instrumenta vix et perpauci in eorum imagines accedentes eius quod assimilatur genus aspiciunt. [xxviii = 250B] At pulchritudinem tunc licebat videre clarissimam, quando cum beato illo choro felicem visionem contemplationemque secuti cum Iove quidem nos, alii vero cum alio[4] quodam deorum, viderunt et initiati sunt sacris, que phas est dicere sacrorum omnium beatissima; que operamur integri quidem nos et malorum expertes, quot in posterum manebant, integra quoque et simplicia inmobiliaque et beata spectacula initiati inspectantes pura in luce, puri et inmaculati solutique ab hoc quod nunc circunferentes corpus vocamus, in modum ostree huic alligati. Hec autem memorie beneficio sint attributa,

---

[1]quasi vacillans E   [2]breviter E   [3]hic L   [4]aliquo L

propter quam desiderio illorum que quondam vidimus nunc sermonem extendimus. Pulchritudo autem, quemadmodum diximus, *et cum illis progrediens effulgebat tunc, et huc*[1] profecti
percepimus eam per sensuum nostrorum perspicacissimum clar-
issime refulgentem. Visus enim *nobis peracutissimus*[2] est sensuum omnium, qui per corpus fiunt, quo sapientia non cernitur.
Ardentes enim excitaret amores, siquid tale ipsius simulachrum
manifestum oculis proveniret. Eadem est de ceteris que sunt
amabilia ratio. At vero pulchritudo sola hanc habuit sortem, ut
maxime omnium et perspicua sit et amabilis. [xxix = 250E] Qui
ergo non est mysteriis nuper initiatus aut potius est depravatus
haud celeriter hinc illuc ad ipsam pulchritudinem excitatur,
similitudinem hic quandam que ab illa denominatur aspiciens.
Quapropter non veneratur dum aspicit, sed quadrupedis ritu
deditus voluptati aggredi *et serere filios nititur*[3] petulanterque
congrediens nec timet nec erubescit voluptatem preter naturam
sectari. Sed qui nuper expiatus est sacris, quive aliquando est
plurima contemplatus, quando vultum divina forma decorum
videt apte ipsam pulchritudinem imitatum, vel aliquam corporis
speciem, primo quidem horret; metusque priscorum aliquis in
eum revolvitur; deinde inspiciens tanquam deum colit, ac nisi
vereretur vehementis insanie crimen, sacra amatis non aliter
quam dei statue faceret. Intuentem vero ipsum velut ex horrore,
permutatio, sudor et ardor insolitus occupat. Quando enim pulchritudinis influxum per oculos accipit, calefit, quo pennarum
natura irrigatur, postquam vero incaluit, liquescunt que ad pul-
ulandum spectant, queque diu pre duritie compacta exitum ger-
minis cohibebant. Ubi autem instuxerit[4] alimonia, pennarum
germina iam ab ipsis radicibus tumescentia impetu quodam per
anime speciem totam nituntur erumpere, tota enim erat olim
pennis suffulcta. Fervet itaque tunc omnis et prosilit, atque ut
infantes cum dentes emictunt pruritu et dolore gingivarum vex-
antur, ita et pennas emictentis anima fervet et titillatione moles-
tiaque afficitur. Itaque cum pueri speciem intuetur, cupidinem-
que inde effluentem inbibens irrigatur calescitque, dolere iam
desinit atque letatur. Cum vero procul abfuerit[5] exaruerintque

---

[1] et cum illis effulgebat tunc incedens et huc E   [2] nobis acutissimus E   [3] et concumbere
nititur L E; et concubere nititur Fc V   [4] instruxerit L   [5] abierit L; abuerit V

meatus, qua parte scaturire nititur ala, aridi et constricti, pennarum germen cohibent. Hec intus una cum cupidineo illo influxu obclusum tumescentiumque more resiliens, ipsum sibimet
suos meatus undique obstruit pungitque. Tota igitur anima undique saucia stimulo concitatur et angitur, rursusque memor
pulchritudinis delectatur. Ex utrisque vero permixtis[1] passionis
huiusmodi vehementia et novitate vexatur, et anxia furit atque
insanit. Sic affecta pre furore neque nocte dormire potest,
neque die usquam consistere, sed passim discurrit desiderio pulchri videndi perculsa. Videns autem et influxum illum cupidineum hauriens, abstrusa prius et conclusa iam aperit et resolvit.
Cum vero iam respiraverit stimulis angustiisque liberatur. Hac
utique suavissima voluptate in presenti usque adeo delinitur, ut
numquam ab eius illecebris sponte discedat, neque aliquem
pluris facit quam amatum, sed parentes, fratres, amicosque
omnes oblivioni tradit; ac dissipato per incuriam patrimonio
minime conmovetur, patrias quoque consuetudines et dignitates
quibus gloriari solebat penitus aspernatur, et servire et iacere
parata ubicumque permictitur, modo igniculo suo inhereat.
Non enim colit solummodo et veneratur formosum, sed medicum etiam hunc gravissimorum morborum sibi solum invenit.
Hunc utique affectum, ingenue adolescens, ad quem meus est
sermo, homines **erota** id est amorem apellant. Quo autem modo
dii nominant, si audieris, merito propter iuventutem ridebis.
Tradunt enim Homerici quidam, ut arbitror, ex reconditis carminibus, in amorem carmina duo, quorum alterum valde petulans neque satis concinnum. Sic autem aiunt.

Hunc quidem mortales **erota** id est amorem vocant volatilem;
Immortales autem **pterota** id est alationem propter *volandi necessitatem.*[2]

His partim licet credere, partim non licet. Atqui causa affectio-
que amantium hec ipsa est. [xxx = 252C] Quotcumque igitur
ex Iovis pedissequis capti fuerint, gravius constantiusque ala-
tionis onus ferre possunt. Qui vero Martem coluerunt, cumque
illo circumvagati sunt, amore illaqueati, siquam ab amato sibi
inferri iniuriam putant, in cedem facile provolant, precipitesque
tum ad seipsos, tum ad amatos necandos feruntur. Atque ita
secundum quemque deorum cum quo quilibet chorum egit,

---

[1]permixtus L V   [2]necessitatem natura volatilem E

eundem honorat imitaturque semper in vita pro viribus quoad
permanet incorruptus; et hoc pacto primam hic vite generationem ducit, talemque seipsum ad amatos et alios exhibet.
Amorem ergo pulchrorum ex suo quisque deligit[1] more, et tanquam deus sibi ille sit quasi statuam fabricat et exornat utpote
honoraturus atque sacrificaturus. Iovis itaque cultores eum
sibi amandum querunt, cuius Iovialis sit animus. Quare con-
siderant utrum ad philosophiam et imperium natura sit aptus,
et quando illum amant inventum, omni opere contendunt quo
ille talis evadat. *Ac nisi prius quod exoptant ingressi fuerint*
studio suo tunc[2] contendunt admodum, discuntque undecum-
que aliquid possunt, atque ipsi etiam ad hoc opus progrediuntur. Investigantes ex seipsis dei sui naturam, voti tandem com-
potes fiunt, ex eo quod summa quadam attentione mentis aciem
in deum erigere compellantur; deinde cum per memoriam illum
attingant, divinitate afflantur, atque ex eo mores et studia,
quatenus homini licet dei participem fieri, capiunt.[3] Quoniam
vero horum omnium causas referunt in amatum, dilectione
ardentius accenduntur. Ac si ab Iove hauriant, baccantium
sacerdotum more, in amati animum transfundentes proprio
deo quoad possunt simillimum reddunt. Quicunque vero Iunonem secuti sunt regium querunt, quo invento similiter affecti
eadem erga illum omnia faciunt. Apollinis preterea reliquo-
rumve cultores deorum singuli deos singulos imitantes eodem
modo affectum natura adolescentem querunt. Eoque com-
parato et ipsi imitantes et adolescentibus persuadentes moder-
antesque in numinis ipsius studium et ideam pro viribus agunt.
Non invidia non illiberali malivolentia in adolescentes suos
utuntur, sed omni studio illos ad perfectam tum sui, tum dei
quem colunt similitudinem formare conantur. Cura igitur finis-
que vere amantium, si modo quod cupiunt fuerint assecuti,
talis est profecto qualem descripsimus; et insignis admodum
felixque ab amico propter amorem furente, dilecto suo si captus
fuerit, provenit. [xxxi = 253C] Comprehenditur autem quisquis
capitur hoc pacto. Quamlibet animam ab initio huius fabule tri-
fariam divisimus; atque equorum quidem formas geminas duas

---

[1]diligit L   [2]Ac nisi prius ingressi studium fuerint tunc E   [3]cupiunt L

quasdam species posuimus, *aurigam vero*[1] speciem tertiam;
eademque nobis in presentia maneant. Equorum autem alter
bonus, alter non. Que autem aut boni equi virtus aut mali pravi-
tas sit, nondum plane diximus, nunc vero dicendum. Bonus
excellentiori in statu situs est,[2] specie rectus, et articulatim dis-
tinctus, ardua cervice, *aquilinis naribus, nitido colore,*[3] nigris
oculis, honoris cupidus, temperantie pudorisque particeps, ac
vere opinionis amicus, nullis stimulis indigens, *scilicet cohorta-
tione sola*[4] rationeque regitur. Alter intortus et multiplex *temer-
eque delatus,*[5] rigenti et dura cervice atque demisso collo, simo
vultu, fusco colore, oculis cesiis sanguineque suffusis, morosus
et contumax, irsutis auribus atque surdis, vix flagello stimulis-
que obtemperans. Quando igitur auriga amatorium *aspiciens
oculum,*[6] totamque sensu inflammans animam titillationis et
desiderii stimulis concitatur, tum qui aurige obediens est equorum ut consuevit pudore cohibitus seipsum continet ne prosiliat
in amatum. Alter neque stimulis neque verberibus coherceri
potest, sed exultat; ac violentia delatus coniunctum sibi equm
aurigamque perturbat rapitque ad veneris voluptatem. At illi ab
initio adversantur, indignati quod ad gravia et iniqua trahantur.
Tandem cum malum id minime cesset, compulsi feruntur,
ceduntque iam et consentiunt quod iussi sunt facere. Hinc
herent igniculo, aspectumque ipsius coruscum inspiciunt. Quem
intuitus auriga, pulchritudinis ipsius naturam memoria repetit,
rursusque illam cum temperantia cernit, in casto fundamento
firmiter collocatam. Videns autem metuit, ac 'pre reverentia
recidit resupinus, *ubi simulque*[7] cogitur usque adeo habenas
retrahere, ut equi *ambo natibus*[8] humi resideant; sed alter quidem sponte, quia minime reluctatur, procax autem equs alter
prorsus invitus. Longius vero discedentes, alter quidem propter
verecundiam admirationemque sudore totam animam made-
facit, alter vero, a dolore liberatus quem et frenum et casus
incusserat, vix tandem respirat, atque resipiscens indignatione
motus aurigam equmque coniunctum increpat quod timiditate

---

[1]aurigalem vero E   [2]excellentiori habitu est L E; excellentiori habitu situs est Fc V
[3]naribus modice aquilinis, nitido colore L Fc V E   [4]cohortatione sola E   [5]fususque et
confuse compositus Fc E; *add.* L V   [6]aspiciens vultum L Fc V E   [7]simulque E
[8]ambo femoribus aut natibus L Fc V E

atque ignavia constitutum ordinem deseruerint. Rursusque no-
lentes accedere cogens, vix tandem concessit illis differri in posterum exorantibus. Accedente autem statuto tempore, cuius
esse inmemores illi quidem simulant, hic vero illis commemorat
vi illata inniens trahensque compellit iterum iisdem verbis amatos affari; postquam vero prope accesserunt, inflexus incli-
natusque extensa cauda[1] frenum mordet, et impudentissime
rapit. Sed auriga multo magis eadem passus *veluti a carceribus
retrogressus magis etiam*[2] *quam petulans equs e dentibus violen-
ter trahit frenum,*[3] atque impuram linguam maxillasque cruen-
tans crura natesque humi defigit, ac penas dare compellit.
Quando vero idem sepe pravus equs ille perpessus lascivire des-
titit, mansuefactus iam aurige obtemperat providentie; atque
etiam cum videt pulchrum formidine contremiscit, adeo ut
quandoque contingat amatoris animam iam cum reverentia
quadam et metu adolescentum vestigia sequi. [xxxii = 255A]
Utpote igitur omni cultu tanquam deo equalis adolescens obser-
vatus ab amatore haud quidem simulante sed revera sic affecto,
presertim cum et ipse honoratus natura colentis sit amicus, in
idem postremo cum amatore conspirat, ac etiam si antea a
familiaribus suis condiscipulisque et aliis per calumniam decep-
tus fuerit, dicentibus turpe esse amanti herere, ideoque amantem reiecerit, tandem vero procedente tempore etas et nature
debitus ordo eum in consuetudinem amantis inducunt. Nunquam enim fato decretum est vel malum amicum malo, vel
bonum bono non amicum esse. Ergo cum adolescens colloquio
et consuetudine receperit amatorem, tunc amantis illius benivo-
lentia iam facta propinquior amatum ipsum ammirari compellit, animadvertentem necessariorum amicorumque omnium aliorum benivolentiam, si cum amico divinitus afflato conferatur,
nullius fore momenti. Ac si senior ille diu sic pergat hereatque et
in gymnasiis ceterisve similibus tangat, tunc iam fluxus liquoris-
que illius fons quem **himeron**, id est, cupidineum influxum Iupiter Ganymedis amore captus vocavit, quive in amantem uber
influxit, partim in ipsum infusus est partim extra ipso exuber-

---

[1]causa L	[2]*quoted for correction as* autem Fc	[3]*et quasi de termino flectens resupinus*
habenas longe vehementius trahit [et *add.* L Fc V] dentes equi flagitiosi reprimit L Fc V E

ante effunditur. Atque ut flamen et echo a lenibus[1] solidisque
repulsa corporibus eodem unde venerunt iterum reflectuntur,
ita pulchritudinis ille livor rursus in pulchrum per oculos reflu-
ens qua penetrare in animam consuevit adeo pennarum meatus
irrigat ut et possint iam et incipiant pululare; atque ita amati
animum mutuo implet amore. Amat igitur, quid vero diligat
ambigit, affectumque suum nec novit, nec eloqui potest, sed
perinde ac si lippi alicuius aspectu oculos similiter sit infectus,
presentis morbi assignare causam nescit, nec animadvertit quod
seipsum amatore[2] tanquam in speculo respicit. Itaque presente
illo, dolere ut ille similiter desinit; absente vero desiderat vicissim desideratus, mutuum amorem tanquam amoris simulachrum possidens; nec amorem ipsum, sed amicitiam et vocat et
putat. Cupit ergo ferme ut ille quamvis moderatius videre atque
assidua consuetudine perfrui; et ut par est post hac protinus hec
facit. In ipsa igitur consuetudine amatoris quidem intemperans
equs aurigam compellans brevem efflagitat pro multis laboribus
voluptatem, adolescentis autem *equs eidem,*[3] quid dicat ignorat,
sed percitus anxiusque amantem mutua prosequitur benivolen-
tia amantissimo suo congratulatus. Atque in ipsa familiaritate
paratus est pro viribus amatoris desiderio obtemperare. Coniu-
gatus autem equs simul et auriga cum pudore et ratione his in
rebus huic adversantur. [xxxiii = 256A] Quare *si secundum rectam vite*[4] institutionem et philosophie *studia meliores*[5] cogitationis partes obtineant, beatam atque concordem presentem
vitam agunt, sui ipsorum domini atque modesti ea parte subiecta cui anime vitium inest; ea contra liberata ad quam probitas
pertinet. *In huius autem vite fine recuperatis*[6] alis prepetes *evolant cum trium certaminum*[7] vere Olympicorum *unum pervice-
rint,*[8] quo quidem nullum prestantius bonum aut humana temperantia aut divinus furor hominibus afferre potest. *Quod si
impudentiorem*[9] quandam vitam philosophie expertem alioquin
ambitiosam secuti sint, forte in ebrietate aut alia quavis desidi-
osa licentia intemperati illorum equi incautas animas invadunt,
easque in idem conducentes illud oblectamenti genus sectari

---

[1] levibus L   [2] seipsum amatorem L; seipsum in amatore E   [3] equus idem E
[4] si ad rectam vite E   [5] studia ducentes meliores E   [6] Hac autem vita functi recuperatis E
[7] evadunt triumque certaminum E   [8] unum pervicerunt E   [9] Quod si inferiorem E

compellunt, quod vulgo beatissimum iudicatur, inque eius desiderii expletione nonnumquam deinde versantur. Hac tamen idcirco raro utuntur, quia non omnis in hoc consentit animi cogitatio. Amici ergo et isti, licet minus quam illi superiores, tum fervente amore tum restincto degunt, fidem sibi invicem firmissimam et dedisse et accepisse putantes, nephas enim esse ducunt fidem frangere, et inimicos quandoque ex amicis evadere. Demum cum nature *sic concesserint, affecti*[1] abeunt ut alati quidem nondum sint, sed pennas emictere[2] quodammodo ceperint. Quamobrem premium amatorii furoris non parvum reportant. Nam in tenebras locumque sub terram descendere illos, qui iam iter sub celis agere ceperant, lex prohibet, sed claram vitam agentes beatos fieri iubet dum una pergunt et simul alas emictunt; atque hec amoris gratia fiunt. Tot igitur ac talia, o puer, tanquam divina amatoris tibi amicitia conferet. Eius autem qui non amat familiaritas, temperantie mortali coniuncta, mortalibusque et exilibus ministeriis[3] dedita, illiberalitatem illam que vulgo virtus habetur in sodalis sui animo generabit; efficietque ut novem annorum milia super terram et sub terram demens pererret.

---

[1]concesserint, sic affecti E   [2]amittere L V   [3]mysteriis L

Texts II   Commentarium in Phedrum
A Critical Edition and Translation

Headnote

This critical edition of the three chapters of Ficino's *Phaedrus*
argumentum and of the subsequent eight chapters of his commentary proper is based on the final version, printed in the
Commentaria in Platonem (Florence, 1496), the *editio princeps*.
It has been collated throughout with the only other complete
fifteenth-century version, that recently found by Kristeller in a
Prague manuscript, which almost certainly dates from the early
1490s, perhaps 1493 (see the Appendix for a full description).
Additionally, the argumentum's text has been collated with the
nearly identical versions in the first two editions of Ficino's *Platonis Opera Omnia* (Florence, 1484, and Venice, 1491), and also
with those in the three extant manuscript versions of the *Phaedrus* translation: the Laurentian Library's Pluteo 82. 6, the
Ghent Rijksuniversiteit Library's MS 354, and the British
Library's Harleian 3481 (see Kristeller, *Sup. Fic.* 1:xi, xxix,
xxxii, clv; *Studies in Renaissance Thought and Letters* [Rome,
1956], p. 159; and "First Printed Edition," p. 33n.). Kristeller
has argued that, while the Laurentian Library's manuscript was
probably transcribed a little before 1484 (but see Texts I, headnote, above), the Ghent and London manuscripts were derived
from the 1484 or 1491 editions. A glance at the variants in the
apparatus below nevertheless shows some interesting, if minor,
differences.

The corrigenda from the 1496 edition have been incorporated
without comment (the 1491 edition has no corrigenda at all, and
the 1484 none, it so happens, for the argumentum). Nonsub-
stantive, typographical errors have been corrected and the spell-
ing regularized (with the u/v distinction), abbreviations and
diacritics have been silently expanded, and the punctuation has

been modernized. The paragraphing throughout is that of the
1496 edition, with individual instances of no paragraphing in
the Prague manuscript noted in the apparatus. Observe, however, that the 1496 edition is alone in dividing the argumentum
into paragraphs and that it and the Prague manuscript are alone
in dividing the argumentum into three chapters, with headings
and numbering. As with my edition of the *Philebus* commentary, the texts in the three editions of Ficino's *Opera Omnia,*
1561, 1576, and 1641, have been dismissed as too corrupt to be
of any value, even though bibliographical references must continue for the most part to be to the 1576 edition (the superior
one anyway) since it is generally available in the Turin reprint
of 1959.

Some particulars in the translation:

1. *Mundanus* and *super-* or *supramundanus* are used to
describe different ontological levels and the gods occupying
them, as are *celestis* and *supercelestis,* though the two pairs are
not completely parallel. We must first understand the basic
structure of Ficino's metaphysical cosmology, Iamblichan and
Proclan in inspiration but simplified and adapted to his own
Christian Platonism and keyed here to what he considered a
Plotinian interpretation of the *Phaedrus.* Central to his analysis
is the meaning of the word *ouranos* ("heaven") in the passage
extending from 246E to 248C, which speaks of the flight of the
Jovian cavalcade up to "the vault of heaven," thence to its
highest point or "arch" (which Ficino had already translated as
celi summum), and finally out upon its "back" (*celi dorsum*) to
gaze upwards at "the superheavenly place" (in Greek the *hyper-
ouranios topos*). Chapter 11 and summae 19-22 argue against
the normally accepted astronomical sense of "heaven," and
maintain (on the authority ultimately of Plotinus, Iamblichus,
and Proclus, but not, curiously, of Hermias) that Plato is referring to the "concave," the arch, and the "convex" of the intellectual realm, the realm of the three Proclan orders of intelligible, intelligible-intellectual, and intellectual gods existing
between "the supercelestial place" of the Ideas and the lower
animate and sensible realms. Hence Ficino can summarily

observe in his *Parmenides* commentary: *Ibi* [= *in Phaedro*] *enim per locum sub coelo sensibilem vel ad summum animalem designat naturam; per locum vero coelestem, intellectualem; per supercoelestem intelligibilem*—"In the *Phaedrus* Plato means by the place beneath heaven the sensible, or at its height the animate, nature; by the celestial place, the intellectual nature; and by the supercelestial, the intelligible" (*Op.*, p. 1175.2). We thus have what would seem to be a three-tier model formulated in terms of subcelestial, celestial, and supercelestial places, where the celestial signifies the intellectual "nature" or realm.

In chapter 11 of his *Phaedrus* commentary, however, Ficino not only works with a four-tier model (by making the obvious and traditional distinction between the animate and sensible worlds) but also calls upon the equation that the *Timaeus* makes at 28B and 30C-32B between the terms *world* and *heaven*. Thus he arrives at a sensible or corporeal world or heaven; an animate (led by the ruling gods of the four elemental spheres, of the seven planetary spheres, and of the fixed stars, that is, the Olympian twelve, all under the supreme sovereignty of Jove, the world-soul and primum mobile); an intellectual world or heaven; and an intelligible. In describing the gods occupying the first two realms (or, for that matter, their circuits, vehicles, or spheres), Ficino uses *mundane* or else *celestial* and *subcelestial,* depending on whether he is referring to the gods in the animate realm or to local, particular, sublunar gods under the lordship of Pan. Similarly, in referring to the gods in the third highest, the intellectual, realm (or to their circuits), he uses either *supermundane* or *supercelestial* (though the latter used of the gods only appears appears thrice: at the conclusions of summae 25 and 53, and in Texts IV, extract VII below). The highest, the intelligible, realm is also *supermundane* or *supercelestial,* but is the realm of the Ideas in the prime intellect, not of gods (at least in Ficino's present analysis). Indeed, used nominatively in the plural, the word *supercelestials* always refers to the Ideas, though the Ideas are usually called the intelligibles, or, occasionally, the supernals.

One might anticipate, given the *Timaeus*'s equation, that the

realms themselves, the "places," would be similarly designated, the two higher being the supermundane or supercelestial, the two lower, the mundane or celestial and the subcelestial. As we have seen, however, the *Phaedrus*'s special deployment of the word *heaven* prevents Ficino from doing this—except, of course, in non-Phaedran contexts, or, as in the case perhaps of Texts IV, extract VII, where he has not yet matured his insights into the text. Hence, while the two lower realms are called mundane, as we might expect, and the two higher, supermundane, like their respective gods, only the highest realm is called supercelestial; for the third realm in the mythical hymn is called celestial. Consequently, the animate and corporeal realms are collectively thought of as subcelestial, meaning "beneath the intellectual heaven."

The situation may seem complicated, not to say thoroughly confusing. It does, however, reflect Ficino's precise response to the implications of the Plato text. Though indebted to the *Cratylus* 396BC and to various Neoplatonic, and notably to Proclan, sources, he has individually tailored the distinctions to his own interpretation. The Proclan denotations for supermundane, supercelestial, and so forth differ, radically, for instance, from Ficino's, as Ficino himself noted (see H. D. Saffrey, "Notes platoniciennes de Marsile Ficin dans un manuscrit de Proclus [Cod. Riccardianus 70]," *Bibliothèque D'Humanisme et Renaissance* 21, 1 [1959]: 161-184, and specifically 168-174). The key for us is to recognize that the *Phaedrus*'s reference at 247C to "the supercelestial place" compelled Ficino, as it had others in antiquity, to think of the next, the intellectual, world as "the celestial place," and then of the animate and sensible worlds beneath it as "the subcelestial place." When not referring explicitly to the Phaedran topography, however, Ficino reverts to the more usual meaning of *celestial* and uses it to signify the gods presiding over the eight heavenly spheres (or what concerns them), plus the four leader gods of the four elemental spheres; similarly with *supercelestial* to signify all that is above these animate gods and their spheres, and with *subcelestial* to signify all below the Moon. These various meanings are critical

if we are to understand Ficino's interpretation of the dialogue, and under no circumstances can *celestial* be taken in the ecclesiastical or modern senses or associated with the notion of paradise.

2. *Anima* and *animus* have consistently been rendered as "soul." The distinctions between their meanings (which is partially preserved to this day in Italian and Spanish) is clear-cut in classical Latin, especially in Lucretius's, and was wholly familiar to Ficino (see *Marsilio Ficino: Lessico greco-latino, Laur. Ashb. 1439,* ed. Rosario Pintaudi [Rome, 1977], s.v. *psyche, thymos, dianoia,* and *nous*). Nevertheless, he treats the two as absolutely free variants; logically so, since his fundamental conceptions of man's psychological, mental, and spiritual makeup require a unitary *soul* dominated by its *mens* or *intellectus.*

3. While Ficino occasionally equates *intellectus* with *intelligentia,* more frequently, as in the second paragraphs of chapters 9 and 10, he works with nice distinctions among the intelligence as a faculty, the process of understanding, and what is understood. I have kept to these distinctions by translating *intelligentia* as "understanding," even when it refers to the understanding ruling a cosmic sphere (traditionally referred to as an intelligence).

For Ficino's sensitiveness to other terminological refinements, see his three sections on the *proprietas* of Plato's, of Proclus's, and, in part, of Plotinus's philosophical lexicons (edited by Saffrey in the article cited above, pp. 169-170, 174-178). See also his translation of Speusippus's *Definitiones* (in *Op.,* pp. 1962-1964) and his apprentice Greek-Latin lexicon (edited by Pintaudi with *indices verborum* and cited above).

4. Normally the Greek *archē* requires several different equivalents in English, depending on context; but as long as we bear in mind that Ficino's choice, *principium,* always denotes, among other things, that it is a cause, then we can consistently render it as "principle," as in "the principle of motion."

5. *Jovian, Venerean, Saturnian,* and the like have been chosen as less connotative forms than *jovial, venereal, saturnine,* and so on.

6. *Prophetic, hieratic, poetic,* and *amatory* have been used for the sequence of divine madnesses, rather than *mantic, telestic, poetic,* and *erotic* or *vatic, initiatory, poetic,* and *erotic.* While the last two sets may come closer to the Greek, the first has Christian overtones that Ficino intended. The most difficult of the four is *mysterialis,* which might, alternatively, have been rendered as "priestly."

Lemmas, when distinguishable from paraphrase and summary, are set in boldface. Superscript numbers in the translation (running consecutively from 1 to 60) are keyed to references gathered in a separate section on pp. 238-245, while superscript letters in the Latin text refer to textual variants, which are footnoted on each page. Bracketed numbers in the Latin indicate the pagination of the Prague manuscript, while bracketed numbers in the translation, followed by A, B, C, D, or E, indicate the conventional Stephanus pagination of the *Phaedrus* and thus the sections to which the commentary chapters or the *summae* refer.

ARGVMENTVM MARSILII FICINI IH PHEDRV.

Dispositio libri. Allegorica Precepta moralia : Duo in nobis duces
atq̃ Demones.   · Caput primũ·

LATO Hoster poeticæ muse, quam a tenera
ætate, immo ab apollinea genitura sectatus est, furore grauidus primum peperit Liberum totvm pene poeticvm et candidissimvm. Candidissimus et de
pulchritudine simul atq̃ amore vir pulcherrimvs omniumq̃
amore dignissimus. Vt merito ceteros quoq̃ liberos deinceps
ediderit venustatis et gratiæ plenos a venerea musa exordiu
foelix auspicatvs solus q̃ omniвm iienustatem vbiq̃ cvm dignitate coniunxerit. Quoniam iiõ plurima huiꝰ libri mýste-
ria in theologia et libro de amore exposuiṃꝰ argumentṽ huiꝰ
breuiter perstringemvs. Symposivm de Amore quidem præ-
cipue tractat: consequenter iiõ de pulchritudine. At Phedrus gratia pulchritudinis disputat de amore. Heqꝫ ab re
omnino inserta est oratio Lysiæ atq̃ oratoria disputatio. Pulchritudo enim et ad mentem et ad visum auditvmq̃ pertinet
quo fit vt vbi de animorꝫ numinvmq̃ pulchritudine agi-
tvr. Itemq̃ de pulchritudine corporis, merito de orationis
pulchritudine disputetvr. Statim iiõ in ipso exordio Socra-
teſ inter iocandvm seria numivin tradit precepta, omnia ob
sapientiæ studivm penitvs contēnenda. Potissimꝰ sapientiæ
studivm consyderare se ipsum: Inter hec artificiosissima
loci descriptio allegorice significat academiam. Platanus

**Marsilio Ficino's introduction to and commentary on the Phae-
drus. Chapter 1. The book's arrangement, allegory and moral
injunctions. Our two internal leaders and two demons.**

[i] Our Plato was pregnant with the madness of the poetic
Muse, whom he followed from a tender age or rather from his
Apollonian generation.[1] In his radiance, Plato gave birth to his
first child, and it was itself almost entirely poetical and radiant.[2]
This most beautiful man, the worthiest of all for love, wrote
simultaneously about beauty and love; so that, quite properly,
he then brought forth the rest of his children too, and they were
full of loveliness and grace. Having made a happy start under
the auspices of the Venerean Muse, he was unique among men
in joining loveliness everywhere with excellence. Since I have
already explained many of this book's mysteries, however, in
my *Theology* and in my book *On Love,* let me make the introduction brief.[3]

[ii] The *Symposium* treats of love principally and of beauty as
a consequence; but the *Phaedrus* talks about love for beauty's
sake.[4] Nor is it totally irrelevant that Plato inserts Lysias's
speech and the argument over oratory; for beauty pertains to
the intelligence, to sight, and to hearing. Consequently, in dealing with the beauty of souls and of divinities and likewise with
the body's beauty, Plato is correct to discuss the beauty of
speech. At the very beginning, amidst his joking, Socrates gives
us some exceedingly important injunctions. To study wisdom
we must utterly despise all else: to examine one's self is wisdom's most perfect study. Among the ingenious aspects of the
dialogue are the following: the description of the spot stands
allegorically for the Academy; the plane tree for Plato; the
agnus castus bush for the chastity of Platonic and Socratic love;
the fountain for the overflowing of the wisdom to be shared;
and the rest of the embellishments stand for the oratorical and
poetic flowers that fill Plato's Academy. Lysias is justly re-
buked for asking what kind of effect love has before he has first
defined or distinguished it.

[309] **Argumentum et commentaria**[1] **Marsilii Ficini**[2] **in Phedrum.**[3] **Dispositio libri, allegoria,**[4] **precepta moralia. Duo in nobis duces atque demones. Cap. I.**[5]

Plato noster poetice Muse, quam a tenera etate immo ab apollinea genitura sectatus est, furore gravidus, primum peperit liberum[6] totum pene poeticum et candidissimum candidissimus, et de pulchritudine simul atque amore vir pulcherrimus omniumque amore dignissimus. Ut merito[7] ceteros quoque liberos[8] deinceps ediderit venustatis et gratie plenos, a venerea Musa exordium felix auspicatus, solusque omnium venustatem ubique cum dignitate coniunxerit. Quoniam vero plurima huius libri mysteria in Theologia et libro De Amore exposuimus, argumentum huius[9] breviter[10] perstringemus.[11]

Symposium de amore quidem precipue tractat, consequenter vero de pulchritudine. At Phedrus gratia pulchritudinis disputat de amore. Neque ab re omnino inserta est oratio Lysie atque oratoria disputatio. Pulchritudo enim et ad mentem et ad visum auditumque pertinet. Quo fit ut ubi de animorum numinumque pulchritudine agitur itemque de pulchritudine corporis, merito de orationis pulchritudine disputetur. Statim vero in ipso exordio Socrates inter iocandum seria nimium tradit precepta. Omnia ob sapientie studium penitus contemnenda. Potissimum sapientie studium considerare se ipsum. Inter hec artificiosissima loci descriptio allegorice signat[12] Academiam, platanus[13] [310] Platonem, castum arbustum amoris platonici et socratici[14] castitatem, fons in communicanda sapientia largitatem, ornamenta cetera oratorios poeticosque flores quibus Academia Platonis abundat. Reprehenditur iure Lysias quod qualis sit amoris effectus inquirat, neque prius amorem ipsum definierit[15] neque distinxerit.[16]

---

[1]et commentaria *om.* PGHLFV   [2]Florentini *add.* L   [3]Phedro G; Platonis de pulchro *add.* L   [4]allegorica P   [5]*no. ch. heading* GHLFV   [6]librum G   [7]merito *om.* G [8]libros G   [9]eius GHLFV   [10]brevissime GHLFV   [11]*no* ¶ PGHLFV   [12]significat PGHLFV   [13]Platanas G   [14]platonici et socratici *transp.* H   [15]defuerit V [16]destiterit P; *no* ¶ PGHLFV

[iii] In all this, take note of the modesty of Socratic love; for Socrates begins with his head veiled since he is about to say something less than honorable. Immediately he invokes the Muses to grace his less-than-honorable speech with the splendor at least of their delivery. But before blaming the base lover and in order not to commit the same offense as Lysias had, Socrates defines base love as a certain passion or lust that rebels against the reason; it overwhelms the opinion, which is trying to do what is right, and enraptures it instead with the pleasure of shape. In pursuing the definition, Socrates assigns us two leaders: one is our inborn appetite for pleasure, the other is a certain legitimate opinion that we gradually acquire through learning and that directs us towards what is honorable. Two external leaders move these two internal ones in us: the airy demon moves the opinion, and the watery demon, desire. Having completed his definition, Socrates introduces a number of reasons for keeping young men away from base lovers. Meanwhile, take note of this marvelous mystery, which resembles the Mosaic mystery: at the very beginning some demon immediately mingled pleasure with a number of evils. But since Socrates here plays not a philosophical so much as a poetical role, he adds that he has been seized by a demon because he has disparaged Love, the name of a god; he does this so that, in the process of dividing love, he may divide poetically rather than dialectically. In this you will notice that the gravest sin is to offend against the name of a god and that one's soul is warned beforehand not to do it.

Chapter 2. The distinctions among the various madnesses and loves. The orders of gods, demons, and souls. The fall of the demons and souls. The allegory on the soul's powers.

[i] Socrates next distinguishes human skill from madness by using some poetic ambiguities. He divides madness into the divine and the human; the divine he separates into four: prophecy, the hieratic art, poetry, and love. He affirms providence

Considera inter hec amoris[1] socratici pudicitiam, nonnulla enim minus honesta pronuntiaturus obvoluto capite exorditur. Mox invocat Musas, ut rem minus honestam ipse suo saltem splendore elocutionis honestent. Sed antequam turpem vituperet amatorem, ne in eodem sit quo et[2] Lysias crimine, turpem amorem definit esse cupiditatem quandam sive libidinem a ratione rebellem, que superet opinionem ad recta tendentem, et ad forme rapiat voluptatem. Sed dum ad definiendum pergit, duos nobis tribuit duces: unum quidem appetitum voluptatis ingenitum, alterum vero legitimam quandam opinionem acquisitam paulatim per disciplinam et ad honesta ducentem. Verum hos nobis intrinsecos duces extrinseci duo movent: demon quidem aereus opinionem, aqueus vero libidinem. Postquam vero definivit, multis rationibus adolescentes a turpibus amatoribus segregat. Tum[3] vero interea mirabile nota mysterium mosaico mysterio simile. Malorum plurimis in ipso statim principio demon aliquis immiscuit voluptatem. Quoniam vero non tam philosophicam quam poeticam agit personam, subdit se correptum a demone, quod amorem dei nomen vituperaverit. Idque facit ut distincturus amorem poetico potius quam dialectico more distinguat. In his [311] animadvertes gravissimum peccatum esse in dei nomen delinquere, rursus in animo esse presagium.

Distinctio furorum amorumque. Ordines deorum, demonum, animarum. Casus animarum demonumque. Allegoria de viribus anime. Cap. II[4]

Deinde poeticis quibusdam ambagibus artem a furore secernit. Furorem in divinum dividit et humanum: divinum in quatuor scilicet in vaticinium, mysterium, poesim atque amorem. Providentiam religionemque confirmat. Sapientiam divino

---

[1]amori E   [2]a GFV; *om.* L   [3]Tu PHL   [4]*no ch. break or heading* GHLFV

and religion. He places the wisdom imparted by divine madness far in front of human wisdom. Before he can complete his treatment of particular souls, Socrates introduces the universal souls, that is, the world-soul (which he calls Jupiter) and under it the twelve souls of the twelve world spheres. To these he adds twelve demonic orders and twelve orders of particular souls. He provides all of these individually with chariots, that is, with celestial, sempiternal bodies. He discusses the rational souls, divine and human, and the circuit that each makes; and why men's souls may not only accompany the celestial souls' contemplation in heaven but also follow the angels' intuition above heaven. In the *Theology* I explain the meaning of the chariot [or] vehicle, the wings, charioteer, and horses in the soul and its fate and fall into the body; I also explain the meaning of great Jupiter in heaven and the rest of the gods who follow him.[5] For the present it suffices if you understand there are twin wings, a double impulse innate to the intelligence and lifting the soul to supernals: one is the impulse in the intellect which turns back with all its strength towards the divine truth, the other, the impulse in the will which turns back with all its strength towards the divine good. When they are relaxed and the inclination of the vegetable nature to govern corporeals is intensified, then the Pythagoreans hold that the souls, now their wings are broken, descend to the elements. Next Socrates distributes the soul when it falls from heaven into nine degrees. Throughout he uses poetic license and describes Pythagorean notions rather than his own.[6]

[ii] Note here the similarity between the Pythagoreans' account of the souls' fall and the Prophets' account of the demons' fall. Notice too that the number nine is used alike of the angelic choirs and of the demons who fell from them. And here I'll not go into Pherecydes of Syros's comparable description of the demons' fall: how Ophioneus, the demonic serpent, led the army that rebelled against the divine intelligence to an outcome similar to that in the divine mysteries, namely Jupiter's hurling of the lower demons down to hell.[7] But let me return to the dialogue.

furore[1] infusam humane sapientie longissime anteponit. Antequam peragat animarum tractatum particularium, animas in medium communes adducit scilicet mundi animam, quam nominat Iovem, atque sub ea duodecim animas spherarum duodecim mundanarum; quibus subdit totidem ordines demonum, totidemque particularium animarum. Singulis vero currus accommodat id est celestia corpora atque sempiterna. De rationalibus animabus disputat divinis atque humanis, de circuitu utrarumque, et qua ratione hominum anime tam in celo animarum celestium contemplationem comitentur quam super celum angelicum sequantur intuitum. Quid vero in anima currus, vehiculum, ale, auriga, equi, fatum casusque in corpus; quid iterum Iupiter in celo magnus ceterique dii sequentes, in Theologia exponimus. Satis vero tibi fuerit in presentia intelligere geminas alas esse geminum instinctum menti ingenitum ad superna animum elevantem: in intellectu[2] quidem instinctum ad divinum verum, in voluntate vero instinctum [312] ad divinum bonum pro viribus convertentem. Quando vero hi quidem remittuntur, inclinatio autem vegetalis nature intenditur ad corporea gubernanda, animas fractis iam alis in elementa descendere Pythagorici putant. Post hec cadentem de celo animam in novem distribuit gradus. In his omnibus et poetica licentia utitur et pythagorica potius quam propria narrat.[3]

Inter hec animadverte similem animarum describi casum a Pythagoricis atque demonum a[4] Prophetis; numerum quoque novenarium tam choris angelicis quam lapsis[5] inde demonibus convenire. Mitto nunc quod similem quendam casum Pherecides Syrus[6] narrat demonibus accidisse. Additque Ophioneum[7] id est serpentem demonicum fuisse caput exercitus rebellantis a[8] mente divina; huic et simile, quod in mysteriis divinis continetur, Iovem scilicet inferiores demones ad inferos deturbasse. Sed ad dialogum redeamus.[9]

---

[1]rore *add.* GF   [2]intellectum GF   [3]*no* ¶ PGHLFV   [4]a *om.* H   [5]lapis E
[6]Syrius P   [7]Ophinoeum E   [8]a *om.* PH   [9]*no* ¶ PGHLFV

[iii] When a man's intelligence has been purged and he is dedicated to God, he is filled [Socrates says] with every good. He alone is wise, although, beside himself as it were, he may be derided by the crowd as insane. Next Socrates descends to the divine madness of legitimate love; he maintains that it is kindled in the soul when the soul, in regarding the body's beautiful shape, with ease recalls the divine beauty it had once contemplated and flames and rages with desire to recover it. He describes the madness opposite to this as bestial, not ascending from the body's shape to divine intuition but descending shamefully to sexual union. He also describes a peculiarly human madness that is midway between the divine and the bestial; it is enkindled in the soul of the man who is busy admiring bodily shape but who neither surrenders the divine form entirely to oblivion nor recalls it entirely; consequently he is neither entirely intemperate nor entirely temperate, but seems, as it were, now incontinent, now continent.

[iv] Next Socrates inquires into the causes as to why some people love others more and others less. He has recourse to the stars, which have souls accompanying them from the beginning; for in the *Timaeus* Plato posits as many orders of human souls as there are stars in heaven.[8] Thence Socrates returns to dividing the soul's powers again: he calls reason the charioteer, the twin appetites, the paired horses; and the rational appetite he calls the good horse, the irrational appetite, the bad. The irrational appetite is less bad when it inclines to wrath; worse when it declines to concupiscence. But I shall treat more carefully of this later. Like a poet Socrates then depicts the passions of both continent and incontinent lovers and the love they share. You should not indulge in allegorizing the details here, therefore, in any other way than you would with the Song of Solomon.[9]

Chapter 3. Oratory, the orator, dialectic, and the use of writing.

[i] Having said this, and having dealt with the beauty pertaining to intelligence and the beauty pertaining to sight, Socrates

Denique virum purgata mente deo deditum omnibus inde bonis impleri solumque sapientem esse, quamvis quasi extra se positus vulgo derideatur velut insanus. Post hec descendit ad divinum legitimi amoris furorem, quem accendi putat in animo, quando, pulchram aspiciens corporis formam, divine pulchritudinis quam quondam contemplatus fuerat facile recordatur, illiusque recuperande desiderio inflammatur et furit. Sed contrarium huic describit furorem quasi ferinum, a forma corporis non ad divinum intuitum ascendentem sed ad venereum congressum turpiter descendentem. Describit rursus humanum quendam furorem inter divinum atque ferinum, in eius accessum[1] animo, qui admiratione [313] forme corporee occupatus, neque oblivioni divinam tradit omnino, neque penitus recordatur. Quo fit ut neque intemperatus sit[2] omnino neque etiam temperatus, sed modo quasi incontinens modo continens videatur.[3]

Querens postea causas ob quas alii alios[4] magis minusve ament, confugit ad sidera, quorum ab initio sint comites anime. Tot enim animarum ordines humanarum in Timeo disponit, quot in celo sunt stelle. Hinc revertitur iterum ad vires anime dividendas, et rationem quidem aurigam vocat, geminos vero appetitus[5] equos geminos: appetitum rationalem equum bonum, appetitum irrationalem equum malum; sed in hoc genere appetitum vergentem ad iracundiam minus malum, declinantem vero ad concupiscentiam magis malum.* Sed de his in sequentibus diligentius.** Deinde passiones amantium tam continentium quam incontinentium mutuumque amorem quasi poeta depingit. Quo fit ut non aliter his[6] allegorice indulgendum sit quam canticis Salomonis.

De oratione et oratore et dialectica usuque litterarum. Cap. III[7]

His actis, cum de pulchritudine que ad mentem et que ad visum pertinet tractaverit,[8] iam[9] ad examinandam orationem

---

[1]accensum PGHLFV   [2]fit EV   [3]*no* ¶ PGHLFV   [4]aut *add.* PGHLFV
[5]appetitos L   [6]his *om.* P   [7]*no ch. break or heading* GHLFV   [8]tractavisset PGHLFV
[9]iam *om.* P   *-**om.* GHLFV

now proceeds to examine Lysias's speech and to describe the
orator's function in order to show what kind of beauty there is
in a speech that pertains to hearing. He locates a speech's beauty
in the order: that is, it must have a beginning differing from the
end and have middle sections necessarily joined to the beginning, to the end, and to each other. This is the order he tells the
orator to observe preeminently. He proves that no one can be a
true orator, however, unless he has special knowledge of souls
and human affairs; and in order for the orator to be able to
acquire such knowledge, Socrates tells him to learn the ability to
divide and compound from the dialectician. This ability, he
maintains, is the best instrument for pursuing and finding the
truth; in the *Philebus* he calls it God's gift because, just as it's
the eternal office of God to divide and compound in the world,
so it's the dialectician's to do so in art.[10] Thus Socrates declares
that the most perfect dialectician, namely the metaphysician,
should be worshiped like a god.

[ii] Next he compares various orators and censures those who
deceive the people and themselves by putting the appearance of
truth before the real truth. Stupidly, they believe they can know
what most resembles the truth without even being acquainted
with the truth. Now take note of some excellent precepts. First,
the orator needs three things: natural ability, instruction, and
practice. To perfect each important human art and skill we need
philosophy. By practicing dialectic and contemplating sublimities, we eventually acquire intellectual sublimity and effective
power to act; and we need these two in particular to perfect the
major human arts and skills.

[iii] Next Socrates compares the illegitimate orator to cooks
and sycophants (as in the *Gorgias*) and the legitimate to a doctor.[11] He tells us the rule by which to know the nature of both
the soul and the body, or rather of everything, and then returns
to the orator's function. On the function of writing, he adds
that letters were invented in Egypt along with the other disciplines by a certain demon called Theuth. Socrates laughs at the
person who studies writing in the belief that through letters he
can reveal indubitable truth to posterity. In the manner of the

Lysie pergit atque oratoris officium demonstrandum, ut pateat qualis orationis pulchritudo sit que pertinet ad auditum. Pulchritudinem orationis in ordine collocat: videlicet ut caput habeat a fine differens, habeat et media capiti et fini et invicem necessario copulata. Huiusmodi ordinem in primis ab oratore precipit observari. Probat autem neminem oratorem verum esse [314] posse, nisi rerum presertim humanarum animorumque scientiam habeat. Quo autem orator id assequi possit, precipit, ut a dialectico facultatem discat dividendi atque componendi; quod[1] esse vult precipuum veritatis indagande inveniendeque instrumentum, et in Philebo dei nuncupat donum, propterea quod, sicut in mundo perpetuum dei officium est dividere atque componere, ita et dialectici est in arte. Ideoque[2] consummatum dialecticum id est metaphysicum iudicat tanquam deum esse colendum.[3]

Comparat post hec invicem oratores vituperatque eos qui verisimile vero anteponentes populum fallunt atque se ipsos stulteque confidunt quid veri potissimum simile sit etiam absque veri ipsius notitia posse cognoscere. Mox optima quedam nota precepta. Tria primum oratori necessaria sunt: ingenium, doctrina, exercitatio. Philosophia opus est ad ipsam maxime cuiusque artis perfectionem. Ab exercitatione dialectica rerumque[4] contemplatione sublimium tandem mentis sublimitas visque ad agendum efficax comparatur; que quidem duo in artium maximarum perfectione magnopere necessaria sunt.[5]

Deinde comparat oratorem non legitimum coquis adulatoribusque, quemadmodum in Gorgia, legitimum vero medico. Proinde regulam tradit qua tam animi quam corporis immo rei cuiusque natura sit cognoscenda. Statimque redit ad oratoris officium. Subdit ob[6] ipsum scribendi officium litteras in Egypto a demone quodam Theuthe una cum ceteris disciplinis inventas fuisse. Deridet preterea scribendi studium in eo videlicet qui per litteras indubitatam posteris confidat patefacere veritatem.

---

[1]qui GHLFV   [2]Itaque L   [3]*no* ¶ PGHLFV   [4]utrumque PGHLFV   [5]*no* ¶ PGHLFV   [6]id *add.* P

Pythagoreans, he affirms that the contemplation and transmission of truth occurs in souls rather than in books.[12] Plato also asserts this in his *Letters*.[13] Finally, Socrates praises only the orator who can be a philosopher through ability and study; and he concludes the dialogue with a speech and prayers entreating the soul's beauty from God. Take note here that Socrates, having utterly despised all else, is content with the soul's beauty alone, that is, with wisdom; but note too that he declared that this beauty was acquired not so much through human study as by a divine gift. Up till now this has been a summary of the whole dialogue.

Chapter 4. The poetic madness and the rest of the madnesses; their order, affinity, and usefulness. [245A-C, 265B]

[i] Next it seems worthwhile to explain some of this book's principal mysteries a little more fully. Let me first say something about poetry and the other madnesses that I have neglected in the *Phaedrus* and not dealt with elsewhere. To achieve poetic madness (the madness that may instruct men in divine ways and sing the divine mysteries), the soul of the future poet must be so affected as to become almost **tender** and **soft** and **untouched** too. The poet's province is very wide, and his material is varied; so his soul (which can be formed very easily) must subject itself to God. This is what we mean by becoming "soft" and "tender." If the soul has already received alien forms or blemishes because of its ability to be formed so easily, then it certainly cannot be formed in the meantime by the divine forms; and this is why Socrates added that the soul must be completely "untouched," that is, unblemished and clear.

[ii] Why did Socrates put poetry third in the degrees of madness—for he reminded us that prophecy was first, the hieratic art second, poetry third, and love fourth. It's because prophecy pertains mainly to knowing, the hieratic art to volition (so it succeeds prophecy), but poetry already declines to hearing. The ancient poets did not compose divine hymns until, admonished

Atque Pythagoreorum more[1] [315] probat contemplationem traditionemque veritatis in animos potius quam in libros. Quod in Epistolis quoque confirmat. Denique solum oratorem laudat qui ingenio sit studioque philosophus. Concludit vero dialogum oratione votisque pulchritudinem animi a deo petentibus. In qua considera Socratem ceteris omnino spretis sola pulchritudine animi id est sapientia esse contentum; verumtamen iudicare[2] hanc ipsam non tam humano studio quam divino munere comparari.

Hec fuerit hactenus totius dialogi summa.[3]

De furore poetico ceterisque furoribus et eorum ordine, coniunctione, utilitate. Cap. IIII

Opere pretium vero post hec fore videtur mysteria quedam huius libri precipua paulo latius explicare, ac primo que de poesi ceterisque furoribus hic et in Phedro pretermisi nec alibi declaravi. Oportet ad furorem poeticum consequendum, quo et homines divinis moribus instruantur mysteriaque divina canantur, animum futuri poete sic affectum esse, ut sit quasi **tener** atque **mollis,** preterea ut sit **intactus.** Amplissima enim est poete provincia omniformisque materia. Animus igitur se ipsum formatu facillimum formatori deo subicere debet. Quod quidem per mollem teneritudinem est expressum. At vero si ob eiusmodi facilitatem alienas iam formas[4] maculasve susceperit, certe divinis interim formari non poterit; propterea subiunctum est a Socrate intactum id est immaculatum vacuumque prorsus esse debere.

Sed curnam poesim gradu furorum tertio numeravit? Primo enim [316] vaticinium, secundo mysterium, tertio poesim, quarto amorem commemoravit. Quoniam vaticinium quidem ad cognitionem precipue pertinet, mysterium ad affectum[5] (mysterium igitur sequitur vaticinium), poesis autem ad audi-

---

[1] amore LV [2] indicate GHLFV [3] *this postscript om. and the* Phaedrus *translation beings* GHLFV [4] *for* iam formas P *reads* informas [5] effectum P

by the prophets and priests, they had first thought to celebrate the gods, to pray to them, to intercede, and to give thanks. The amatory madness, however, will be placed fourth; for it is usually excited through sight, which we naturally use after hearing. Besides, through prophecy and priestly mysteries we know God as the good, so we immediately worship divine things and sing [of them] poetically. We have not yet conceived of the amatory madness. After we have gazed at sensible beauty more attentively, however, and known the divine beauty, then we finally love God as the beautiful, having long ago cherished him as the good. In [commenting on] the *Symposium* and *Ion* I arranged the four madnesses in the order pertaining to the soul's restoration; here I have arranged the order insofar as it looks to the actual origin of madness.[14]

[iii] But it is pleasant to indulge the poets a little more. Whoever experiences any kind of spiritual possession is indeed overflowing on account of the vehemence of the divine impulse and the fullness of its power: he raves, exults, and exceeds the bounds of human behavior. Not unjustly, therefore, this possession or rapture is called **madness** and **alienation.** But no madman is content with simple speech: he bursts forth into clamoring and songs and poems. Any madness, therefore, whether the prophetic, hieratic, or amatory, justly seems to be released as poetic madness when it proceeds to songs and poems. And since poetic song and verse demand concord and harmony and every harmony is entirely included in the scale of nine (as I show in the *Timaeus* with music), the number nine seems rightly to have been consecrated to the Muses.[15]

[iv] Finally, having already described three species of madness, Socrates added that divine madness has **further remarkable results,** namely the wonderful effects of the amatory madness; for the remaining madness was love. Indeed, only love restores us to our celestial homeland and joins us with God, as will be apparent subsequently. The apostle Paul absolutely and incontrovertibly confirms this when he puts charity before all the divine gifts, however great.[16] But before Socrates can affirm that love restores us to heaven, he has to examine a number of

tum preterea iam declinat. Neque prius antiqui poete divinos hymnos composuerunt quam per vates sacerdotesque admoniti celebrare deos, precari, deprecari, gratias agere cogitarent. Quartus vero gradus furori dabitur amatorio. Hic enim per visum incitari solet, quo naturaliter utimur post auditum. Preterea per vaticinium mysteriaque deum agnoscimus tanquam bonum. Itaque mox divina colimus et poetice canimus. Furorem vero nondum concepimus amatorium. Sed postquam attentius sensibilem pulchritudinem spectaverimus, agnoverimusque[1] divinam, deum tandem amamus ut pulchrum quem iam pridem dilexeramus ut bonum. In Convivio quidem et Ione furorum quatuor ordinem quantum pertinet ad reductionem anime disposuimus, hic autem quantum spectat ad ipsam furoris originem.

Sed iuvat poetis paulo ulterius indulgere. Quicunque numine quomodolibet occupatur, profecto propter ipsam impulsus divini vehementiam virtutisque plenitudinem exuberat, concitatur, exultat, finesque et mores humanos excedit. Itaque occupatio hec sive raptus **furor** quidam et **alienatio** non iniuria nominatur. Furens autem nullus est simplici sermone contentus, sed in clamorem prorumpit et cantus et carmina. Quamobrem furor quilibet, sive fatidicus sive mysterialis seu amatorius, dum in cantus procedit et carmina, merito in furorem poeticum videtur [317] absolvi. Quoniam vero poeticus cantus atque versus exigit concentus harmonicos, harmonia vero omnis intra novenarium prorsus includitur, quod in Timei musica declaramas, merito novenarium Musis numerum consecravisse videntur.

Denique Socrates tribus furoris speciebus iam narratis addidit **plura** se habere divini furoris **preclara opera,** id est miros amatorii furoris effectus, amor enim erat reliquus. Solus certe nos amor patrie celesti restituit[2] copulatque[3] cum deo, quemadmodum in sequentibus apparebit. Quod quidem per Paulum Apostolum summopere confirmatur, ubi caritatem donis omnibus quantumlibet divinis extra controversiam anteponit. Sed Soc-

---

[1]cognoverimusque P   [2]restitituit E   [3]-que *om.* P

things concerning the condition of the soul, both divine and human. He must show first that the rational soul is sempiternal in order to prove that it gazed at one time upon the divine beauty along with the heavenly host, and that here it recalls the divine beauty through sensible beauty, and that, excited by love, it is recalled hence to sublimities and beatified.

Chapter 5. The soul is self-moving; so it is the principle of motion; so it is always being moved; so it is immortal.
[245C-246A]

[i] Since the *Theology* proved that the soul is the first to be moved in the universal hierarchy and is therefore self-moving and moves others,[17] it is agreed that the soul is the principle of motion and that its motion, being the first and most natural, is the most perfect motion in motion as a class; and, further, that this motion is universal, complete, circular, and sempiternal. But the soul's motion consists in life, and, in turn, the soul's life is engaged in perpetual motion. The soul is therefore immortal. This argument is further confirmed as follows. If that which is moved by another is moved for just so long as it is attached to its mover, surely that which is self-moved must always be engaged in motion, that is, always supplying itself naturally with life's motion and never forsaking itself.

[ii] Let me explain this a little more. Just as there are three main powers in the substance of fire—heat, light, and weightless thinness—so the soul's essence has three similar powers: first, the power of life, second, the power of understanding, third, the power of desiring. So, just as with fire the internal heat, light, and rising precede the external heating, lighting, and lifting, so the powers of understanding and desiring in the soul also perform their acts internally before producing them externally. Even more, the vital nature [i.e., the power of life], which is that which both propagates externally and is the inmost part of the soul's essence, performs its vital activity internally before it produces the effects of imparting life to the body. This vital

rates, antequam affirmet nos per amorem celo reddi, cogitur de
conditione anime tum divine tum humane multa disserere; primoque demonstrare rationalem animam sempiternam, ut pro-
bare possit hanc olim cum celicolis divinam pulchritudinem
inspexisse, eiusque hic per sensibilem pulchritudinem reminisci,
atque hinc amore concitam ad sublimia revocari efficique
beatam.

**Animam ex se moveri. Ergo motus esse[1] principium. Igitur
moveri semper. Esse igitur immortalem. Cap. V.**

Cum probatum in Theologia fuerit animam in universi gradibus esse primum quod movetur ideoque ex se moveri aliaque
movere, constat eam motus esse principium, motumque ipsius
tanquam primum maximeque naturalem esse in suo genere per-
fectissimum; propterea universalem absolutumque et circularem atque sempiternum. Motus autem anime consistit in vita,
vicissimque vita eius versatur in perpetuo motu. Est igitur immortalis. Quod [318] quidem hinc preterea confirmatur, quia si
illud quod[2] movetur ab alio, tamdiu movetur, quamdiu heret
motori, profecto quod ex se movetur, semper versatur in motu;
videlicet semper vitalem motum naturaliter sibi suppeditans nec
unquam deserens semet ipsum.

Sed hoc paulo latius explicemus. Sicut in substantia ignis tres
precipue vires sunt, calor et lux levisque subtilitas, sic tres in
ipsa anime essentia similes: prima quidem vis ipsa vitalis,[3]
secunda vero cognoscendi virtus, tertia est appetendi potentia.
Sicut igitur in igne prius est intus calere, lucere, ascendere,
quam exterior calefactio vel illuminatio vel elevatio, sic et in
anima cognoscendi et appetendi vires actus suos interiores
edunt, antequam in externa producant. Multo magis natura
vitalis que et propagatrix est et intima essentie sue, prius quam
effectus vivificandi producat in corpus, vitalem actum exercet
intrinsecus; eumque[4] temporaliter, alia videlicet semina alias

---

[1]est P   [2]*for* si illud quod P *reads* siquod   [3]vitalis *om.* P   [4]eumve P

activity takes place in time: that is, the soul brings forth internally various seeds at various times more or less in profusion,
and the sequence of notions in the understanding and the variety of choices in the appetite imitate this motion in time.

[iii] This is the reason why the soul's three powers also have
three internal motions. Just as the power of understanding
when it ponders incorporeals declares a realm exists within itself
which is free from the body, so the power of desiring when it
wishes for incorporeals and chooses many things that are contrary to the promptings of the corporeal condition is demon-
strating free will exists. Similarly, a realm flourishes within the
power of life (which is the foundation, as it were, of the other
two powers); that is, the power of life brings forth from itself a
certain vital act and effectual motion. By these means, therefore, the rational soul is self-moved and exists as the principle
of its own motion. This becomes fully apparent when the soul
makes progress in its life and studies together, and exercises its
free will to improve itself. For, in showing itself the good life, it
indicates that it has, in a way, first shown itself life and also,
since it can never forsake itself, perpetual life. To the extent
that the soul turns towards itself and towards divine things and
shows that it has its own motions, which may surmount the corporeal condition, it testifies too that it does not depend on the
body and that it agrees with divine things and that therefore,
separated from the body, it can live united with divinity.

[iv] The argument that before we can go from bodies, which
are all moved by another, to reach intellectuals, which are completely unmoving, we have to proceed via the soul's nature,
which is self-moving, this and other arguments pertaining to the
same problem I have dealt with sufficiently in the *Theology* and
in [an introduction to] the tenth book of the *Laws*.[18] I have also
proved that the irrational life subject to the body is not the
soul's true substance, nor is it freely self-moving or self-acting.
In part it depends on the rational soul (whether particular or
universal) as a mirror image depends on the face; in part it is
excited by natural influences; in part it is impelled by external
objects. But the substance of the rational soul is properly alone
in being freely and absolutely self-moving in its own particular

intus magis minusve proferens. Temporalem eiusmodi motionem imitatur tum in cognitione discursio notionum, tum in appetitu varietas[1] eligendi.

Hac igitur ratione circa tres anime vires tres quoque sunt intimi motus. Atque sicut ipsa cognoscendi virtus liberum a corpore principatum in se ipsa declarat quando cogitat incorporea, sic et appetendi potentia liberum demonstrat arbitrium, ubi vult incorporea multaque eligit contra quam incitet conditio corporalis. Similiter in virtute vitali, que harum quasi fundamentum est, viget aliquis principatus, videlicet ex se ipso actum quendam vividum motumque proferens efficacem. His itaque modis anima rationalis ex se ipsa movetur principiumque sui motus [319] existit. Quod quidem plane confirmat quando proficit in vita simul et disciplina, et pro arbitrio se efficit meliorem. Dum enim sibimet exhibet bene vivere, indicat et vivere sibi prius quodammodo prebuisse, et cum nunquam se deserat, vivere quoque semper. Presertim quia, quatenus ad se ipsam et ad divina se convertit ostenditque proprios se motus habere, qui conditionem superent corporalem, eatenus quoque testatur se a corpore non pendere cumque divinis congruere, iccirco posse separatam a corpore vivere divinitati coniunctam.

Quod autem oporteat super corpora omnia que moventur ab alio, antequam perveniamus ad intellectualia que omnino stabilia sunt, procedere per naturam anime que sit mobilis ex se ipsa, et cetera ad eiusmodi materiam pertinentia, satis in Theologia et decimo Legum libro tractavimus. Probavimus etiam irrationalem vitam corpori mancipatam nec esse veram anime substantiam nec ex se ipsa libereve moveri vel agere; sed partim ab anima rationali sive particulari sive universali pendere, sicut a vultu imaginem specularem, partim a naturalibus influxibus agitari, partim ab externis obiectis impelli. Soli vero rationalis anime substantie convenire ut ex se libere et absolute suo quodam pacto moveatur et moveat atque agat. Itaque omnis ratio-

---

[1]veritas P

way and in being able to move and act on others. So every rational soul, human and divine alike, can be said to be the principle of motion. Every such soul Socrates adjudges immortal, for he promised he would talk about the rational soul alone.

[v] If somebody objects that the irrational soul appears to be the principle of motion in that it introduces from itself vegetative activities and vital qualities to the body, I will reply that it is not the principle, but an instrument. For in so doing the irrational soul is moved by the world-soul and the soul of its sphere. Similarly, the Platonists argue that the elements are drawn upwards and downwards by the soul of their sphere and that the elemental qualities in their actions also are instruments of the universal nature, as I describe in the *Theology*.[19] Indeed, since in the irrational soul the superior power (which pertains to knowledge and desire) does not act but is acted on and is drawn along by the nature's instinct and the impulse of externals, so it follows that the inferior power (which looks to vegetative activity and motion) does not act as the principle but is acted on as the instrument.

Chapter 6. What soul is all and totally soul and how it is the principle of motion. Also how the principle of motion is sempiternal. On the first principle and the rest of the principles. [245C-246A]

[i] It is worth noting that Socrates said, not that every soul is immortal, but that **all soul is immortal**: that is, only that soul is immortal which is all and totally soul. I am talking not only about the world-soul (for Socrates himself clearly considers a number of souls immortal) but about any soul that is whole and has, as it were, all souls within itself (since it has all the powers of the soul within itself) and is the universe, so to speak (since it possesses all the innate forms). Such is any rational soul, for it is one through its universality with the world-soul: it participates of a like immortality and is included in the same demonstration of immortality. For the same reason any rational soul can be said to be the principle of motion (as I said above),

nalis anima tam humana quam divina motus principium dici potest, omnisque talis anima immortalis a[1] Socrate iudicatur. De hac enim sola dicturum se esse promisit.

Siquis autem obiciat animam irrationalem videri principium motus quatenus ipsa ex se vegetales actus vitalesque qualitates edit in corpus, respondebimus non habere veram principii rationem [320] sed instrumenti. In hoc enim opere sic ab anima mundi atque sphere sue moveri sicut Platonici putant elementa sursum deorsumque ab anima sue sphere trahi, immo et qualitates elementales in actionibus quoque suis esse nature universalis organa, quemadmodum in Theologia tractamus. Profecto cum in anima irrationali vis prestantior que ad cognitionem appetitumque pertinet non tam agat quam agatur trahaturque instinctu nature externorumque impulsu, merito vis inferior ad vegetationem motumque spectans non quidem agit ut principium sed agitur ut instrumentum.

Que sit anima omnis atque tota et quomodo principium motus. Item quomodo principium motus sit sempiternum. De principio primo ceterisque principiis. Cap. VI.

Animadversione dignum est Socratem non dixisse omnis anima est immortalis, sed **anima omnis est immortalis**: id est illa quidem anima dumtaxat immortalis est que est omnis totaque anima. Non inquam anima mundi sola—ipse enim Socrates multas proculdubio numerat immortales—sed quecunque anima integra est et in se quasi omnes animas habet, cum omnes anime vires in se possideat, et quasi est universum, cum formas omnes ingenitas habeat. Quelibet rationalis anima est eiusmodi. Hac enim universitate convenit cum anima mundi, similisque immortalitatis est compos atque eadem immortalitatis demonstratione comprehenditur. Eadem ratione quelibet rationalis anima (ut supra diximus) motus principium dici potest, etsi non

---

[1]P *begins the paragraph here instead of at* Siquis

though not every rational soul is the first and universal principle of motion, as this is the office of the world-soul. Other rational souls—those of the spheres, the stars, the demons, and men—are the principles of their own movement, their bodies, their lives, their provinces of activity. Also, any rational soul's power is so great that any one soul in a way may be the universe. Whenever it withdraws into its own fullness, it will unfold all the varieties of notions and powers in itself; and it will pursue the universal providence as if it were the colleague of any celestial soul and even of the world-soul. This is the reason, therefore, that the offices Socrates refers to are appropriate mainly to the world-soul. Then, of course, they are also in accord with celestial souls, and they are certainly common in a way to all rational souls, or at least can be common to them at some time. So the reasons for the world-soul's immortality appear to confirm the other rational souls' immortality also.

[ii] Here we have to remember that Socrates speaks, not about every principle, but particularly about the principle of motion, the producer of all the species of motion. If motion itself as a species is sempiternal like the rest of the species, then a fortiori the cause of motion is sempiternal, namely the soul, which is called the **fountain** and **principle** of movements: fountain, since as universal motion it perpetually flows out of itself, into itself, and into others; principle, since it effectively controls what is in motion. As the soul performs all the species of motion and is thus the origin of generation, it is necessarily **ungenerated** itself. Otherwise, since generation also pertains to motion, the soul would be moved by another and would not exist as the principle of motion.

[iii] Any principle whatsoever, with regard to the nature or property in which it is the primary instance and of which it is the principle, cannot be caused by another at all. The sun is the primary light-giving object. So it is self-shining, formally and sensibly, and nothing else lights it. But, insofar as it is a substance and body and the sun, these properties are all allotted it from a higher principle. Insofar as it already exists as the sun, it shines naturally through itself; and because it shines, it lights others. For the sun was established with the condition that it would

omnis anima primum motionis et universale principium; hoc enim anime [321] mundane munus.[1] Sed relique rationales anime spherarum, stellarum, demonum, hominum, principia sunt movendi circa se ipsas et corpora propria et vitas provinciasque suas. Tanta quoque potestas est cuiuslibet rationalis anime ut quelibet quodammodo sit universum; et siquando in suam[2] amplitudinem se receperit, omniformes in se notiones et vires explicatura sit, providentiamque universalem prosequutura, quasi collega celestis cuiuslibet anime atque mundane. Hac igitur ratione munera que tangit Socrates in primis mundane anime propria, mox etiam celestibus competentia, nimirum et rationalibus omnibus quodammodo vel iam sunt vel saltem quandoque possunt esse communia. Iccirco rationes pro immortalitate anime mundane reliquarum quoque rationalium animarum immortalitatem confirmare videntur.

Meminisse vero oportet Socratem hic non de omni principio loqui, sed proprie de principio motus quod sane omnes motionum species efficit. Profecto si species ipsa motus quemadmodum et cetere species sempiterna est, multo magis sempiterna est ipsa causa motus, id est anima que motionum **fons** et **principium** appellatur: fons quidem quoniam ex ipsa in ipsam et in alia iugiter motus profluit universus; principium vero quia mobilibus efficaciter dominatur. Iam vero cum omnes species motus agat ideoque generationis sit origo, necessario est **ingenitum**; alioquin, cum ad motum generatio quoque pertineat, ab alio moveretur neque principium motus existeret.

Omnino vero principium quodvis, secundum naturam illam vel proprietatem [322] in qua primum est et cuius est principium, effici non potest ab alio. Sol lucentium primum est. Ita igitur ex se formaliter sensibiliterque lucet, ut non illustretur ab alio. Ut autem est substantia quedam et corpus et sol, id totum a principio superiore sortitur. Qua vero ratione sol iam existit, eadem naturaliter per se lucet; et qua lucet, illustrat. Hac enim conditione institutus est sol ut suapte natura luceret. Similiter

---

[1]munus *om.* P   [2]summam P

shine of its own nature. Similarly, the first intellect is the principle of intellectual offices and of many-sided understanding and is naturally intelligent of itself. From elsewhere it acquired the property of being one living, perfect, and preeminently knowing entity. But it produced the property of many-sided understanding naturally in itself and then offered it to those below. A variegated cloud, having received the ray of the sun, may likewise produce various colors in itself. So the simple fact of the cloud's shining derives effectively from the sun; the fact of the cloud's reflecting a particular color derives, at least formally, from itself.

[iv] The soul derives from its own nature the ability to move itself and others; and it depends on nothing else for this property of motion. As long as this principle of motion is not moved by another, then in justice it neither is born nor dies; for generation and death occur through a motion.

[v] Socrates did not deny that the soul exists and understands from another; for it exists from the good, and it has many-sided understanding from the prime intellect. But Socrates did deny that the soul becomes, is born, dies; for these three pertain to motion. The principle of motion, since it may not be moved by another, in justice may not become, be generated, or die; and it is impossible to imagine it being self-generated, since it would then exist before it existed.

[vi] Were you to imagine the principle of motion dying, then all motion would cease and every moving thing would stop; for they depend alike on the principle of motion. This would certainly happen in the future, in brief, were the world-soul to perish, and, likewise, were every soul to perish communally. It would certainly happen too if every soul perished singly, this or that soul separately. Indeed, if our soul perished, the entire generation of men together with the species itself would perish simultaneously. If the soul of this or that celestial sphere were destroyed, all generation subject to that sphere as its province would simultaneously be destroyed. Finally, if you could conceive of any one of the rational souls being destroyed, then you would be, necessarily, conceiving of the destruction of the rest of the souls; for all souls have been created by the same eternal

intellectus primus intellectualium munerum et intelligentie mul-
tiformis est principium, naturaliter intelligens ex se ipso. Et aliunde quidem nactus est, ut sit ens unum et vivum atque perfectum eminentissimeque cognoscens, intellectualem vero proprietatem eiusmodi atque multiformem naturaliter peperit in se
ipso, et in sequentia protulit. Quemadmodum varia nubes
accepto solis radio colores in se varios procreat. Nubes igitur ut
simpliciter luceat efficienter habet a sole; ut autem tali quodam
colore refulgeat habet saltem formaliter ex se ipsa.

Anima ut moveatur et moveat possidet suapte natura; atque
in hac ipsa motionis proprietate non aliunde dependet. Hoc itaque principium motus, dum non movetur ab alio, merito neque
generatur neque interit. Generatio enim et interitus motu quodam accidunt.

Non negavit Socrates hoc ab alio existere vel intelligere; existit enim ex ipso bono, intelligit quoque multiformiter ex intellectu primo. Sed negavit fieri, nasci, interire; hec enim ad
motum pertinent. Principium vero motus, cum non moveatur
ab alio, merito neque fit neque generatur neque interit. Ex se
ipso vero gene[323]rari ne fingi quidem potest, alioquin esset
prius quam esset.

Quod si interire fingatur, mox desinet omnis motus, desinet
et omne mobile; utrumque enim dependet ex principio motus.
Id quidem futurum summatim certum est si forsan interierit
anima mundi, item si omnis communiter anima; certum etiam
singulatim, si hec anima seorsum perierit aut illa. Nempe si desinat anima nostra, simul tota hominum generatio speciesque
peribit. Sin anima huius globi celestis vel illius tollatur e medio,
tota simul generatio sibi subiecta per provinciam suam aufere-
tur. Denique si unam quandam rationalium animarum disperdi
cogites, simili ratione perire ceteras cogitabis. Omnes enim ab
eodem eterno patre similibus proportionibus sunt absque medio
procreate. Sic igitur ad[1] anime cuiusvis interitum quodammodo

---

[1] ab P

Father without an intermediary and with similar proportions. So the consequence of any soul thus perishing would seem, in a way, to be the downfall of the world's machine, that is, the corporeal machine. For the order of stable things proceeds, not from the mobile soul, but from a higher principle.

[vii] Finally, insofar as the meaning of a principle is concerned, it is one thing to compare certain principles to their respective orders, another to refer all principles to the principle of principles in every possible way. As I said [in commenting] on the *Parmenides,* the principle of principles excels them by an interval that is far greater than that separating them from their subordinate orders.[20] For both the principles and their subordinate orders possess the condition of being finite, and both derive from the one principle that mutually reconciles them all. The principle of principles is infinite and not subject along with them to any [higher] principle by whose law it could be connected with the [other] principles in any way. Although we can find something similar between the subordinate orders and their respective principles, something that shares at least the same name if not the same reason for it, yet we cannot conceive of anything in the orders or their respective principles which is like the principles' principle. So, although any excellence at all either in the principles or in things eventually derives from the first principle, I can maintain nonetheless that many individual properties emanate internally, as it were, from themselves. This is because, as Plato says, nothing similar is found in the first principle, upon which they all depend entirely as their maker and end.[21] Meanwhile they formally bear in themselves many individual properties that are worthy of them but not of the first principle.

Chapter 7. The idea of the soul. The classes of being. The charioteer, horses, wings, wheels, and chariot. [246AB]

[i] You must understand that in approaching the task of depicting **the idea of the soul,** Socrates is concerned, not with its

videtur consequenter machina ruitura; corporalis inquam machina. Rerum namque stabilium ordo non ab anima mobili sed ab altiore quodam principio proficiscitur.[1]

Denique quantum ad rationem principii pertinet, aliud quidem est propria quedam principia ad suos ordines comparare, aliud autem principia cuncta ad ipsum principiorum principium quoquomodo referre. Ut enim diximus in Parmenide, hoc illa longiore admodum supereminet intervallo quam illa sibi subditos ordines. Nam et principia illa et ordines finitam conditionem habent, et utraque[2] sunt ab uno invicem cuncta conciliante. Principium vero principiorum infinitum est, et nulli subest una cum illis per cuius legem possit ullo pacto cum principiis coniugari. Quamobrem etsi possumus inter ipsos rerum [324] ordines propriaque ordinum principia quasi simile aliquid invenire, eiusdemque saltem nominis si non rationis eiusdem compos, tamen nihil vel in ordinibus vel in principiis ordinum simile ad ipsum principiorum principium cogitari potest. Itaque etsi quicquid usquam optimi principiis atque rebus inest a primo tandem provenit, nihilominus asserere possumus multa intus ex ipsis quasi propria quedam emanare. Quandoquidem, ut inquit Plato, nihil tale reperitur in primo, a quo tanquam efficiente prorsus atque fine cuncta dependent. Que formaliter interim peculiaria secum multa ferunt digna quidem ipsis sed non digna primo.

Idea anime; genera entis; auriga, equi, ale, rote, currus. Cap. VII.

Ubi Socrates **ideam anime** aggreditur effingendam, tu ideam anime hic intellige non supernum eius exemplar, sed formam

---

[1]*no* ¶ P   [2]*-que om.* P

supernal model, but with its inner form, the disposition of its powers, and its shape, as it were. The soul as divine is known only to divine beings. But we use comparisons at least to think about it. Take these six conceptions: first the unity that is essence's particular crown, then essence itself, then the remaining four classes of being—motion, rest, difference, and identity. The **charioteer** is the intellect and equals the essence. The **charioteer**'s **head** is the power that unites him to the universe's principle, and rules over the intellect, and equals the unity. The **better horse** is the rational power, which may examine either universals or particulars. Its companion, the [irrational] appetite, is also called a horse. In ourselves and the gods alike, the better horse and the charioteer participate in identity more than in difference, in rest more than in motion. The **worse horse** is the imagination together with the nature (that is, the vegetative power), and the appetite, the companion of both. In us this worse horse presumably participates in motion and difference more than their opposites, but in the gods these opposites are tempered. In us the worse horse (that is, the less good) is said to be **contrary**, not because it is bad or wicked, but because it would rather follow the opposite elements [of motion and difference]. So it is called the contrary horse because it is constituted in the main from the contrary—that is, the opposite—elements. Both powers are called horses because of motion. The wing is the upward-drawing power: through this power the divine souls are said to be **winged**, meaning "on the wing," for they are always uplifted; but our souls are **winged**, meaning "fledged," for they can at least be uplifted. Preeminently the wings are the charioteer's, then the better horse's, and only finally the worse horse's, since the worse horse can be raised by the better and can share a certain blessedness with it. Each horse's power [or wing] is akin, for both horses were generated simultaneously by the world's author and are sempiternal. They are said therefore to be **yoked** and **paired**, so to speak: one thinks of them as making up what one might call a two-horsed chariot (hence my use of the term *yoke*). Strictly speaking, by a **chariot** I mean a celestial body—sempiternal, spherical, and by

ipsius intimam dispositionemque virium suarum et quasi figuram. Que quidem tanquam divina solis nota est divinis. Nos
autem hanc per comparationes excogitamus. Accipe sex termi-
nos: primo quidem unitatem que apex quidam est essentie,
deinde essentiam, cum quatuor reliquis generibus entis, motu,
statu, alteritate, identitate. **Auriga** quidem est intellectus con-
gruens cum essentia. **Caput** autem **aurige** est unifica virtus ad
ipsum universi principium, intellectui presidens, cum unitate
conveniens. **Melior equus** est virtus ipsa rationalis, sive per uni-
versalia discurrat, sive per singula. Dicitur equus etiam[1] appetitus eius comes. Est autem equus eiusmodi sicut et auriga tam in
nobis quam in diis identitatis magis quam alteritatis particeps,
statusque [325] magis quam motus. **Equus** vero **deterior** est
imaginatio una cum natura, id est vegetali potentia, appetitus-
que utriusque comes. Equus eiusmodi in nobis quidem motus
alteritatisque[2] magis quam oppositorum compos existimatur, in
diis autem adequat opposita. Ideo equus deterior id est minus
bonus dicitur in nobis **contrarius,** non quia malus vel turpis, sed
quia opposita potius sequitur elementa. Dicitur ergo contrarius,
quoniam ex contrariis scilicet ex oppositis elementis est potius
constitutus. Ambe vires nominantur equi propter motum. Ala
vero est potentia sursum ducens; per quam anime quidem divine
dicuntur **alate** quoniam semper sunt elevate, nostre vero **sub-
alate,**[3] quoniam saltem elevari possunt. Ale potissimum sunt
aurige, mox melioris equi, consequenter vero deterioris, quoniam per meliorem attolli potest atque cum ipso beatitudinis
cuiusdam esse particeps. Equi utriusque potentia est connata;
uterque enim simul est ab opifice mundi genitus atque sempiter-
nus. Ideo dicuntur et **coniugati** et quasi **bigas** vel (ut ita dixerim)
bigam conficere iudicantur, quam ego coniugii appellatione
interpretatus sum. **Currum** vero proprie corpus celeste vocamus
cum immortali qualibet anima sempiternum sphericumque

---

[1]et P   [2]-que *om.* P   [3]sublate P

nature swiftest in motion—with any kind of immortal soul. I can also call the soul a chariot because of motion: the two wheels are the soul's turning back to itself and its conversion again to higher things.

[ii] But I think we should return for a short while to that head of the charioteer; for it is double. I have sufficiently described one aspect as able to join with the principle; but the other is that which is immediately proximate and unites completely with the intelligible world, and this is the highest act of the understanding and instant intuition. The understanding's circuit comes next, which is swiftest, and then the reason's circuit immediately, which is, so to speak, slower; then comes the imagination's [period], and then the nature's. The charioteer's two heads are like the two poles of the sphere. The understanding's swiftest circuit resembles the firmament's diurnal motion and the whole celestial machine's. The reason's slower circuit resembles the planets' motions: its more universal and contemplative circuit resembles Saturn, Jupiter, and the Sun; its more particular and practical circuit, Mars, Venus, Mercury, and the Moon. The imagination's period is like the aether's subcelestial revolution; the nature's period, like air and water's revolution.

Chapter 8. How all soul cares for all that is soulless. The soul's sublime state. The soul's fall. The plane and solid body. The mortal and immortal animal. [246B-D]

[i] When he says **all soul cares for all that is soulless,**[22] Plato perhaps means, not that this or that soul takes care of the whole world as the world-soul does, but that every part of the world is cared for by some one of the souls. Thus everything eventually is cared for by all the souls. Perhaps he also means (as his subsequent arguments signify) that any rational soul can both betake itself by degrees through all the world's spheres and then be taken back sometime into heaven to the universal providence dwelling there. The soul has been formed to do this, he says, **at different times in different species.** The particular soul of a man

natura motuve celerrimum. Animam quoque currum appellare possumus propter motum, rotas autem duas conversionem anime ad se ipsam conversionemque iterum ad superna.[1]

Sed redeundum parumper[2] arbitror ad illud aurige caput. Est enim geminum: unum quidem quod satis expressi unificum cum principio; alterum vero huic subinde contiguum uniens maxime cum intelligibili mundo, summus videlicet [326] actus intelligentie intuitusque subitus. Cui mox succedit circuitus intelligentie velocissimus; huic subinde rationis circuitus quasi tardior; huic imaginationis; huic vero nature. Duo quidem capita duobus sphere polis similia sunt. Circuitus autem intelligentie velocissimus similis [est] diurno firmamenti totiusque celestis machine motui. Circuitus rationis tardior similis est motibus[3] planetarum: universalior quidem magisque contemplativus Saturno, Iovi, Soli, particularior vero magisque practicus Marti, Veneri, Mercurio, Lune; imaginationis periodus revolutioni etheris sub celo similis, periodus vero[4] nature revolutioni aeris atque aque.[5]

Quomodo anima omnis totius inanimati curam habeat. De statu anime sublimi. De casu anime. De corpore plano atque de solido. De animali mortali atque immortali. Cap. VIII.

Quando dicit **anima omnis totius inanimati curam habet** forte non vult ita hanc vel illam curare mundum totum quemadmodum anima mundi, sed omnes mundi partes ab aliqua animarum coli adeo ut omne tandem colatur ab omnibus. Forte etiam vult, quod per sequentia significatur, quamlibet animam rationalem posse tum per omnes mundi spheras gradatim se conferre, tum etiam in celo habitantem ad universalem ibi providentiam quandoque recipi. Inquit autem **alias in aliis speciebus constitutam** id efficere. Id quidem pro anima particulari vel hominis vel inferioris demonis dictum puta que pluribus peragit

---

[1] *no* ¶ P   [2] parum P   [3] motui P   [4] rationis *add.* P   [5] aqua E

or lower demon, for instance, does this by acting through a number of points in time and space; the celestial soul does it with a disposition that stays the same. Therefore, in this species of body and life, our soul lives now on earth. At another time, in a purer body and life, it inhabits, by degrees, the higher spheres. Eventually, in seeking celestial things again with its celestial body, not only does it return to its own star someday, but in the presence of any star it can live the life conformable to that star. Any planet governs the whole, but with its own property: Jupiter gives something Jovian to all, the Sun something Solarian, and the rest likewise. The absolutely universal providence alone gives everything to all. So, in devoting itself to Jupiter or the Sun, our soul seems to receive, in a way, a providence like the whole's and like the world-soul's; when, that is, it has been completely restored to the amplitude of its reasons, powers, and notions.

[ii] So it was correct for Socrates to say, not that every soul, but that all soul takes care of the whole machine [of the world]; for he is referring to the rational soul, which has all the soul's powers and the forms of things in itself. While it preserves its universality by action and affection, the rational soul inhabits heaven along with the universal souls of the celestial beings; in the interim it can gaze on the whole intelligible world with the speculative intellect and simultaneously regard the whole sensible world with the practical. It performs this office of the universal providence either with the universal reason in its simplicity, as the world-soul does, or with the universal reason in the manner of Saturn, Jupiter, the Sun, or the others.

[iii] So the rational soul is said to retain its wings as long as it undertakes these sublime activities in the highest degree. But whenever its wings (the powers recalling it to its sublime activities) become less free, whenever, so to speak, it has neglected the world's universal form and gazes more diligently on some particular province of the world and loves its life more ardently —being attracted to it by the imagination and vital power simultaneously—then the soul, in a way, contracts. Moreover, it acquires under heaven a more contracted body, that is, an airy

intervallis et vicibus quod celestis anima eodem efficit habitu. Quapropter anima nostra nunc quidem in [327] hac specie corporis atque vite colit terram, alias autem in corpore vitaque puriore gradatim spheras sublimiores habitat. Denique cum celesti corpore suo celestia repetens non solum ad suam quandoque stellam revertitur sed penes quamlibet stellam potest vitam agere stelle conformem. Planeta quilibet gubernat totum sed proprietate sua. Iupiter quidem dat omnibus aliquid ioviale, Sol omnibus quoque solare ceterique similiter. Sola providentia prorsus universalis dat omnibus omnia. Nostra igitur anima, se Iovi accommodans aut Soli, similem quodammodo totius providentiam sortiri videtur, similem quoque cum anima mundi, quando[1] videlicet in amplitudinem rationum et virium notionumque suarum penitus restituta fuerit.

Quamobrem merito non dixit Socrates omnis anima, sed anima omnis totam colit machinam, id est anima rationalis que in se omnes habet anime vires rerumque formas. Hec quidem, dum suam actu et affectu conservat universitatem, celum habitat cum universalibus[2] celestium animabus; potestque interim et intellectu speculativo totum mundum intelligibilem contueri et practico simul totum sensibilem circunspicere; sive id universalis providentie munus agat universali simpliciter ratione sicut anima mundi, sive universali quidem ratione, sed more Saturni vel Iovis aut Solis vel aliorum.

Eatenus igitur alas dicitur retinere dum videlicet sublimia hec eminenter attingit. Siquando vero alas id est vires ad sublimia revocantes minus habeat expeditas, id est quando universali mundi forma quasi iam neglecta particularem quandam mundi pro[328]vinciam diligentius intueatur et eiusmodi vitam amet ardentius, alliciente videlicet ad eandem imaginatione simul potentiaque vitali, mox animus quodammodo fit angustior; corpusque preterea sub celo quoddam adsciscit angustius id est aerium, donec etiam factus angustior in angustissimum descen-

body. The soul continues contracting until it descends into the most contracted body of all, the earthy. But its prime name everywhere is man: in heaven, celestial man; in the air, airy man; and on earth, earthy man.

[iv] When Socrates calls the body **solid**, Hermias wants it to refer to the material body under heaven (and heaven not to possess matter).[23] So he wants to call the celestial body "plane" and the elemental body "solid." Hence the Platonic precept: Don't add depth to plane.[24] Hence too Zoroaster's magical saying: Don't weigh down spirit, don't at some time assign depth to what is plane.[25] It's as if the soul's ever-familiar celestial body were called, because of its purity at least, "spirit" and "plane." But because of its inclination towards the elements, and having already acquired a material, that is, a thicker, body, the soul immediately appears to acquire depth.

[v] The human animal can be called both **immortal** and **mortal**: immortal insofar as it consists of a rational soul and its celestial body, mortal insofar as it is joined to an elemental body. But any mundane god is an absolutely immortal animal. Socrates therefore warns us lest we perhaps be deceived when we consider the composition of an immortal animal. We suppose that a mundane god is an animal with a soul and body naturally and perpetually joined. This is true up to a point, but we do not comprehend it with any certain reason, particularly if we ever conceive of this union in terms of the intercourse between the soul and the mortal, earthy body. For the latter is not utterly ready for life. Instead of the body approaching the soul, the soul is borne down to the body in a headlong fall and sustains it only with effort and governs it with care. Yet this does not happen with the soul and the celestial body. For the latter turns towards the soul with a sort of wonderful readiness in the same way as the soul turns towards it, as Plotinus frequently maintains.[26] The elemental body does not possess the power to receive life to the degree that the soul has to bestow life; so it does not live forever, nor is it entirely nor perfectly whole. The celestial body, however, does possess the power to the same degree; so it seizes the whole life equally and wholly and preserves it forever.

dat atque terrenum. Ubique vero in primis nominatur homo, sed in celo quidem homo celestis, in aere aerius, in terra terrenus.

Ubi vero Socrates nominat corpus **solidum** Hermias materiale sub celo vult intelligi, celumque non habere materiam; ideo celeste corpus dici planum, elementale vero solidum. Hinc preceptum illud Platonicum: noli addere plano profundum. Hinc et magicum illud a Zoroastre[1] dictum: noli gravare spiritum, vel quod planum est reddere quandoque profundum; quasi celeste corpus anime semper[2] familiare saltem propter puritatem nominetur spiritus atque planum, sed propter inclinationem animi ad elementa iam addito materiali id est crassiore[3] quodam corpore mox profundum fieri videatur.[4]

Humanum hoc animal et **immortale** dici potest atque **mortale**: immortale quidem quantum ex anima rationali et celesti suo corpore constat, mortale vero quantum elementale corpus est adiunctum.[5] Deus autem quilibet mundanus est animal simpliciter immortale. Admonet ergo Socrates ne forte de compositione animalis immortalis cogitantes decipiamur. Fingimus quidem mundanum deum esse quoddam animal habens animam et corpus naturaliter perpetuoque copulata; et vere quidem hactenus, sed id nulla ratione certa comprehendimus, presertim siquando de hac copula sentiamus quem[329]admodum de commertio anime cum corpore mortali atque terreno. Hoc enim non omnino aptum est ad vitam, nec tam hoc accedit ad animam quam anima precipiti quodam lapsu defertur ad ipsum et labore substinet curaque gubernat. Nec tamen ita contingit circa celeste corpus et animam. Hoc enim sic ad eam mira quadam preparatione quasi se confert, sicut hec ad ipsum, quod sepe Plotinus inquit. Corpus quidem elementale non tantam habet potentiam, ut vitam accipiat, quantam anima, ut prestet vitam. Ideo non semper vivit neque totum penitus neque perfecte. Celeste vero corpus habet equalem. Quamobrem totum eque totam rapit vitam semperque conservat.

[1] *em.;* Zoroaste EP   [2] super- P   [3] *for* id est crassiore P *reads* vel saltem   [4] *no* ¶ P
[5] advinctum E

[vi] Heaven is so close to soul and vice versa that what is vital motion in soul proceeds in heaven as dimension and circuit; and what is understanding in soul proceeds in heaven as light. So, if heaven has no matter at all, as many believe, dimension alone has to be subtracted, and it becomes soul. The soul has only to be extended into dimension (and you can imagine this happening easily, since it is always in motion), and it immediately becomes heaven. So the power in heaven to be easily formed is commensurate with the soul's power to form heaven. Every celestial vehicle under its soul therefore sustains life with a wonderful ease and retains it forever: it is a sort of life extended out from the soul.

[vii] What among mathematicians is a unity, point, line, plane, solid, in the universe is the one, mind, soul, heaven, and the subcelestial region. Just as a point results from unity with the simple addition, so to speak, of position, so mind seems to proceed from the one with an addition of essence. Again, just as a line is the product of extending a point through motion, so soul comes from motion added, as it were, to mind. Again, just as a line extended to a line produces a plane, so soul proceeds as heaven when, as it were, it swells. Finally, just as a plane moved through depth becomes a solid, so when heaven in a certain descent, so to speak, submits to matter, or a state resembling matter, it seems to become elemental body.

Chapter 9. How everything divine is good, wise, and beautiful. Again, on beauty and love. [246DE]

[i] There is a power in the soul dragging it downwards towards sensibles, namely the power responsible simultaneously for imagination and vegetative functions; there is also a power higher than this lifting the soul towards divine things. If the worse power can sometimes lead away the better, then the better can certainly lead the worse back again. In the same way the sun's power lifts dampness upwards, which otherwise naturally descends. The elevating power in the soul's intellect or reason is

Profecto celum est adeo propinquum anime atque vicissim, ut quod est motus vitalis in anima in celo evadat dimensio atque circuitus; quod rursus in anima intellectus est idem in celo lumen. Celum itaque, si nullam habet materiam ut multi putant, sola dimensione subducta fit anima. Atque hec in solam porrecta dimensionem, quam facile fingitur subitura quia semper est in motu, fit e vestigio celum. Quanta igitur potentia est in anima ad formandum[1] celum tanta est in celo facilitas ut formetur. Omne itaque celeste vehiculum sub anima sua mira vitam facilitate suscipit retinetque semper; atque est quasi vita quedam ex anima porrecta foras.[2]

Itaque quod apud mathematicos est unitas, punctum, linea, planum, solidum, id in universo ipsum unum, mens, anima, celum, regioque sub celo. Sicut enim punctum simplici positione quasi ex unitate resultat, sic intellectus positione quadam essentie provenire videtur ex uno. Item sicut ex puncto per motum producto fit linea, [330] sic menti quasi addito motu fit anima. Rursus quemadmodum linea in lineam velut extenta facit planum, sic anima quasi tumens evadit celum. Denique sicut planum commotum per profunda fit solidum, ita celum quasi descensu quodam subiens vel materiam vel conditionem materie similem elementale corpus videtur evadere.

Quomodo divinum omne sit bonum et sapiens atque pulchrum. Item de pulchritudine et amore. Cap. VIIII.

Est in anima potentia deorsum ad sensibilia trahens, scilicet imaginalis simul atque vegetalis, est item hac superior virtus elevans ad divina. Si potentia deterior meliorem potest quandoque deducere, multo magis melior deteriorem reducere potest, sicut et solis virtus humorem sursum attollit alioquin naturaliter descendentem. Virtus autem elevans in intellectu vel ratione anime

---

[1] formantdum E   [2] *no* ¶ P

called a **wing**: it lifts the soul to love, contemplate, and worship
the divine. The divine that is attained through this wing is called
the good, wise, and beautiful. The soul can become a participant of it, they say, through the understanding. This divine is
not the absolute good, but the essential and intelligible good;
for the absolute good exists above wisdom and beauty, whereas
the essential and intelligible good is simultaneously good, wise,
and beautiful. This wise and beautiful good is present to all the
gods, supramundane and mundane, under the first god. By contemplating it any contemplative intellect is nourished.

[ii] In the gods what is **good, wise, and beautiful**? In any god
exist intellect, the process of understanding, and the intelligible.
The intelligible exists as good, for it is perfect there, sufficient,
and desirable (the **Philebus** tells us that these are the good's
three attributes).[27] In concerning itself with the intelligible, [a
god's] understanding is called wise. Hence his intellect, ablaze
with the splendor of the forms, is called beautiful. So goodness
in any god is united—compared with the rest—and hidden: it is
the essential and vital perfection, the fertile power and intelligible capacity, containing in itself all the hidden intelligible species comprehended in the intelligible light. Wisdom in any god
is the process of understanding which brings forth the intelligible light and unfolds the intelligible species inwardly. Beauty,
finally, is the completed unfolding of the intelligible light and
the intelligible species. Although beauty is the last to proceed,
as it were, in any god, it is the first to confront those ascending
to that god. Since beauty manifests itself most and appears first
and is, so to speak, the splendor emerging from all those lights,
Plato often calls it **the clearest and most obvious** of all divine
things.

[iii] The light that flows out of the good through intellects
and intelligibles Plato calls in the *Republic* the truth.[28] As the
Philebus says, we cannot gaze on this, the good's light and
nature, with a simple glance:[29] we divide it among ourselves by
our particular condition. So we call this light good insofar as it
proceeds from the good itself as something desirable and leads
intelligences back to the good; we call it wise insofar as it causes

nominatur **ala**: erigit hec animam ad divinum amandum et contemplandum atque venerandum. Ipsum vero divinum quod per hanc attingitur appellatur **bonum** et **sapiens** atque **pulchrum**. Cuius sane per intelligentiam animus fieri dicitur posse particeps. Id autem non ipsum simpliciter bonum, sed essentiale et intelligibile bonum. Illud enim super sapientiam pulchritudinemque existit. Hoc autem et bonum est simul et sapiens atque pulchrum. Eiusmodi bonum sapiensque et pulchrum omnibus sub primo deo diis inest supramundanis atque mundanis; cuius contemplatione alitur intellectus quilibet contemplator.

Quidnam est in diis bonum? Quid sapiens? Quid pulchrum? Nempe in deo quolibet est intellectus, intelligentia, [331] intelligibile. Intelligibile quidem tanquam bonum exstat, quia videlicet perfectum[1] illic est et sufficiens atque appetendum. Que quidem tria Philebus docet esse munera boni. Circa hoc intelligentia sese versans sapiens appellatur. Hinc intellectus ipse formarum splendore refulgens appellatus est pulchrum. Quamobrem bonum in quolibet deo unitum est pre ceteris et occultum: essentialis videlicet ipsa vitalisque perfectio, fecunda[2] potestas intelligibilisque facultas, occultas in se continens[3] species intelligibiles omnes intelligibili lumine comprehensas. Sapientia vero illic intelligentia est que lumen intelligibile parturit, speciesque intelligibiles intrinsecus explicat. Denique pulchritudo est consummata luminis intelligibilis specierumque intelligibilium explicatio. Que quidem, etsi illic quasi provenit ultima, prima tamen ascendentibus illuc occurrit; et quoniam se maxime offert apparetque prima, atque ex cunctis luminibus illis resultat ut splendor, iccirco sepe Plato pulchritudinem appellat **clarissimam** atque divinorum omnium **patentissimam**.[4]

Preterea lumen ex ipso bono per intellectus et intelligibilia profluens appellat in Republica veritatem. Hoc lumen naturamque boni non possumus (ut Philebus inquit) intuitu simplici contueri, sed apud nos ipsi nostra quadam conditione partimur. Dicimus ergo bonum quantum ab ipso bono provenit expeten-

---

[1]per effectum P   [2]facunda P   [3]contines E   [4]*no* ¶ P

other things to be known and to know; and we call it beautiful,
finally, because it fills knowers and known with a marvelous
splendor and fashions them with grace. Here Plato calls this
beautiful [light] most clear for the reason described; in the *Symposium* he calls it, in addition, soft, delicate, and charming, as
it delights those contemplating it in wonderful ways.[30] Both
there and here he calls it **lovable** too, since it causes love, and
with utmost effectiveness and gentleness alike it incites those
contemplating it with absolute grace and wonder to itself.[31]

Chapter 10. How the gods may be compounded in four ways. [246E-247A]

[i] Since Plato here introduces as many gods as possible, perhaps it might be worthwhile to say something about the number
of gods. Just as Christian theologians observe four senses in the
divine Scriptures, the literal, moral, allegorical, and anagogical,
and since they pursue mainly one sense here and another there,
so Platonists have four ways of compounding the gods and spirits; and they pursue one way here, another there, according to
the occasion. I too have been accustomed to interpreting and
distinguishing the spirits similarly in my commentaries, using
one way here, another there, as occasion requires.

[ii] The first method of compounding the gods is to distribute
them through various substances, as, for example, when we call
the first god the good itself or the one; the second god, Saturn,
that is, the intellect, the good's son (as Saturn is the first intellect, so is he the first intelligible and the intelligible world); and
the third god, that is, the world-soul sprung from Saturn, great
Jupiter, the leader in heaven. Thus in the *Republic* the first principle is called the good, and the first intellect, the good's son;
the *Cratylus* names the latter Saturn (for Saturn there is the
intellect, pure and full—*satur*), and Jupiter, the great understanding's son.[32]

[iii] Platonists locate three orders of supramundane gods between the prime intellect and the world-soul: some are next to

dum redigitque mentes ad bonum. Dicimus et sapiens qua ratione causa est ut alia cognoscantur atque cognoscant. Dicimus denique pulchrum quia cognoscentes et cognita splendore mirifico replet et gratia condit. Pulchrum hoc Plato, ea quam diximus ratione, hic nominat [332] lucidissimum. Addit in Convivio mulcens et delicatum atque blandum, quia miris modis contemplatores oblectat. Subiungit ibi et hic **amabile**, quoniam causa est amoris, et contemplatores ad se gratia prorsus admirationeque tam efficacissime quam blandissime provocat.

Quomodo dii quatuor modis multiplicentur. Cap. X.

Quoniam vero Plato hic deos quam plurimos introducit, opere pretium forte fuerit non nihil de numero deorum confabulari. Sicut Christiani theologi in divinis eloquiis quatuor sensus observant litteralem, moralem, allegoricum, anagogicum, et alibi quidem hunc, alibi vero illum precipue prosequuntur, ita Platonici quatuor habent multiplicandorum deorum numinumque modos; aliumque multiplicandi modum alibi pro opportunitate sectantur. Ego quoque similiter in commentariis meis alibi aliter, quatenus locus exigit, interpretari et distinguere numina consuevi.[1]

Primus igitur multiplicandi modus est deos per substantias varias distribuere, ut quando primum nominamus ipsum bonum vel ipsum unum; secundum vero Saturnum id est intellectum boni filium, qui sicut est intellectus primus sic intelligibile primum intelligibilisque mundus; tertium autem id est mundi animum Saturno genitum, Iovem magnum in celo ducem. Sic primum in Republica principium dicitur ipsum bonum, intellectus autem primus boni filius, qui nominatur in Cratylo Saturnus. Illic enim Saturnus asseritur intellectus purus atque satur, Iupiter autem magne intelligentie filius.

Sed inter intellectum primum animamque mundi tres supra-

---

[1] *no* ¶ P

that intelligible world, others to this sensible world, and others are in between. The Platonists mostly call the highest the intelligible gods, the lowest the intellectual gods, and those in between the mixed gods.[33] Just as the first sphere in the world's corporeal fabric is simply called Heaven, the second sphere Saturn, the third Jupiter, and their souls similarly, so with this class of intellects beneath the intelligible world we can perhaps call the first intellect Sky, the second Saturn, the third Jupiter, and then the remainder by the names of the planets and of the souls presiding over the elements (and so named in my *Theology*).[34] These names, I repeat, are appropriate for the twelve gods who lead the supermundane gods. Although the first [god] in this dodecade is called Sky or Heaven, the supermundane gods as a class are called heaven, that is, the intellectual heaven.

[iv] Following them are the mundane gods. Their prince is mundane himself, the world-soul. In the *Philebus* Plato calls the world-soul Jupiter, the highest intellect's offspring. In Jupiter's nature is royal intellect and royal soul, that is, a twin power, the intellectual and the vital; each is royal because in the world it exercises the universal sovereignty that presides over all the mundane gods.[35] The twelve mundane leaders, namely, the souls of the spheres, immediately follow this Jupiter. I am assuming that there are only twelve spheres. For just as Aristotle postulated as many world rulers as [spherical] motions but left it to a wiser man to establish the actual number of motions and spheres, so Plato, too, having first granted that there are twelve spheres, then shows that there are twelve rulers, the spheres' souls.[36] In other words, Plato is very willing to concede any other number to wiser men. The stars' souls and the invisible spirits distributed through the twelve spheres follow the twelve leaders. These spirits are called particular leaders, gods, demons, and heroes.

[v] So far I have arranged the gods in Platonic custom, according to the differences of substances. The second way of dividing them is mainly through the ideas: thus, however many ideas of the species the intelligible world contains, this constitutes the number of gods there. According to such usage you

mundanorum deorum ordines Platonici collo[333]cant: alios quidem illi mundo intelligibili, alios autem huic sensibili mundo proximos, alios vero medios; et supremos quidem precipue vocant intelligibiles, extremos illorum intellectuales, medios vero mixtos. Forte vero sicut in machina mundi corporea prima sphera vocatur simpliciter Celum, secunda Saturnus, tertia Iupiter similiterque illarum anime, sic in hoc intellectuum genere quod est sub intelligibili mundo primus intellectus nominari potest Celius, secundus Saturnus, tertius Iupiter, et reliqua deinceps planetarum nomina animarumque elementis presidentium, quas nominamus in Theologia. Hec inquam nomina diis duodecim supermundanorum deorum ducibus competunt. Etsi in hoc duodenario primus appellatus est Celius, totum tamen id genus nominatur celum, scilicet intellectuale celum.[1]

Hos dii mundani sequuntur. Quorum princeps ipse quoque mundanus est anima mundi, quam in Philebo Iovem Plato nominat intelligentie summe progeniem, in cuius natura sit regius intellectus et anima regia id est virtus gemina, intellectualis scilicet atque vitalis; et utraque regia id est principatum in mundo tenens universalem mundanis diis omnibus presidentem. Hunc Iovem sequuntur proxime duces mundani duodecim, anime scilicet spherarum, si modo sint sphere duodecim. Sicut enim Aristoteles tot esse mundi rectores voluit quot et motus, numerum vero motuum spherarumque certum sapientiori concessit, sic et Plato semel admisso[2] duodenario spherarum numero duodecim mox rectores adhibet spherarum animas; numerum videlicet alium quemlibet sapientioribus facile concessurus. His utique succedunt stellarum [334] anime distinctaque per duodecim spheras invisibilia numina, que quidem numina duces particulares cognominantur diique et demones atque heroes.

Hactenus deos per substantiarum differentias more platonico disposuimus. Secundus autem distribuendi modus est potissimum per ideas; ut quot speciales idee mundo intelligibili contin-

---

[1] *no* ¶ P   [2] amisso E

were permitted in the old days to swear even by animals, trees,
and lower things [—that is, to regard them as gods—] provided
that, in using their names, you were thinking of their ideas. It
is still more fitting to call the ideas of all the spheres and stars
gods.

[vi] The third method of compounding the gods is to proceed
with ampler, more general properties than the species. In this
manner first we distinguish the gods as they are distributed
through the intelligible world; for in it the first distinction is
through formal properties. So the divine mind's unity and head
could perhaps sometimes be given the name of the first god,
whether the good or Demogorgon[37] or else particularly the absolutely first. Consequently I would prefer first to name what is in
second or third place. Following [the unity] in the intelligible
world is the intellect. We consider two properties [or under-
standings] in this intellect. First is the contemplator, and it
stands apart as if content with truths alone. Insofar as it regards
the good itself, the Platonists call it Sky (for Plato in the *Cratylus* interprets Uranos, Heaven, to mean the glance upwards to
things above);[38] and insofar as it turns itself towards its own
essence, the Platonists certainly call this [first] understanding
Saturn. The second understanding is, however, the practical, so
to speak: it regulates everything in the manner of an architect
and father, and is Jupiter—not simply **great Jupiter,** but Jupiter
the greatest and first. Hence, having called the first intellect
Jove in his third book on queries concerning the soul, in his
book on the three principles Plotinus later called it Saturn;[39]
that is, he contemplated it in alternate ways, as I said. But his
words in the book on queries concerning the soul make it clear
that he is introducing a twin Jupiter: the first is the world architect, who is separated in a way; the second is the world leader,
that is, the world-soul.[40] This is the Jove whom Plato calls the
leader in the *Phaedrus,* and in his letter to Hermias, moreover,
the leader of all present and future things:[41] secretly he is putting the intellect as cause before Jupiter and the good as lord
and father before both (but for this see the letter). Here let me
proceed with the order of division I established just now. In the

entur dii illic totidem numerentur. Quo quidem usu fas erat quondam etiam per animalia et arbores inferioraque iurare, modo nominibus his horum idee cogitarentur. Itaque multo magis deos nominare decet ideas spherarum omnium et stellarum.

Tertius autem multiplicandi modus est per generaliores amplioresque proprietates incedere quam species. Quo quidem pacto deos per mundum intelligibilem primo distinguimus. Prima enim per formalia distinctio est in eo. Unitas igitur illa caputque divine[1] mentis cognomento primi dei quandoque forsan poterit appellari, sive bonum, sive Demogorgon sive aliter precipue quidem[2] ipsum simpliciter primum;[3] consequenter autem quod in secundo vel tertio primum nominare placuerit. Sequitur intellectus in ipso intelligibili mundo. In hoc autem intellectu proprietates due considerantur. Prima quidem contemplatrix et segregata quasi solis contenta veris: hanc ut suspicit ipsum bonum Platonici vocant Celium (Plato enim in Cratylo Uranon id est Celum interpretatur aspectum ad superiora); eam deinde intelligentiam quatenus ad essentiam propriam se convertit proculdubio nominavere[4] Saturnum. Secunda vero intelligentia est quasi practica et architecti patrisque more [335] cuncta dispensans; hanc precipue **Iovem** non simpliciter **magnum**, immo maximum atque primum. Hinc Plotinus, cum in libro de dubiis anime tertio intellectum primum appellavisset Iovem, post in libro[5] de tribus principiis Saturnum cognominavit; aliter videlicet et aliter ipsum quemadmodum diximus contemplatus. Manifestis autem verbis in libro de dubiis anime Iovem geminum introducit: primum quidem Iovem mundi architectum quodammodo separatum; secundum vero mundi ducem id est animam. Quem Plato Iovem **ducem** appellat in Phedro; in epistola quinetiam ad Hermiam appellat ducem rerum omnium presentium atque futurarum. Cui clam intellectum preponit ut causam, ipsum vero bonum utrisque preficit ut dominum atque patrem. Sed de his ibi. Hic iam institutum

---

[1]divinis P   [2]quod P   [3]primum *om.* P   [4]nominare P   [5]librum P

intelligible world Rhea is the vital power perhaps. The Saturnian and Jovian intellect lies upon her (the first as husband and the second as son). Accompanying or following the intellect is the quickening power, Juno: she is the daughter of [its] first under-standing and sister and spouse of [its] second. Neptune is the active, moving power for completing work and the distributor too of a like property in [its] effects. Pluto (and Vesta) is the fixed and fixing property. Neptune has his own spirits accom-panying him, and Pluto has his.

[vii] I return briefly to the vital, quickening power. Corres-ponding to it most of all is the world-soul. It can also be called Venus. Perhaps this is why Plotinus says Venus is the world-soul and perhaps what is comparable to the world-soul in the intelligible world.[42] The power is called Venus insofar as it is always disposed towards beauty through both intellects to which it is subject: through the contemplative intellect [the Saturnian] to gazing at beauty, through the active [the Jovian] to imitating it. But being so disposed may be Love or Cupid/ Desire [rather than Venus].

[viii] To my way of thinking too, the fact that Latin often uses the alternative *venustas* ("loveliness") for beauty and derives the term from Venus helps us on occasions to be able to call beauty Venus,[43] though beauty seems to be not the maternal so much as the paternal principle for love and desire. As I have often stated elsewhere, I think that in the intelligible world beauty pertains to the completely unfolded series of the ideas.[44] In this series I am considering in the main three things: grace, splendor, and power (or virtue). We can call the first Venus, the second Apollo, and the third Pallas.

[ix] But why does the *Symposium* refer to a twin Venus, per-taining to both Saturn and Jupiter?[45] Perhaps because she per-tains to Saturn, as I described, and to Jupiter whether she is the vital power or the ideal grace. As the latter, insofar as she is her-self worthy of admiration, she seems to look more to Saturn; but as she is worthy of imitation in effect, rather, more to Jupiter.

[x] When I call Apollo and Minerva Jupiter's children, there-fore, in a way I have already distributed into parts Jupiter's

modo nobis distinctionis ordinem prosequamur. Rhea forsan in mundo intelligibili est virtus illa vitalis; cui incubat[1] intellectus saturnius atque iovius, primus quidem ut maritus, secundus ut filius. Iuno vivifica virtus que comitatur vel sequitur intellectum: prime quidem intelligentie filia, secunde vero soror atque coniunx. Neptunus autem agilis motrixque virtus ad opificium[2] peragendum, similemque proprietatem effectibus quoque distribuens. Pluto Vestaque firma proprietas atque firmans. Neptunum comitantur numina sua, sua quoque Plutonem.

Redeo parumper ad virtutem vitalem atque vivificam. Cui respondet potissimum anima mundi. Venus etiam illa vocari potest. Unde forsan Plotinus Venerem mundi animam esse dicit, et forte quod huic est in ipso intelligibili mundo [336] proportionale. Nominatur autem Venus quatenus per utrumque cui subest intellectum ad pulchritudinem semper afficitur: per contemplativum ad intuendam, per activum ad imitandam. Affectus autem ille sit Amor atque Cupido.

Interea cogitanti mihi usum loquendi latinum, qui pulchritudinem sepe nominat venustatem et hanc deducit a Venere, succurrit posse etiam pulchritudinem quandoque Venerem appellari, tametsi pulchritudo ad Amorem atque Cupidinem non tam ut maternum quam ut[3] paternum principium esse videtur. Pulchritudinem ibi, quod alibi sepe diximus, ad ipsam idearum seriem penitus explicatam pertinere putamus; in hac tria potissimum cogitantes, gratiam et splendorem atque virtutem. Illam quidem Venerem, istum vero Apollinem, hanc denique Palladem possumus nominare.

Sed curnam in Symposio Venus gemina nuncupatur ad Saturnum videlicet attinens atque Iovem? Forte quoniam Venus sive virtus sit vitalis ad Saturnum (ut diximus) Iovemque pertinet, seu sit gratia idealis: hec ipsa ut spectabilis est ad Saturnum magis, ut effectu potius imitabilis magis ad Iovem spectare videtur.

Proinde quando Apollinem et Minervam Iovis filios appellamus, amplissimam illam Iovis providentiam omnia tam sensi-

---

[1] incumbat P   [2] officium P   [3] ut *om.* P

most ample providence, which regulates all sensibles and intelligibles equally. Besides the other names, I usually call the part that provides for sensibles Mars and Vulcan, and the part that gives and rules over intelligibles Minerva, Apollo, Dionysus, Mercury, and the Muse. As Mercury it bestows on minds and wits a sort of motion for inquiry (one might say). As Apollo it bestows the light for finding and seeing clearly. As Minerva it bestows the power to attain along with the light. As the Muse it reveals or gives a harmonious order to inventions and prepares the inventor. Finally, as Dionysus it brings it to pass that minds seem to overreach their ends, as it were, in seeing and in loving also.

[xi] But let me return briefly to the part providing, so to speak, for sensibles. As Mars it brings motion, as Vulcan, the effect, and here, too, as Dionysus, ecstasy.

[xii] In all this recall that you can use the same rationale behind compounding the gods in the prime intellect through particular formal properties (and the same system of names too) for then enumerating the gods in the world-soul and thereafter in the souls of the spheres and stars. In any of these souls, I repeat, remember to enumerate all the spirits equally. Hence Orpheus not only locates all the gods in one Jupiter as both the creator and the soul of the world, but also often calls to mind all the spirits in any one god.[46] I gladly copied him in my book *On The Sun.*[47] I have said a lot too about divine names in my exposition of the *Cratylus,* where I also say that in any one god Sky is the name for looking to higher things (whether properly this is the function of the understanding or of the unity superior to the intellect), Saturn is looking selfwards, Jupiter is looking to the ordering of lower things.[48] In Plato, then, Sky is clearly not the universe's first principle, since not only does it look at something, but it looks up at something higher; and both actions are totally foreign to the first principle, if we believe Plato.[49] Wherever I may perhaps have said that the first principle is called Sky I have been talking in a sense that is not the Platonic one.

[xiii] In any one of the world's spheres, however, many individual divinities follow the gods: these are commonly called

bilia quam intelligibilia pariter dispensantem iam in partes quodammodo distribuimus. Et partem quidem sensibilibus providentem preter cetera nomina Martem atque Vulcanum nominare solemus; partem vero intelligibilia tribuentem atque regentem Minervam Apollinemque et Dionysum et Mercurium atque Musam. Ut enim est Mercurius mentibus ingeniisque mo[337]tum quasi quendam prestat (ut ita dixerim) ad querendum; ut Apollo lumen ad inveniendum et perspicaciter intuendum. Ut Minerva cum lumine vim prestat ad consequendum. Ut Musa ordinem harmonicum monstrat vel dat inventis inventoremque concinnat. Ut denique Dionysus efficit, ut quasi fines suos tum videndo tum etiam amando mentes excedere videantur.

Sed revertamur parumper ad illam quasi partem sensibilibus providentem. Hec quidem ut Mars motum affert, ut Vulcanus effectum, ut hic etiam Dionysus excessum.

Inter hec vero memento qua ratione deos in intellectu primo per formales quasdam proprietates multiplicavimus, eadem ratione et appellatione mox in anima mundi numerare posse, atque deinceps in animabus spherarum atque stellarum; in qualibet inquam eque numina cuncta connumerare. Hinc Orpheus non solum deos omnes in uno collocat Iove tam opifice mundi quam animo mundi, verum etiam in quolibet deo sepe numina cuncta commemorat. Quem nos in libro De Sole libenter imitati sumus. Multa preterea de divinis nominibus in nostris in Cratylum expositionibus declaravimus. Ubi etiam dicitur in quolibet deo Celium appellari aspectum ad superiora, sive per intelligentiam proprie fiat, sive per unitatem intellectu superiorem; Saturnum vero aspectum ad se ipsum; Iovem autem aspectum ad sequentia dispensanda. Hinc apparet Celium apud Platonem non esse primum universi principium, quippe cum non solum aspiciat, sed suspiciat etiam superius aliquid. Utrumque summatim, si Platoni credimus, alienum est a primo. Sicubi vero forte primum [338] dixerim nominari Celium alio quodam potius more quam platonico sum loquutus.

Post hec autem sequuntur particularia numina in quibuslibet

demons. Though Iamblichus, Syrianus, and Proclus distribute them into particular orders, into gods, archangels, angels, demons, principalities, and heroes,[50] yet all these particular divinities are, I repeat, commonly named demonic. They follow the universal gods. The demons have already received among themselves the ample providence in the gods' possession (after its distribution). Various demons minister to various gods; or, if many serve the same gods, yet different demons perform the different offices of the same god. In this manner Saturn exists among the demons, therefore, and Jupiter, Neptune, Pluto, and each of the gods likewise. This is the fourth way of compounding the gods I had promised you at the start: namely, through their attendants, the demons. Not only does one Saturn or one Jupiter exist among these demons, but many Saturns and many Jupiters in each sphere minister to the offices of Saturn and Jupiter. Similarly, the rest of the demons serve the rest of the gods.

Chapter 11. The four worlds. The supercelestial place. The twelve gods. [247A-E]

[i] There are four worlds; for, as the *Timaeus* says, [a] world or heaven is the universe of forms.[51] The universe of forms is not only in the world's corporeal fabric, the world called the corporeal, but also in the world-soul and souls as a universal class, the world called the animate. Above the animate world is the intellectual world in the pure intellects above heaven; this is the third world or third heaven, the plenitude of all the intellectual forms (third, that is, in order of ascent). The fourth world is in the prime intellect, where the first intelligible is; it has in itself the universe of intelligible forms and is called the intelligible world. Since the first, intelligible, and ideal species exist in this world, they are the preeminent objects for the intellectual eyes of all intelligences.

[ii] Four worlds also seem to exist in the soul; for the universal forms exist in a way in the soul's vegetative nature and in its imagination, reason, and intellect.

mundi[1] spheris plurima, que communiter demonia nominantur. Quamvis apud Iamblicum et Syrianum atque Proclum in quosdam ordines digerantur, scilicet in deos, archangelos, angelos, demones, principatus, heroes, hec inquam omnia particularia numina communiter demonico nomine nuncupata, deos illos sequuntur universales; providentiamque penes illos amplam ipsi iam demones apud se sortiti sunt distributam. Aliique demones diis aliis subministrant, vel si eisdem multi serviunt, varii tamen ad varia dei eiusdem[2] officia conferunt. Sic igitur inter demones Saturnus est et Iupiter, Neptunus et Pluto, et similiter quisquam deorum. Atque hic est quartus quem promiseram ab initio multiplicandi modus, videlicet per pedissequos deorum demones. Inter quos sane demones non solum est Saturnus vel Iupiter unus, sed multi in qualibet sphera Saturni, multi Ioves, videlicet Saturni vel Iovis officiis ministrantes; ceterique ceteris similiter servientes.

De quatuor mundis. De loco supercelesti. De diis duodecim. Cap. XI.

Quatuor mundi sunt, sicut enim in Timeo dicitur, mundus sive celum est universitas ipsa formarum. Universitas eiusmodi non solum est in machina mundi corporea, qui mundus corporeus appellatur, sed etiam in anima mundana universoque genere animarum, qui mundus dicitur animalis. Super animalem mundum est intellectualis mundus in [339] intellectibus supra celum puris, qui tertius mundus est sive celum tertium, intellectualium omnium plenitudo formarum, tertium videlicet in ascensu. Quartus est in intellectu primo ubi est intelligibile primum, in quo formarum intelligibilium universitas; mundus intelligibilis appellatur, quoniam in hoc prime[3] intelligibiles idealesque species extant, mentium omnium intellectualibus oculis obiecta precipua.

Videntur quoque in anima esse mundi[4] quatuor. Nam in

---

[1]mundis P   [2]eiusmodi E   [3]prime *om.* P   [4]esse mundi *transposed* P

[iii] So the bond between the four worlds is at least as strong as the union between the four elements: the corporeal world is thus completely united through its highest member with the lowest member of the animate world; the animate world is similarly united with the intellectual world, and the intellectual with the intelligible. In the *Phaedrus* and the *Symposium* the highest object of contemplation is the intelligible world, since in both we ascend only to the extent that we reach beauty through the love of beauty; but the highest beauty formally exists in the intelligible world.

[iv] When Socrates says that the mundane gods **climb heaven**, he intends it to mean the intellectual heaven, the unclouded intellectual sky. For through their souls these gods are already higher than the corporeal world, and they are always in the animate world. First and most easily they ascend to the intellectual heaven, for they also possess intellects. Then they proceed to the intelligible heaven with the intellect [alone], which is proportionate with the intelligible.

[v] The corporeal world is perceived through the senses and the imagination, the animate through the reason (with the intellect), the intellectual through the intellect (with the reason), and the intelligible with the intellect alone, as the *Phaedrus* says. The good itself is higher than the intelligible world, and no intellect can perceive it (as the *Parmenides* demonstrates), and it cannot, strictly speaking, be called [a] world or heaven. So **heaven** for the mundane gods and their followers, in their ascent, consists of the purest class of intellects and of the formal, intellectual universe in it. The highest order of intellectual beings there is called in the *Phaedrus* the heaven's **convex**; the middle order, the heaven's **height**; and the lowest order, the heaven's **concave**. For the mundane gods and their followers, however, the universe of the intelligible world exists in a way above [this intellectual] heaven, and for them it is called the **superheavenly place**.

[vi] Since it is called place, essence, being, knowledge, the knowable, truth, the true, the ideas' series, certainly a degree such as this is not the universe's absolutely first principle. For

natura anime vegetali et in imaginatione rationeque et intellectu anime quodammodo forme sunt universe.

Proinde quanta est inter quatuor elementa connexio, tanta saltem est inter quatuor mundos copula. Mundus ergo corporeus per summitatem suam cum mundi animalis infimo est summopere copulatus; similiter animalis mundus cum intellectuali; similiter quoque intellectualis cum intelligibili mundo. Mundus intelligibilis in Phedro et Symposio contemplationis summum tenet, siquidem utrobique eatenus ascenditur, quatenus per amorem pulchritudinis ad pulchritudinem pervenitur, summa vero pulchritudo formaliter est in illo.

Quapropter ubi Socrates inquit mundanos deos **celum scandere**, intelligi vult intellectuale celum scilicet intellectuale purum. Sunt enim ipsi iam per animas suas corporali mundo superiores atque in animali mundo semper. Ascendunt vero primum atque facillime ad intellectuale celum, habent enim intellectus et ipsi. Progrediuntur deinde ad intelligibile celum, ipso scilicet intellectu proportionem cum intelligibili possidente.[1]

Mundus corporeus sensu et imaginatione percipitur, animalis [340] autem ratione cum intellectu, intellectualis vero intellectu cum ratione, intelligibilis autem intellectu solo, quemadmodum[2] declaratur in Phedro. Nam ipsum quidem bonum intelligibili mundo superius nullo capitur intellectu, ut in Parmenide patet, nec rite mundus aut celum appellari potest. **Celum** igitur mundanis diis deorumque pedissequis est in ascensu ipsum purissimum intellectuum genus et universitas illa[3] formalis et intellectualis in eo. Ubi summus intellectualium ordo in Phedro dicitur **convexum** celi; medius vero celi **profundum;**[4] tertius[5] denique **concavum**. Verum ipsa mundi intelligibilis universitas extat mundanis diis pedissequisque[6] deorum quodammodo supra celum, diciturque illis **locus ille supercelestis**.

Quoniam vero nominatur locus, essentia, ens, scientia, scibile, veritas, verum, series idearum, certum est eiusmodi

---

[1]possidentem P   [2]quendammodum E   [3]illa *om.* P   [4]profundu P   [5]tertium P   [6]-que *om.* P

the latter is free of these and like [predications], as I maintained
at length in [commenting] on the *Parmenides*,[52] where Plato
everywhere provides confirmatory proofs.

[vii] The universe's first principle is absolutely one and absolutely above everything. So the intelligible intellect that is immediately born from it is one in the highest degree and universally
the universe. So it is sufficiently one itself numerically and is
[punningly] called the *uni*verse. No one mind, soul, or sphere
under it, however, is thus universally the universe, but is the
universe only with a manner and a property of its own. So none
is so properly called [a] world as this first [intelligible] intellect
uniquely is. But the class of such intellects is denominated the
intellectual world; the class of souls, the animate world; and the
class of bodies, likewise, the corporeal world. Let me return,
however, to the intelligible world, which is the first universe and
therefore universally the universe and is called the supercelestial
place.

[viii] Certain facts are denied and affirmed about this intelligible place above heaven. **Touch** is denied, that is, every condition and property proper to the corporeal world; **shape** is
denied, that is, the animate world's quality, which the *Timaeus*
describes through figures and numbers;[53] and **color** is denied,
that is, a certain participated light proper to the intellectual
world. For this higher place is pure [and not participated] light,
and pure light is seen not in color but in a transparent medium.
Guided by Plato, finally, we usually use the innermost light of
the sun to describe the good itself, which is higher than the intelligible place.[54] The text sufficiently sets forth what is affirmed,
however, about the intelligible place.

[ix] Since Plato delights in the number twelve both here and
in the *Laws* and the *Republic*,[55] and since the majority of Platonists have dedicated the dodecade not only to the mundane
gods but to the higher gods also,[56] perhaps the following can
seem probable. Those intellectual gods I located between the
intelligible and animate worlds are the princes—twelve in
number—of the [other] intellectual gods there and comprise
four trinities. The first trinity is next to the intelligible world,

gradum non esse ipsum simpliciter primum universi principium. Illud enim est ab his et similibus absolutum ut in Parmenide latissime declaramus, Platone multis passim testimoniis confirmante.

Primum universi principium est et simpliciter unum et simpliciter super omnia. Intellectus igitur intelligibilis inde proxime genitus est et maxime unum et universaliter universum. Ideo ipse unus numero sufficienter est et dicitur universum. Neque tamen quelibet mens sub ipso vel anima aut sphera ita est universaliter universum sed suo quodam pacto et proprietate quadam. Ideo non quelibet nominatur proprie mundus sicut singulariter ille primus. Sed intellectuum [341] eiusmodi genus mundus intellectualis cognominatur; genus animarum animalis mundus; genus corporum mundus similiter corporalis. Sed ad mundum illum intelligibilem, qui primum universum est et ideo universaliter universum locusque supercelestis dicitur, redeamus.

Iam vero de hoc intelligibili supra celum loco quedam negantur, quedam etiam affirmantur. Negatur quidem **tactus** id est omnis conditio passioque mundo corporeo propria. Negatur **figura** id est animalis mundi qualitas, que per figuras et numeros describitur in Timeo. Negatur **color** intellectuali mundo conveniens scilicet lumen quoddam participatum. Est enim ille superior locus lumen purum, quale non in colore aspicitur sed in diaphano. Ipsum denique bonum intelligibili loco superius per lucem solis intimam indicante Platone designare solemus. Que vero de intelligibili affirmantur satis in textu patent.

Quoniam vero Plato hic et in Legibus et Republica duodenario gaudet numero, et plerique Platonici diis non solum mundanis sed etiam superioribus duodenarium dicaverunt, probabile forsan videri potest deos illos intellectuales, quos inter intelligibilem animalemque mundum disponebamus, esse numero duodecim principes intellectualium ibi deorum,[1] et

---

[1] deos P

the last is contiguous to the animate, and the two middle trinities come together in fit proportion from either side, almost like air and water between fire and earth. Let the intelligible world, that is, the first intellect, be the head of this dodecade and of the rest of the intellects in the intellectual world, just as the world-soul is the leader too of the mundane dodecade. Perhaps the twelve princes above the animate world are the intellects in command of the twelve spheres' souls in the animate order; thus various intellects would rule over and provide for various souls and spheres and be named similarly. Perhaps too various souls look to various intellects (namely those in charge of them) before others and worship and imitate them with all their strength. Perhaps again those twelve intellects look at the first intelligible, the exemplar, in such a way that any one of them contemplates mainly the models there which principally pertain: first to itself, then to the soul and sphere most subject to it, and finally to everything that either rests within this sphere or everywhere proceeds from it. I deal with the rest of the information about the numbers and names of the gods in book 4 of my *Theology*.[57]

[x] Some have supposed that the dodecade celebrated in the *Phaedrus* along with its leader, Jupiter, is supermundane; but I think, with Plotinus, that it is probably mundane.[58] For in the *Phaedrus* Socrates deals principally with the mundane gods: he calls them **divine animals** constituted from a soul and a celestial body. He assigns them charioteers, horses, and chariots, internal circular motions, the ability both to impel the spheres [under them] and to ascend towards higher things, the companionship of Vesta (who is undoubtedly the soul of the earth), and an escort of demons and also of human souls. Socrates also depicts Jupiter himself in terms of motion, that is, leading [others] and advancing [himself] and doing both in heaven, in his own body, as it were, as if he were the world-soul and the world-god.

[xi] That **heaven**, by the contemplation of which great Jupiter and the rest of the world's leaders are themselves made blessed and make their worshipers blessed, you must not equate with

habere quatuor trinitates. Primam intelligibili mundo proximam, ultimam animali contiguam, duas autem medias illinc atque illinc convenienti proportione vergentes, ferme quemadmodum inter ignem atque terram, aer atque aqua. Huius igitur duodenarii et reliquorum illic intellectuum intelligibilis ille mundus [342] intellectus scilicet primus caput esto, quemadmodum duodenarii quoque mundani anima dux est mundana. Forte vero duodecim principes super animalem mundum intellectus animabus spherarum duodecim hoc ordine presunt, ut intellectus alii animabus spherisque aliis imperent atque provideant, ac similiter nominentur. Anime quoque alie alias forte mentes videlicet sibi prefectas pre ceteris speculantur et colunt et pro viribus imitantur. Forsan vero et duodecim ille mentes ita primum intelligibile speculantur exemplar, ut quelibet earum illic potissimum exemplaria contempletur precipue pertinentia tum ad se, tum etiam ad animam spheramque sibi maxime subditam tum denique ad omnia que in hac ipsa sphera consistunt vel ab ipsa passim proficiscuntur. Reliqua de numeris nominibusque deorum in Theologie quarto tractamus.

Quidam existimaverunt duodenarium in Phedro cum suo Iove duce celebratum esse supermundanum. Ego vero cum Plotino probabiliter arbitror esse mundanum. Nam Socrates mundanos in Phedro deos precipue tractat. Appellat enim **animalia divina** ex anima et celesti corpore constituta. Tribuit eis aurigas et equos atque currus, discursiones intimas, agitationes spherarum, ascensiones ad altiora, societatem Veste que proculdubio est anima terre, comitatum demonum et animarum etiam humanarum. Ipsum quoque Iovem vocabulo motionis effingit, ducentem scilicet et incedentem[1] agentemque hec in celo quasi corpore suo, quasi sit mundi anima deusque mundanus.

Neque vero putandum est **celum** illud, cuius contemplatione Iupiter magnus ducesque mun[343]di reliqui beati sunt cultoresque[2] suos beatos efficiunt, esse hoc nobis sensibile celum,

---

[1] incidentem P   [2] -que *om.* P

the heaven we perceive, since [even] we would not be rendered happy by looking only at the latter.[59] The mundane gods and divine souls are far above our heaven; and they are not turned back principally to contemplate it (as if they could become more perfect at some point by gazing at the less perfect). The celestials that we merely see they know in their causes and reasons, having been turned back by their intelligence, not towards them, but towards themselves or to something higher. The world rulers are never under the circumference of our heaven, and they do not make pure souls blessed by the consideration of subcelestials (since Socrates calls souls led astray towards subcelestials **crippled and lame of wing**). To say that the divine souls, which Plato says are more eminent than our heaven and move their celestial [spheres] by their own inmost motion, **are carried around** placed **on the back of that heaven,** and thus look up at the intelligible ideas, would be ridiculous (since the ideas are understood, rather, through the intellect and reasons and the intellectual gods). It would also be ridiculous to so distribute the grades of the divine understandings in threes that they are distributed through the ascent to—or consideration of—the concave, height, or convex of [our heaven's] fabric. And finally, Plato shows us in the *Cratylus* what that heaven truly is when he interprets Uranos, that is Heaven or Sky, to mean the vision that gazes at the supernals.[60] Uranos, therefore, is the intellectual class of gods looking upwards to the intelligibles. The first of these intellectual gods especially is called Sky or Heaven. The mundane gods and their attendants are said, in all probability, to arrive through the intellectual at the intelligible.

The end of the introduction to the *Phaedrus*. Comment follows along with chapter summaries.

quando neque nos sola huius inspectione felices efficeremur. Dii profecto mundani animeque divine hoc celo prestantiores sunt, neque convertuntur ad hoc precipue contemplandum (quasi ex imperfectiore spectaculo perfectiores sint quandoque futuri). Cognoscunt vero celestia hec oculis manifesta in causis rationibusque suis, non quidem ad hec sed ad se ipsos vel ad superius mente conversi. Neque unquam sub huius celi circunferentia sunt mundi rectores, neque consideratione subcelestium puras animas beatas efficiunt (quippe cum Socrates animas ad ista distractas appellet **alis mancas** atque **claudas**). Ridiculum dictu foret divinas animas, que apud Platonem eminentiores celo sunt et celestia sua[1] movent motu videlicet intimo, **in dorso celi** positas **circunferri** ideasque intelligibiles ita suspicere (que per intellectum potius rationesque et deos intellectuales intelliguntur). Ridiculum quoque divinarum intelligentiarum gradus ita tripliciter distribuere ut per ascensum vel intuitum circa molis concavum vel profundum vel convexum distribuantur. Plato denique in Cratylo docet quid revera sit istud celum, cum Uranon id est Celum sive Celium[2] interpretatur visionem superna spectantem. Uranos igitur est intellectuale deorum genus intelligibilia sursum spectans. Precipue vero intellectualium primus Celius nominatur sive Celum. Mundani denique dii pedissequique deorum probabiliter per intellectuale ad intelligibile per[342(= 4)[3]]venire dicuntur.

Finis argumenti in Phedrum. Sequitur commentum cum summis capitulorum.

---

[1]suo P   [2]celum E   [3]*this mistake in pagination is never rectified* P

Texts III Commentum cum summis capitulorum
A Critical Edition and Translation

Headnote

This critical edition and translation of the *Commentum cum summis capitulorum* is also based on the version in the editio princeps of 1496, collated with that in the Prague manuscript, though the revisions that the former contained for the 1484 Plato edition have been omitted (but see Texts I, headnote and apparatus above). I have again incorporated the corrigenda of the 1496 edition without comment, followed the same editorial and translation principles, and used the same apparatus for indicating references (numbered 61 to 101), lemmas, variants, the Prague-manuscript pagination, and the Stephanus pagination as for the *Commentarium* (see Texts II, headnote above). Note that the Prague manuscript does not supply headings for any of the summae, though it uses the same numbering for them as the 1496 edition does.

Chapter 1. [227A]

Having just left Lysias, Phaedrus is asked by Socrates to repeat Lysias's conversation and speech. Phaedrus pretends he
does not want to, but at length agrees.

Chapter 2. [229A]

The pleasant spot is described; allegorically it stands for the
Academy and Plato. The story of Boreas's rape of Oreithyia.[61]
We should not pay too much attention to stories. The man who
is a slave to the senses is a wild, many-sided, savage animal; but
he who employs reason is a simple, gentle, divine animal. We
must study to learn before all else.

Chapter 3. [230E]

Lysias's speech. The beloved ought to shun his lover's over-
familiarity as a benevolence that is disreputable, harmful,
annoying, and inconstant; for this is the love that ruins us.

Chapter 4. [234C]

We praise a speech when good things are not only said but
said well. Socrates condemns Lysias for repeating the same
things too often, and prefers instead the old writers on love.

Chapter 5. [235E]

In a speech we must beware that we do not overlook what
should come first and pass rashly on to subsequent matters. In
dealing with necessities we should praise the arrangement, with
other things, the invention. By making a vow, Phaedrus com-

Cap. I.

O Amice etce. Phedrus a Lysia profectus rogatur a Socrate ut sermonem et orationem Lysie referat. Dissimulat nolle, tandem concedit.

Cap. II.

Peropportune[1] etce. Descriptio loci ameni. Allegoria pro Academia et Platone. Fabula Erethrie[2] a Borea rapte. Non est fabulis incumbendum. Qui servit sensibus est animal brutum et ferum atque multiplex. Qui ratione utitur est animal simplex, mite, divinum. Discendi studium omnibus preponendum.

[343] Cap. III.

Mearum quidem etce. Oratio Lysie. Amatus debet amatoris sui consuetudinem fugere tanquam infamem noxiamque et molestam instabilemque benivolentiam; quam pernitiosus amor.

Cap. IIII.

Quid tibi videtur etce. Laus orationis est ut non solum bona, sed etiam bene dicantur. Improbat Lysiam quod sepius eadem repetat. Veteres de amore scriptores huic anteponit.

Cap. V.

(So.) Amicissimus es etce. Cavendum in oratione ne prioribus

---

[1] *preceded by* Pau. P   [2] Herethrie P

pels the ironic Socrates to speak. He implores him by invoking
the divinity watching over the trees and ruling the spot, as if
Socrates were a superstitious man. Besides his devoutness, Socrates also openly reveals his sense of modesty and shame.

Chapter 6. The invocation to the Muses. Lovers. Two leaders dwell in us. [237A]

Since he is about to treat of love, Socrates calls upon the
Muses; for they bestow grace and goodwill upon us on account
of their own harmony. One of them is called Erato, that is, lovable. Socrates censures intemperate love, which Lysias had censured too. But he defines it first; for nothing can be known
about something's kind unless we first know what it is by definition. When Socrates mentions Lysias, he is also secretly referring to his own person under the person of Lysias. For each of
them loves Phaedrus, though not in the same way. Each urges
Phaedrus not to indulge his lover intemperately. There are two
leaders in us: the desire for pleasures, and legitimate opinion or
judgment. Intemperate love is defined thus: it is an irrational
desire that attracts us to the pleasure of shape.

Chapter 7. The Nymphs, Dionysus, the Muses. [238C]

The Nymphs are divinities presiding over generation; accordingly, they are said to dwell in streams or woods, since generation is accomplished through wetness and descends to the wood,
that is, to prime matter.[62] Dionysus is their leader; for he is the
god who presides over both generation and regeneration. Thus
perhaps he is supposed twice born. The hymns proper to him
are dithyrambs, for they are inspired, obscure, and complex.
But since both the soul on the one hand and desire on the other
are also inspired by one or other of these divinities, Socrates is
enraptured by Dionysus and the Nymphs; for he is concentrating on the love involved in generation and will soon treat of love

pretermissis ad posteriora temere transeatur. In necessariis laudanda magis dispositio est, in aliis inventio. Ironicum Socratem Phedrus iuramento compellit loqui; tanquam religiosum obsecrat ipsum per numen arboribus providens locoque prefectum. Socrates ultra religionem pudorem quoque suum manifeste declarat.

[344] Invocatio Musarum. Amatores. Duo in nobis duces.[1] Cap. VI.

(So.) Agite o Muse etce. Socrates tractaturus de amore Musas invocat, que propter harmoniam ad gratiam et benivolentiam conferunt. Quarum una Erato id est amabilis nominatur. Vituperat amorem incontinentem, quem vituperavit et Lysias. Sed definit ipsum prius. Non enim quale sit unumquodque cognosci potest, nisi prius quid sit definitione sit cognitum. Socrates dum tangit Lysiam clam sub Lysie persona tangit et suam. Uterque enim amat Phedrum quamvis non similiter. Uterque persuadet non indulgendum incontinenter amanti. Duo in nobis duces: cupiditas voluptatum, et legalis opinio. Amor incontinens definitur ita: irrationalis cupiditas trahens ad voluptatem forme.

[345] Nymphe, Dionysus, Muse. Cap. VII.

Num tibi o amice etce. Nymphe sunt numina que generationi presunt. Ideo dicuntur aquas inhabitare vel silvas, quoniam generatio et per humorem expletur et descendit ad silvam id est materiam primam. Dionysus his est prefectus.[2] Est enim deus generationi regenerationique presidens. Ideo forte bis natus fingitur. Huic conveniunt hymni, dithyrambi inflati, obliqui, multiplices. Quoniam vero animus aliter et aliter affectus aliis quoque aliisque afflatur numinibus, ideo Socrates attentissime trac-

---

[1]NB. P *has no heading for any summa*   [2]profectus E

the regenerator. We need silence for divine inspiration, that is,
freedom from alien motions. But that spot is divine which is
subject to the more outstanding influences and divinities. Socrates is only divinely inspired in Plato when he speaks of love
and beauty; for he is personally more drawn to these, and visible beauty recalls invisible beauty to mind, the love of which
unites us with God. Here Socrates started out inspired by the
more peaceful divinities, the Muses, but he ended in the frenzies
of Dionysus. For contemplations pass on into frenzies.

Chapter 8. [238D]

The familiarity of an intemperate lover can be the cause of
numerous evils to the beloved insofar as it opposes the goods of
his soul, body, and fortune.

Chapter 9. The local demons. How demons can lead souls both upwards and downwards. [240A]

The degree to which the familiarity of an intemperate lover is
not only harmful but annoying. There are many demons distributed through [the world's] provinces. They are allotted to the
various genera of things, animals, and lives. These demons also
detain souls in the provinces they have already chosen. Hence in
the *Republic* Plato describes the demons as the leaders of chosen
lives, of fate, and of chance.[63] They move our imaginations by
means of their own imaginations, powers, and devices to believe
in and to hope for future pleasure someday in such things. They
do this even when we are very young and first make choices;
whence they seem to mix "the bait of pleasure" with evils, that
is, with our inclinations toward lower things, in order that they
may detain us in this their province for a longer time. In a way,
if the good demons do it, they do it so that the universal order
may be fulfilled; if the bad demons, that they might interfere
with it. In the good demons, that is, in the world's rulers, are

tans de amore, qui in generatione versatur, mox tractaturus de amore regenerante nimirum a Dionyso Nymphisque corripitur. Silentio id est vacatione ab alienis motibus opus est ad divinum afflatum. Locus autem ille divinus est qui prestantioribus subest influxibus atque numinibus. Socrates apud Platonem ibi solum divinitus concitatur ubi[1] de amore et pulchritudine loquitur. Ad hec enim et ipse propensior est, et pulchritudo visibilis in memoriam revocat invisibilem,[2] cuius amor copulat nos cum deo. Incepit autem hic a pacatioribus id est a Musis, desivit in bacchanalia. Contemplationes enim perveniunt in furores.

[346] Cap. VIII.

Age igitur o etce. Quot malorum causa[3] sit amato consuetudo amatoris incontinentis, quantum obsit bonis animi et corporis et fortune.

Demones locales. Quomodo demones et elevent animas et deducant. Cap. VIIII.

Sunt alia quoque etce. Quantum amatoris incontinentis consuetudo non solum sit noxia sed molesta. Multi[4] sunt demones per provincias distributi. Alii illic alia sortiti rerum animalium vitarum genera. Hi animas, que talia iam[5] elegerunt, in talibus quoque detinent. Hinc in Republica Plato describit demones electarum vitarum et fati sortisque ductores. Movent igitur[6] imaginationibus et viribus machinisque suis imaginationes nostras ad opinionem spemque voluptatis in eiusmodi rebus quandoque future. Idque faciunt etiam ab initio electionis etatisque humane; unde videntur iocundam escam malis id est inclinationibus ad inferiora miscere, ut in hac ipsorum provincia diutius demorentur. Si boni demones id quodammodo faciunt, ut uni-

---

[1]et *add.* P   [2]invisibilis E   [3]causas E   [4]Multas P   [5]iam *om.* P   [6]in *add.* P

powers with which they may justly detain us in a certain manner
and powers with which they may at some time release us or
recall us to celestial things. Iamblichus proves this when he says
that such demons partly bind us to fate and partly free us from
it.[64] Hence Orpheus often sings that the divinities hold keys with
which they may equally close and open.[65] Having been enraptured by the Nymphs, Socrates therefore can liberate a young
man from desires.

Chapter 10. The Nymphs, Bacchus, the Apollonian Demon. [241D]

Socrates has been inspired by Bacchus mainly to dithyrambs,
by the Nymphs to songs. Through the Nymphs he censures the
intemperate lover, through Bacchus he approves of the temperate; the result is, so to speak, that he brings the young man
forth again. Finally, since he has become ecstatic through Bacchus, perhaps the Apollonian demon immediately enraptures
him (for Apollo is closest to Bacchus) with the result that he
even exceeds the bounds of human behavior and thereafter
treats of the divine love that excites us through some frenzy.

Chapter 11. The way in which a demon can move our imagination and sense. [242B]

Although a demon may indeed frequently move the imagination, which is the universal sense, through his own imagination
and can thus move it through the sight and hearing alike, nevertheless he moves Socrates through the hearing. For Socrates is
the most eager of all for instruction and dedicated, as it were, to
the hearing. But how? Either the demon takes the concept to be
imagined and effectively extends it to or generates it in the inmost hearing; or the demon himself in his own spiritual body
forms the sound by a certain marvelous motion, and with the
same motion strikes as a sound upon the spiritual body of Soc-

versalis ordo expleatur, [347] efficiunt; sin demones improbi, ut officiant. In demonibus quidem bonis id est mundi rectoribus sunt vires quibus ad certum modum iuste detineant, et quibus quandoque solvant ac revocent ad superna, ut probat Iamblicus qui eiusmodi demones inquit partim quidem alligare nos fato, partim vero solvere. Hinc Orpheus sepe numina claves tenere canit quibus videlicet claudant pariter et aperiant. Potest itaque Socrates raptus a Nymphis adolescentem a libidinibus vindicare.

Nymphe, Bacchus, demon phebeus. Cap. X.

Cur[1] ergo etce. Afflatus est Baccho ad dithyrambos precipue, a Nymphis ad carmina. Per Nymphas vituperat amatorem incontinentem; per Bacchum probat continentem, ut adolescentem quasi regeneret. Denique quoniam per Bacchum fit excessus, mox demon forte phebeus (Phebus enim Baccho proximus) corripit, ut etiam mores humanos excedat tractetque [348] posthac de amore divino per furorem aliquem excitante.[2]

Quomodo demon moveat imaginationem atque sensum. Cap. XI.

(So.) Cum flumen etce. Demon profecto cum imaginatione sepius imaginationem moveat, que sensus est universus ideoque possit ita movere per visum ut per auditum, Socratem tamen discipline studiosissimum et auditui deditum quasi per auditum movet. Sed quomodo? Sane vel conceptum imaginabilem efficaciter ad intimum propagat auditum, vel format ipse demon in suo corpore spiritali vocem motu quodam miro eodemque motu pulsat corpus Socratis spiritale (quasi voce quadam), quo quidem vibrato excitatur ad idem et auditus Socratis intimus. Sed

[1]*preceded by* Pausanias. P   [2]excitantes P

rates. When this vibrates, Socrates's inmost hearing is excited to the same. But Socrates here makes it plain that dwelling in his soul is a presentiment that is quite apart from the reminder he receives from his demon.

Chapter 12. How love is a god or godlike. The kinds of love dwelling in a god and in other beings. [242D]

It is most dangerous to offend not only against a god but even against a divine name. This crime is atoned for through penitence, but late penitence is dangerous. Love is a god or something godlike. Indeed, something divine is that love that is the longing to contemplate divine beauty or even to imitate it, whether this longing is in a divine intelligence, in a celestial soul, or in a particular soul like ours. Such a love is everywhere Venus's son, that is, son of the vital and effective power that strives towards the intelligible forms. It is ignited by a certain abundance and dearth equally, as we explain in [the commentary] on the *Symposium*.[66] In addition to being something divine, love is also a god, that is, the god in whose presence love flourishes. Or rather he is the highest god, for just as he can be called beauty in Plotinus, being the fountain of beauty, so he can be called love, too, as the author of the love that attains beauty.[67] For when Plotinus puts the will first, he is about to deny, not love itself, but assuredly the love that is poor.[68]

Chapter 13. The kinds of loves, frenzies, and oracles. [243E]

Love is threefold: intemperate, temperate, and divine. The first hurls the soul down towards corporeal beauty; the second turns it back towards animate beauty, that is, to morality and wisdom; the third recalls it to intelligible and ideal beauty. Socrates and Lysias have openly censured the first; Socrates has secretly praised the second; and now at last Socrates is about to praise the third. Anyone who absolutely disapproves of love necessarily errs; and anyone who condemns intemperate love on

preter demonicam admonitionem inesse presagium animo Socrates hic plane declarat.

[349] Quomodo amor sit deus aut divinus. Qualis amor in deo qualis in aliis. Cap. XII.

(So.) Gravem o Phedre etce. Periculosissimum est peccare non solum contra deum sed etiam contra divinum nomen. Crimen per penitentiam expiatur; sed periculosa est penitentia sera. Amor autem deus est aut divinum quiddam. Profecto divinum quiddam est amor ille, qui est desiderium divine pulchritudinis contemplande vel etiam imitande; sive hoc desiderium sit in mente divina, sive¹ in anima celesti, sive particulari quadam atque nostra. Eiusmodi Amor ubique est filius Veneris, id est vitalis et effective potentie ad formas intelligibiles annitentis. Conflaturque ex copia quadam pariter et inopia, quemadmodum exponimus in Convivio. Est quoque deus amor, id est ille deus penes quem viget amor; immo et deus ipse summus, ille enim sicut apud Plotinum appellari pulchritudo potest tanquam fons pulchritudinis, sic et amor tanquam auctor amoris pulchritudinem consequentis. Ubi enim Plotinus in primo voluntatem ponit, non negabit amorem, sed inopem certe negabit.

Species amorum, furorum, oraculorum. Cap. XIII.

(So.) Sic ergo o egregie etce. Triplex amor est, incontinens, continens, divinus. Primus ad formam corporis precipitat animum; se[350]cundus convertit ad pulchritudinem animi, mores scilicet atque sapientiam; tertius ad intelligibilem idealemque revocat pulchritudinem. Primum Socrates Lysiasque palam vituperavere. Secundum Socrates clam laudavit, deinceps iam tertium laudaturus. Erret necesse est quisquis amorem simpliciter improbaverit. Erret quoque quisquis amorem incontinentem

---

¹sine P

the grounds that it is a frenzy, that is, an alienation of the intelligence, also errs. For the love that alienates a soul, which has been seized by a god and raised above man, is also a frenzy, though a frenzy we should venerate since it comes from a god, makes us godlike, and is both the cure of the greatest evils and the cause of the greatest goods. It is therefore more excellent than human temperance or prudence, which are neither the cures of such great evils nor the causes of such great goods.

We have discussed sufficiently the definition of *frenzy* and the order of the four frenzies in [the introduction to] the *Ion* and [the commentary on] the *Symposium*.[69] And we have dealt sufficiently with prophecies, oracles, and the power of sacrifices in our work on Iamblichus and in the [*Platonic*] *Theology*.[70] It must be enough at this point for us to understand that both Plato and the Platonists openly affirm prophecies, oracles, miracles, and atonements for crimes.[71] They also put the divine frenzy far before human wisdom (as the apostle Paul also declares),[72] and affirm that divine prophecy is to be wholly preferred to men's predictions, which proceed from craft and skill.

The oracle at Dodona came from Jupiter, at Delphi, from Apollo: both were operated by Jovian and Apollonian demons and perhaps by men and instruments of a Jovian or Apollonian character. At Dodona they gave the replies to a woman crowned with oak leaves, whereas at Delphi to a woman on a tripod. Socrates mentioned both of them together as if they were kin, so to speak. For in the heavens [the planets] Jupiter and the Sun are totally in accord in their hidden power: the Sun is the principal minister of Jupiter the craftsman, and his illuminating power accompanies Jupiter's power to fabricate.

Chapter 14. How the four divine frenzies are joined together. The mundane gods. The divine and human souls. [245A]

In describing any one frenzy, Socrates in a way recalls the others: not unjustly so, for they are mutually joined. In the intelligible world the illuminating power of Apollo possesses the related inciting [or producing] and, as it were, heating power of

hac propria ratione damnaverit quia sit furor quidam id est alienatio mentis. Est enim preterea et furor aliquis per quem animus alienatur deo raptus super hominen elevatus; hic venerandus est, quoniam est a deo facitque divinum, atque est maximorum tum malorum medicina tum bonorum causa. Est ergo prestantior quam humana temperantia vel prudentia, que non tam ingentium vel malorum remedia sunt vel bonorum cause.[1]

De furoris definitione ac de quatuor furorum ordine satis in Ione et Convivio loquimur. De vaticiniis et oraculis sacrificiorumque virtute una cum Iamblico et in Theologia satis egimus. Satis esto nunc intelligere vaticinia et oracula et miracula[2] expiationesque criminum palam a Platone et Platonicis affirmari; divinumque furorem humane sapientie, quod et Paulus Apostolus ait, longe preponi, vaticiniumque divinum artificiosis hominum presagiis summopere preferendum.[3]

Dodoneum oraculum ab Iove, Delphicum ab Apolline, per demones videlicet iovios et phebeos hominesque forte consimiles et instrumenta conformia. Ibi quidem femine quercus frondibus coronate[4] responsa dabant; hic in tripode respondebant. Connumeravit utraque Socrates quasi cognata. Iupiter enim et Sol in celo virtute occulta maxime consonant, et Sol opificis Iovis precipuus est minister, et virtus [351] illustratoria virtutem opificiam comitatur.

Quomodo quatuor divini furores sunt invicem copulati. Dii mundani. Anime divine atque humane. Cap. XIIII.

Tertia vero a Musis etce. Non immerito in furore quolibet[5] describendo furorem quemlibet quodam pacto commemorat. Sunt enim invicem coniugati. Nam in mundo intelligibili illuminatoria. Phebi virtus coniugatam habet provocantem et quasi calefactoriam Bacchi virtutem. In virtute quidem illuminatrice

---

[1] *no* ¶ P   [2] *et miracula om.* P   [3] *no* ¶ P   [4] coronante E   [5] quodlibet E

Bacchus. The power for prophecy and poetry flourishes in the illuminating power, the power for love and [priestly] prayer in the inciting. In the heavens there is a similar bond in the Sun and near the Sun. For light and heat refer to both Apollo and Bacchus. Furthermore, the Sun's power incites us via Mercury to the Muses [that is, to poetry], and via Venus to love. But how the Sun's power may signify prophecy and priest-craft may be left at this point to the astrologers. Finally, in us the understanding and the will are kin: prophecy and poetry pertain to the former, but priestly prayer along with love to the latter. Accordingly, we often flee from prophecy to prayers, and often from prayers we acquire prophecy. On the one hand we sing divine hymns with the Muse [that is, with poetry]; on the other we are incited to the love of divine things. In turn, by always loving such ardently, we prophecy many matters and perform mysteries effectively and sing hymns of admiration. Poetry of this last kind, which is poured into us from on high, Plato prefers even to philosophy, while the poetry of men he drives far from the city.[73]

The debate to be is not only about the soul but about almost all divine matters. Though it may seem unbelievable perhaps to the argumentative, nevertheless it is believable to the divine, that is, to the wise. The debate is principally about the divine and human soul. Divine souls are either mundane gods—the souls of the spheres and stars—or souls that always follow these gods—the sublime souls that rule in the world's spheres, angels, demons, heroes. Summarily I am glad to call these animate beings demonic. After them come our souls: sometimes they follow the gods, sometimes not. Inferior demons, if any, are also of this kind. The nature of divine souls is revealed in the main through their works, the nature of our souls through their desires, now for temporal things, now for eternal too.

Chapter 15. Two syllogisms on the soul's immortality. [245C]

All soul is immortal, that is, all rational soul human and divine alike, as premised a little earlier. Since Socrates, like

viget virtus ad presagium et poesim; in provocatrice vero ad amorem atque vota. Simile quoddam in celo coniugium est in sole penesque solem. Lumen enim calorque Apollinem referunt atque Bacchum. Solaris preterea virtus per Mercurium quidem ad Musas per Venerem vero provocat ad amorem. Sed quomodo vaticinium sacerdotiumque significet nunc astrologis concedatur. In nobis denique intelligentia voluntasque sunt germane. Ad illam quidem vaticinium cum poesi, ad hanc autem mysteriale votum pertinet cum amore. Quamobrem ex vaticinio sepe ad vota confugimus, ex votis sepe consequimur vaticinium. Et utrobique divinos cum Musa canimus hymnos, utrobique ad divinorum incitamur amorem, atque vi[352]cissim divina semper ardenter amando multa vaticinamur, mysteria efficaciter operamur, hymnos canimus admirandos. Eiusmodi poesim divinitus nobis infusam Plato etiam philosophie preponit, humanam vero procul ex urbe propulsat.[1]

Futura disputatio non solum de anima sed etiam de divinis ferme omnibus; quamvis contentiosis forte incredibilis videatur, divinis tamen id est sapientibus est credibilis. Disputatur de anima divina et humana potissimum. Anime divine sunt vel ipsi dii mundani scilicet spherarum stellarumque anime, vel anime que semper sequuntur hos deos scilicet sublimes animi in spheris mundi rectores, angeli, demones, heroes. Hec equidem[2] animalia summatim demonica libenter appello. Post hec sunt anime nostre que aliquando sequuntur deos, aliquando non sequuntur, et siqui inferiores demones sunt eiusmodi. Patet vero maxime natura animarum divinarum per opera, nostrarum vero per affectus tum ad temporalia tum etiam ad eterna.

[353] Syllogismi duo de immortalitate anime. Cap. XV.

Anima omnis immortalis etce. Anima omnis est immortalis; omnis inquam paulo ante premissa[3] scilicet rationalis, tam humana quam divina. Quoniam vero Socrates tanquam furore

---

[1] *no* ¶ P   [2] quidem P   [3] promissa P

someone incited by frenzy, does not arrange the parts of the syllogisms entirely in order, let me briefly present them as follows.
Since through the soul's presence bodies reach the point of
seeming to be self-moved in a way, we can agree that the soul
naturally possesses the quality of being able to move and act of
and through itself. Hence two syllogisms are woven primarily
from the same premise. First: the soul is mobile through itself.
What is mobile through itself is always moving; because it never
forsakes itself, it is never deserted by the moving power. That
is, if it is always moving as a result of an internal motion, it is
always alive. Therefore the soul is immortal. The second syllo-
gism is thus: the soul is mobile through itself. Therefore it exists
as the principle of motion. The principle of motion is unbegotten. What is unbegotten is immortal. Therefore the soul is
immortal.

**Chapter 16. Charioteers and horses in divine or human souls—
their quality. [246A]**

In divine souls the charioteer and [his] horses are all called
good. They are always good because they are never corrupted;
and they are constituted from good things—from the better
genera of being, or, rather, from the five genera possessed by all
things but which they possess in a more outstanding manner.
But our charioteer and horses have a disordered and obvious
contrariety, since they can become bad at times even though
they derive from good things; this is especially because our inferior horse turns aside towards the worse genera of being,
motion, and difference. Our charioteering is said to be **difficult**
because, while the superior horse's motion is towards intelligibles, the inferior's inclines towards sensibles and descends to
generation. In this life our soul is not capable of both contemplating and providing at the same time, but a divine soul is capable, and so will our soul be when it has been eventually restored
to its native land.

concitus syllogismorum partes non omnino disponit in ordinem, nos ita breviter componemus. Cum per ipsam anime presentiam corpora consequantur, ut appareant quodammodo per se moveri, constat animam naturaliter hoc habere, ut ex se ipsa et per se ipsam moveatur et agat. Hinc syllogismi duo precipue ex eodem capite contexuntur. Primus: anima per se mobilis est. Quod per se mobile semper movetur; quia nunquam se ipsum destituit nec unquam a virtute motrice deseritur. Si semper movetur scilicet motu quodam intimo, semper vivit. Anima igitur immortalis. Secundus vero syllogismus: anima per se mobilis est. Igitur principium motus existit. Principium motus ingenitum. Quod ingenitum, immortale. Anima igitur immortalis.

Qualitas aurigarum et equorum in animabus divinis vel humanis. Cap. XVI.

De immortalitate anime etce. Auriga in animabus divinis et equi[1] dicuntur omnes boni, id est semper boni quia nunquam depravan[354]tur, et ex bonis id est constant ex melioribus generibus entis; immo ex eisdem communiter quinque generibus sed prestantius se habentibus. Nostri vero permixtam habent manifestam contrarietatem, cum evadere quandoque possint ex bonis mali; presertim quoniam equus noster inferior ad deteriora entis[2] genera id est motum alteritatemque declinat. Dicitur autem aurigatio nostra **difficilis**, quoniam motus quidem superioris equi[3] ad intelligibilia, inferioris autem ad sensibilia vergit, ad genituramque declinat. Neque potis est anima nostra in hac vita[4] contemplari pariter atque providere; anima vero divina potest, et nostra tandem in patriam restituta.

---

[1]qui P   [2]*em.*; etiam P, entium E   [3]qui *add.* P   [4]vita *om.* P

Chapter 17. The immortal and the mortal animal. [246B]

The immortal animal is composed of a soul and a celestial body, but the mortal animal of an elemental body besides. This mortal animal, man, arises from the soul's fall from life's universal reason to the particular reason, from heaven to earth. It is difficult to understand how wonderfully the immortal animal has been composed.

Chapter 18. The freeing or impeding of the wings in the soul. [246D]

The wing is the lifting power that is divinely implanted in the intellect and reason. When freed, it flourishes and effectively lifts them to the divine. All that is divine is good, wise, and beautiful. Lifting to the divine in this life, therefore, restores the soul to the position of participating in such gifts and prepares it to enjoy them perfectly in another life. But if the soul in this life turns itself towards the contraries—that is, to the bad (which is longing for sensibles), to the ignorant (which is the senses), to the ugly (which is matter)—it binds the wing so that after this life it cannot immediately fly back to the heights.

Chapter 19. Great Jupiter in heaven. The twelve leaders under him and the army of divinities. [246E]

Great Jupiter, the leader in heaven, the world-soul, the soul that has preeminence among the celestial souls, **quickens his winged chariot,** that is, activates the twin motions of conversion in himself (so described in the *Timaeus*).[74] He **proceeds first,** for he is the first to be moved [or he is the primum mobile of astronomy]. He moves his external chariot through his own internal motions; that is, he moves the world's machine through his own internal chariot, which is said to be winged; for while he rules the world he still devotes himself to divine things. So in this way

Immortale animal et mortale. Cap. XVII.

Qua vero ratione etce. Immortale animal est ex anima corporeque celesti compositum, mortale vero ex corpore insuper elementali. Hoc mortale animal scilicet homo provenit ex lapsu anime ab universali vite ratione ad particularem, ex celo ad terram. Quam vero mirabiliter animal immortale sit conflatum difficile cognitu.

[355] Expeditio vel impedimentum alarum in anima. Cap. XVIII.

Per quam vero etce. Ala, id est virtus elevans intellectui rationique divinitus ingenita, quatenus expedita viget, efficaciter elevat ad divinum. Omne vero divinum est bonum, sapiens, pulchrum. Elevatio igitur ad divinum in hac vita participem animum donorum eiusmodi reddit, preparatque ut in alia vita his perfecte fruatur. Si autem animus in hac vita se transferat ad contraria—id est ad malum quod est affectus ad sensibilia, item ad ignorans quod est sensus, item ad turpe quod est materia—ligat alam ut nequeat post hanc vitam mox ad sublimia revolare.

Iupiter magnus in celo. Duodecim sub eo duces atque exercitus divinorum. Cap. XVIIII.

Magnus utique etce. **Iupiter dux in celo magnus**, id est animi mundi que inter celestes animas principatum tenet, **citans alatum currum**, id est exercens in se geminum conversionis motum in Timeo descriptum, **incedit primus**. Est enim mobile primum, atque [356] ita per interiores motus movet currum exteriorem id est machinam universi per currum interiorem qui alatus dicitur, quoniam dum regit mundum nihilominus divinis incumbit. Sic igitur feliciter exornat universaliter cuncta simulque facillime

he universally adorns all things and simultaneously provides for them with the utmost ease. **Following him,** that is, imitating him through their motion, are the world leaders, the souls of the twelve spheres; and after them come the stars' souls and those of the higher demons. They follow him, I say, in that they move externals through the same internal motions and at the same time contemplate divine things. When Socrates uses the terms **proceed, lead, quicken, follow**—all of which signify progression—he calls upon poetic license to exclude Vesta, the soul of the earth. For such terms seem less appropriate for her, the ruler of a stable mass, while for the other leaders among the twelve they seem more probable. Even so, she enacts her own motions and her mass's more hidden motions; and she enacts them in a fixed order, that is, with the power and providence that have been divinely imposed upon her as her own. The rest of the spheres' souls and the divine souls like them similarly enact [their motions] with their providence, though with a motion more manifest than hers. When they govern their machines with the same ease as Jupiter, then they happily gaze in the intellectual heaven upon the divine things shining from above. These are called **the spectacles** when they pertain more to what they see with a motionless gaze, but **the ways to and fro** when they pertain more to what they see as their gaze moves around. Each of the gods performs the office assigned him from above, in part of contemplating, in part also of providing, neither function hindering the other. Since the beneficent nature of the gods always overflows with goodnesses to all, it is just that any particular soul (of a man or of some lower demon) that is **both willing and able** follows the gods immediately, that is, is again called above by them and rides away a participant in like felicity.

Chapter 20. The banquet in the native land. The way and the steps of contemplation. [247A]

The mundane gods and the souls accompanying them approach **the table** and **the highest feast,** that is, they approach

providet. **Hunc sequuntur,**[1] id est per motum imitantur, duces mundani, duodecim spherarum videlicet anime; deinde anime stellarum sublimiumque demonum. Imitantur inquam per similes motus intimos exteriora movendo et divina interim contemplando. Socrates, dum pronuntiat **incedere, ducere, citare, sequi** (que quasi progressionem significant), interim licentia quadam poetica Vestam id est terre animam excipit. Huic enim molem regenti[2] stabilem cognomenta[3] eiusmodi minus convenire videntur;[4] ceteris autem in duodenario ducibus probabilius convenire. Agit tamen motus ipsa suos, sueque[5] molis occultiores, eosque certo quodam ordine id est proprietate quadam et providentia propria sibi iniuncta[6] divinitus; suaque [providentia] similiter cetere spherarum anime similesque divine, sed manifestiore motu. Dum vero suas ita machinas moderantur ea facilitate qua Iupiter, divina interim feliciter speculantur in celo intellectuali superne lucentia. Ubi profecto **spectacula** nominantur que ad stabilem intuitum magis attinent, **discursiones** vero que ad mobilem circunspectum. Quisque vero deorum institutum sibi divinitus officium peragit, partim quidem contemplandi, partim etiam providendi, neutro neutrum impediente. Cum natura deorum benefica bonis in omnia semper exuberet, merito quicunque particularis animus (sive ho-[357]minis sive inferioris demonis alicuius) **vult atque potest** subito deos sequitur, id est sursum revocatur ab illis, similisque felicitatis compos evadit.

Convivium in patria. Modus atque gradus contemplandi. Cap. XX.

Cum vero ad mensam[7] etce. Dii mundani comitesque eorum animi accedunt **ad mensam epulumque summum,** id est ad contemplationem diis supermundanis convenientem. Mensa qui-

---

[1]*em.*; sequutur E, sequitur P   [2]ingenti P   [3]cognomento P   [4]videtur P
[5]-que *om.* P   [6]invicem P   [7]convivium P

the contemplation that is proper to the supermundane gods. This is called a table insofar as they receive in proportion to their capacity, but a feast insofar as they receive in proportion to the generosity of the givers. In their approach they first attain the concave circumference of the intellectual heaven, that is, the furthest or lowest orders of intellectual beings. Then they ascend through the middle orders to the highest. In this ascent all the chariots of the gods and of the divine souls, since they are obeying the charioteer and are evenly balanced, **proceed with ease;** and by chariots I mean all the internal discursive [that is, rational] powers that follow on the understanding of all and simultaneously contemplate and provide equally. The chariots of particular souls and of our souls, however, proceed on the journey **with more difficulty.** The worse horse is drawn towards generation and even drags the charioteer down with it unless he has trained and mastered it properly. But the divine souls, the constant followers of the gods, when they arrive by contemplation at the height of the intellectual heaven, **halt there**, that is, they do not turn aside to another place. **The circumference**, that is, the fastest intellectual movement or discourse of reason proper to that height, agrees with them there: through this discourse they contemplate the supercelestials, that is, the intelligible heaven. When you hear me say "temporal discourses," take it to mean that, whereas the pure intellects understand motionlessly, the mundane gods and divine souls revolve around and ponder the intelligibles with a perpetual movement or discourse of their reason; when our souls do likewise, however, they need particular intervals of time.

Chapter 21. The supercelestial place. The prime intelligible. The way of contemplation. [247C]

Since Socrates is about to discuss the intelligible world, he declares he is about to speak the truth. For truth, as the *Republic* says, is the light that proceeds from the good and is diffused through both intellects and intelligibles.[75] Primarily it is in the

dem dicitur quantum pro suo modo suscipiunt, epulum vero quantum pro largitate donantium. In hoc autem accessu primo quidem concavam intellectualis celi circunferentiam id est ultimos intellectualium attingunt ordines; deinde ascendunt per medios ad supernos. In hoc autem ascensu omnes deorum divinorumque animorum currus, aurige obedientes equaliterque librati, **facile gradiuntur**—currus id est intime discursive vires omnes que et omnium sequuntur intelligentiam, et simul possunt equaliter [358] contemplari atque providere. Currus autem particularium nostrarumque animarum **difficilius** illud iter agunt: in quibus deterior equus ad generationem inclinatur, et trahit secum etiam aurigam qui non bene hunc educaverit atque domuerit. Animi vero divini assidui deorum pedissequi, cum ad summum intellectualis celi contemplando pervenerint, in eo summo **consistunt** id est nusquam declinant.[1] Ibi **circunferentia**, id est intellectualis discursio velocissima[2] illi summo conveniens, illis competit; per quam supercelestia id est celum intelligibile[3] contemplantur.[4] Tu vero,[5] ubi audis temporales discursiones, intellige puros quidem[6] intellectus stabiliter intelligere, deos vero mundanos animosque divinos discursione perpetua circa intelligibilia[7] se versare,[8] nostros autem per quedam temporum intervalla.

Locus supercelestis. Intelligibile primum. Modus contemplationis. Cap. XXI.

Locum vero supercelestem[9] etce. Socrates de mundo intelligibili loquuturus inquit se de veritate dicturum, quoniam veritas ut dicitur [359] in Republica est lumen ex ipso bono per intellectus intelligibiliaque diffusum; in primis autem in intellectum et

---

[1]declinatur P [2]illa *add.* P [3]intelligens P [4]contemplatur Iuno P
[5]Tu vero *om.* P [6]quidem *om.* P [7]intelligentia P [8]versari P [9]superceleste P

prime intellect and the prime intelligible, where its splendor is the prime beauty. It is called **the supercelestial place**; place because it is the first complex [that is, the first complement and combination] of the ideas. This complex is the first, universal, and perfect essence. Neither tangible to the senses, figurable to the imagination, nor possessed of color for the simple reason, it can be perceived by an intellect alone. Primarily it exists in a supermundane intellect, then in a mundane intellect, the leader of its soul. A celestial soul attains the intelligible world only through its intellect (but it attains God, who is still higher, through its unity). Why does Socrates say that this intelligible world **uses** the intellect contemplating it, not that it is apprehended by it? Because it uses it as its instrument and reveals itself to it with its own light. The genus of true knowledge for a soul is in this place, because, though divine souls have formulas of the ideas implanted in them and turn to these formulas in order to acquire knowledge, nevertheless they do not acquire the highest knowledge through their turning, unless, by means of the implanted formulas, they transfer themselves to the ideas.

Accordingly, the cogitation of a god, that is, the process of acquiring knowledge discursively in any leading mundane god, is nourished by the supermundane gods in [his] intellect and by the knowledge that is inviolable. For the discourse of reason starts from understanding as its beginning and arrives at knowledge as its end. Similarly, the cogitation of any divine soul perpetually accompanying the gods is illumined and nourished by the supermundane and the mundane gods. Such cogitation, in that it is about to receive from the higher gods the limits of contemplation, felicity, and providence proper to itself, always perceives the intelligible entity as their gift. At first sight it loves it as the beautiful, then it contemplates the same more attentively as the true, or rather as truths. For it sees the ideas of all entities in the one entity and, in gazing on it, is nourished and perfected. Hence it possesses well-being and rejoices as in the good. As in the *Philebus,*[76] Socrates here locates felicity in the mixture that results from vision and joy.

The divine souls, however, are said to see the ideas **through**

intelligibile primum, ubi splendor eiusmodi est pulchritudo prima. Illic **locus** dicitur **supercelestis,** locus inquam id est prima complexio idearum. Hec prima et universa perfectaque essentia est, nec sensu tangibilis, nec imaginatione figurabilis, nec ratione simplici colorabilis, sed intellectu solo perspicienda. In primis[1] quidem in[2] intellectu supermundano, deinde in[3] intellectu mundano anime sue duce, per quem solum celestis anima mundum attingit intelligibilem (deum vero superiorem per unitatem). Sed curnam hoc intelligibile dicitur intellectu[4] contemplatore **uti** potius quam apprehendi? Quoniam hoc illo utitur ut instrumento, suoque illi lumine se patefacit. Genus autem vere scientie circa animam hunc habet locum, quoniam, etsi anime divine insitas idearum formulas habent ad quas sese convertunt scientiam adepture, nondum tamen scientiam consummatam per eiusmodi conversionem adipiscuntur, nisi per formulas insitas se transferant in ideas.[5]

Proinde cogitatio dei, id est discurrens illa cognitio in mundano quovis deo principe, a supermundanis nutritur intellectu scientiaque inviolabili. Nam discursio et ab intelligentia incipit velut principio et ad scientiam pervenit velut finem. Cogitatio quoque divine cuiuslibet anime deos perpetuo comitantis similiter a supermundanis mundanisque diis illustratur atque nutritur. Cogitatio eiusmodi, que convenientem sibi contemplationis et felicitatis et providentie modum a superioribus acceptura est, semper eorum munere ens ipsum intelligibile suspicit; primoque aspec[360]tu hoc amat ut pulchrum, mox idem attentius contemplatur ut verum, immo tanquam vera. In uno enim ente entium omnium contuetur ideas; contuendo nutritur atque perficitur. Hinc bene se habet atque gaudet ut bono. Hic Socrates ut in Philebo felicitatem in mixtione quadam ex visione et gaudio collocat.[6]

Dicuntur autem anime divine ideas videre **per tempus,** non

---

[1]primo P   [2]in *om.* P   [3]in *om.* P   [4]intͭͭs [= intellectus] P   [5]*no* ¶ P   [6]*no* ¶ P

time. This is not because they stop seeing them at any point, but because they go from contemplating some ideas to others in a temporal circuit. Having started out from an [idea at the] head of ideas, they begin to proceed through the subsequents and never cease until they return by the same steps back to the same head. That celestial circumference above the visible heaven **rules** this circling in the soul. For the circling of the understanding and the height it attains in the supermundane intellect leads the souls' circuits to the supercelestials, that is, to the intelligibles. What the circling of an intellect completes in a moment, the circling of a soul, however, enacts in time, until it too is brought back to the same head along with the circuit of the intellect. Remember that the intellectual souls, in that they are souls, must act with motion through all their powers, since motion is the natural property of the soul and pertains to its essence. Insofar as they are intellectual in power, however, souls possess a certain motionless intuition in their intellect, an intuition that is beyond the mobile understanding and in accord with those above.

Chapter 22. The objects and grades of contemplation in the homeland. [247D]

Although a divine soul discourses on the intellectual circuit through all the ideas, Socrates makes particular mention of three: **justice, temperance,** and **knowledge.** For these three principally lead to felicity and most pertain to beauty. The knowledge in question is not born from notions, like that which is in the soul; nor is it as one thing in another, as a formal reason exists, as it were, in the intellect; nor is it the knowledge of what we commonly call entities, for it does not look at natural things as objects. Rather it is the unbegotten, simple, and essential power, essence itself. It looks at its own essence as object, and it exists in the prime entity as the true knowledge, the exemplar and cause of all that can be known. The divine soul, therefore, observes not only these three ideas but also the rest of the ideas,

quia quandoque desinant intueri, sed quoniam ideas alias ex aliis temporali quodam circuitu contemplantur; et postquam a quodam idearum capite ceperunt per sequentia progredi, nunquam desinunt donec ad idem caput iisdem gradibus revertantur. Hunc in anima circulum **regit** circunferentia illa celestis super visibile[1] celum. Nam intelligentie circulus atque summitas in intellectu supermundano circuitus animarum ad supercelestia scilicet intelligibilia ducit. Sed quod intellectualis circulus momento complectitur id tempore peragit animalis, donec etiam ad idem caput una cum intellectuali circuitu referatur. Memento intellectuales animas qua ratione anime sunt per omnes vires suas mobiliter agere, siquidem motus est proprietas anime naturalis necessario pertinens ad essentiam; verumtamen qua proprietate intellectuales sunt habere in intellectu ultra mobilem intelligentiam intuitum quendam stabilem superioribus competentem.

[361] Obiecta et gradus contemplationum in patria. Cap. XXII.

In hoc autem circuitu etce. Etsi anima divina intellectuali circuitu per omnes discurrit ideas, tamen de tribus potissimum Socrates mentionem facit, **iustitia, temperantia, scientia**. Hec enim precipue ad felicitatem conferunt et ad pulchritudinem maxime pertinent. Scientia quidem illa non est ita ex notionibus genita sicut que est in anima; nec est ut aliud in alio sicut quasi formalis ratio quedam in intellectu; nec eorum que communiter entia nominamus, non enim res naturales aspicit ut obiecta. Sed est ingenita et simplex et essentialis virtus ipsaque essentia, essentiamque suam aspicit ut obiectum; atque est in ipso ente primo scientia vera scientiarum omnium exemplar et causa. Divina igitur anima non has solum tres ideas sed etiam ceteras

---

[1]visibilia P

which are in truth the entities, being nourished by its observation. For this last is not a "thin" or solitary vision, but a natural disposition or affection that functions by tasting and enjoying no less than by seeing. While the soul is looking at the entities, it immediately **sinks back to heaven again** away from them —for they exist in the superheavenly place—as away from its principles and models; it proceeds, that is, to contemplate intellectuals. Then it proceeds from the intellectuals to considering itself and the things that properly pertain to the nature of soul; and this is **to return home.** We must not suppose that, when divine souls set out from the supercelestial place to proceed to the celestial and thence home, they abandon the higher grade for the lower. They use their highest powers, rather, to act above heaven, their middle to act in heaven, and their lowest to act at home; and they do all three everywhere on the circuit simultaneously. Since the divine soul goes from the contemplation of higher things home to the consideration and exercise of its own property (whence it provides for mundane things), the **charioteer,** the intellect, **stops his horses at the stable,** that is, fills the lower powers (through which providence is enacted) with the goods derived from contemplation. **At the stable,** that is, at the memory and preservation of divine things, **he nourishes them with ambrosia,** with solid sustenance, insofar as he stops them in their causes and goods, **and likewise with nectar,** with liquid, insofar as he strengthens and calls upon them to come forth providing in abundance. This is the life of the gods, that is, of the celestial and of the higher demonic souls, whose number is computed secretly. It is our life too insofar as we contemplate the intelligibles with our utmost attention and our utmost longing equally.

Chapter 23. The causes of the souls' descent. [248A]

Our soul has powers with which it can contemplate divine things and provide for inferiors. If it can always fulfill both tasks, for the good of all and then for itself, then it must do so.

que vere sunt entia speculatur, et speculatione nutritur. Non enim est illic visio tenuis aut sola sed naturalis affectio per modum gustandi non minus quam videndi. Dum illa videt, mox ex illis que in supercelesti loco sunt velut a principiis exemplaribusque **celum subit iterum** procedens scilicet ad intellectualia contemplanda; ex intellectualibus autem ad se ipsam et que proprie ad anime naturam pertinent contuenda, idque est **redire domum.** Neque vero putandum divinas animas, cum a loco supercelesti ad cele[362]stem et ab hoc domum[1] proficiscuntur, superiorem gradum pro inferiore relinquere; sed supremis viribus suis super celum agere, mediis in celo, infimis vero domi, simul quidem tria hec efficere et ubique circuitu. Quoniam anima divina ex contemplatione superiorum accedit domum ad suam proprietatem considerandam atque exercendam unde mundanis providet, ideo **auriga,** id est intellectus, **ad presepe sistit equos,** id est vires inferiores, per quas peragitur[2] providentia, bonis contemplatione profectis implet. **Ad presepe,** id est ad memoriam conservationemque divinorum, **nutrit ambrosia,** solido nutrimento, quatenus eos sistit in causis suis atque bonis, **item nectare,** liquido, quatenus roborat et provocat ut providendo foras exuberent. Atque hec est vita deorum id est celestium demonicarumque sublimium animarum, quarum in numero clam computatur, et nostra, quatenus attentione summa affectuque pari intelligibilia contemplatur.

Cause descensus animarum. Cap. XXIII.

Ceterarum vero animarum etce. Anima nostra vires habet quibus contemplari divina potest et quibus inferioribus providere. Si utrumque [363] semper universo bonum et sibi denique bonum explere potest, ergo[3] debet. Quoniam vero et ipsa est

---

[1]demum P   [2]P *has a colon here and no pointing after* implet   [3]primo P

But since our soul is the lowest of the divinities, and the governing of our body on earth most difficult, and since it thus cannot
fulfill both tasks absolutely simultaneously, it probably fulfills
them alternately, now pursuing the celestial life, now the
earthly. Since the soul should not be forced by divine influence
to come from heaven hither, it descends, rather, as a result of a
natural condition. Since the circuit of its understanding has its
measures, and these will last for certain intervals of time, and
since the vegetative action also has its measures, the activity of
the soul's understanding is gradually in a while remitted, and
similarly its desire. But the remission of intention is soon the
origin of future intermission. And intermission is at length the
cause of future abandonment. Meanwhile, to the extent that the
activity and desire of the understanding are remitted, the activity and desire of the generative power and of the imagination
(which is entirely similar) and also of cogitation are intensified.
All this will be **to lose [one's] wings,** and to sink down to quickening the body (which is still lower) and to governing the province of earth. Thus Socrates touches on the three effects in [the
right] order, namely those of remission, intermission, and abandonment, when he has the charioteer **unperturbed** by the horses
until he remits contemplation, **unconstrained** by them until he
intermits it, and **unconquered** by them until he abandons it.

When Socrates's poetic license invents the souls' **struggling
together** in heaven, it signifies that, when the contemplation of
supercelestials has been abandoned in the consideration of celestials, not only is the concupiscible power that concerns subcelestials aroused, but also the irascible power and warlike pride.
When the souls have thus been finally thrown into disorder, the
prize they ultimately carry off is opinion instead of the knowledge of divine things. Because the soul retains a certain hidden
memory of that beauty, however, when it recalls it in a way, it
chooses to recover it completely. Eventually it will receive that
beauty **from the meadow of truth,** that is, from the fullness of
the ideas in the intelligible world. Since this is so, it is always
justly drawn to the knowledge of all things. Whenever it becomes liberated, it will strive for knowledge zealously.

ultimum divinorum, et hec in terris nostri corporis gubernatio difficillima, ideoque utrumque simul prorsus implere non potest, probabiliter per vices implet, tum quidem celestem vitam agens tum vero terrenam. Sed cum inde[1] huc[2] divinitus compelli non debeat, naturali quadam potius conditione descendit. Siquidem intelligentie sue circuitus mensuras habet suas certis temporum curriculis duraturas, mensuras quoque suas actio vegetalis, remittitur igitur paulatim actus intelligentie sue quodam tempore, similiter et affectus.[3] Intentionis autem remissio future mox intermissionis est origo. Intermissio vero future tandem dimissionis est causa.[4] Interea quatenus actus et affectus ille remittitur, eatenus actus affectusque potentie genitalis consimilisque imaginationis necnon cogitationis intenditur. Id totum erit **amittere pennas** et labi deorsum ad corpus iam inferius vegetandum ac terrenam provinciam gubernandam. Tres igitur illos scilicet remissionis, intermissionis, dimissionis effectus Socrates ordine tetigit, ubi auriga **non** prius **perturbatur** ab equis quam contemplationem iam remittat, **neque cogitur** ab eisdem nisi iam intermittat, **neque superatur** nisi dimittat.[5]

Ubi vero **mutua** animarum **certamina** poetica licentia finguntur in celo, significatur supercelestium contemplatione dimissa in ipsa etiam consideratione celestium vim non solum concupiscibilem circa subcelestia, sed irascibilem etiam pugnacemque superbiam excitari atque ita denique perturbatas pro scientia divinorum opinio[364]nem denique reportare. At quoniam animus latentem quandam beatitudinis illius memoriam retinet, quando illius quodammodo reminiscitur, optat summopere illam recuperare; quam denique **ex ipso veritatis prato** id est intelligibili mundo idearum plenitudine recepturus, merito ad ipsam rerum omnium scientiam semper afficitur, et siquando fuerit expeditus studiose contendit.

---

[1] in E   [2] hunc E   [3] effectus P   [4] *em.*; cauda EP   [5] *no* ¶ P

Chapter 24. The soul's state in its native land. Its descent and return, and its nine lives. [248C]

Does the remission of understanding or the intensifying of the lower nature come first? This is the question. In some places Plato seems to suggest the former, in others the latter; and the Platonists similarly.[77] So, everything considered, perhaps the most likely solution is that both happen simultaneously. For it is impossible for the higher power to be distracted by the lower as long as it thrives in its native land. Nor can one believe that the more eminent power is easily diverted from so much good, unless either its power or its activity is naturally remitted, while the power of the power that is drawn down towards its opposite is intensified. Therefore both occur at the same time, that is, with the harmony of the universe similarly in accord. For the universal harmony is governed **by Adrastia**, that is, by an inescapable law of divine providence. Adrastia decrees laws not only for the mundane [gods] but for the supermundane too and arranges them in their orders.

Under this law, our soul, while it devotes all its attention to contemplating some idea that is the head of a particular circuit and does so in the company of its own god in that grade of supernal contemplation, thus performs the entire circuit (which continues through the ideas consequent on the head idea), as long as it encounters no impediment. Having also performed this, should the head of another circuit arise, it devotes equal attention also to proceeding likewise upon it. Whenever it goes around the head of some circuit a little too negligently, however —the result of its own weakness in that its higher power is now somewhat remitted and its lower simultaneously intensified— then it sinks from its former state to a grade a little worse. It sinks from the intelligible to the intellectual perhaps, thence to the rational, thence immediately to the imaginative and sensual, from a higher sphere to a lower, and at last to the elements. The final descent occurs when it has already constrained its wings, the powers that raise it to the divine. Consequently it forgets divine matters, especially if it has **by some chance** fallen among

Status anime in patria; discessus; reditus; vite novem.
Cap. XXIIII.

Regulaque Adrastie[1] dee etce. Queritur utrum prius sit,
remissione intelligentie an nature deterioris intentio. Plato alicubi quidem prius illud alicubi vero prius hoc indicare videtur
similiterque[2] Platonici. Omnibus igitur pensitatis probabile
forte fuerit simul utrumque concurrere. Neque enim fas est virtutem superiorem, quamdiu in patria sua viget, a deteriore
potentia inde distrahi; neque credibile prestantiorem illam facile
e tanto bono diverti, nisi et vis eius sive actus naturaliter remittatur, et vis interim potentie declinantis ad oppositum intendatur. Itaque pariter utrumque concurrit, harmonia scilicet universi similiter concinente; que qui[365]dem universa regitur **ab**
Adrastia[3] id est inevitabili quadam providentie divine lege, que
non mundanis solum sed etiam supermundanis leges sancit[4]
ordinesque distribuit.[5]

Sub hac igitur lege noster animus, dum in illo contemplationis superne gradu suum comitatus deum ideam aliquam que sit
circuitus alicuius caput attentissime contemplatur, integrum
illum circuitum per consequentes ideas inde continuatum ab
impedimento procul peragit. Hoc quoque peracto si caput alte-
rius exorditur, studio pari pariter quoque prosequitur. Siquando vero circa periodi alicuius caput paulo negligentius agat
—scilicet propter impotentiam suam quia iam vis superior ali-
quantulum remittatur simulque intendatur inferior—ex illo
statu delabitur ad gradum aliquanto deteriorem: forte[6] ab intelligibili ad intellectualem, ab hoc deinceps ad rationalem, ab hoc
subinde ad imaginalem atque sensualem, a sphera quadam
superiore ad inferiorem,[7] ac tandem ad elementa. Id postremo
contingit quando alas id est vires ad divina tollentes iam
coegerit in angustum, unde obliviscitur divinorum, presertim si
casu quodam in demones inciderit ad sensibilia[8] divertentes.

---

[1]Adastrie P   [2]simulque P   [3]Adastria P   [4]scandit P   [5]*no* ¶ P   [6]formam P
[7]interiorem P   [8]sensualia P

those demons who turn away towards sensibles. Nevertheless, the soul that has just descended from heaven cannot be precipitated **into a beast**. For souls are purgatorially dispatched to treat with beasts when, having deviated still further from the celestial property, they have laid aside human characteristics and doffed those of wild animals.

As long as souls in their native land use their intellect alone, with the mundane and the supermundane gods, and contemplate the intelligible world diligently, all there see all things equally although all things in different ways. But when souls have begun to use their intellect with their reason, along with the mundane gods, in order to consider the celestial bodies and their souls, then not all of them now gaze upon all things: some gaze upon more, others on less. From nine differences in their vision nine future lives now make a beginning. Moreover, since there are nine principal celestial souls, the world-soul together with the souls of the eight celestial spheres, and since our souls while they dwelt in heaven were especially accommodated to them, each to his particular god, then, as they devote themselves to celestials having abandoned higher things, they appear in justice to submit to nine differences. This is in order to bring hither the nine mental dispositions for displaying the nine faculties distributed jointly to the nine grades. But when we say that this soul has seen **more** than that soul has seen, you must understand it to mean not only more in a numerical sense, but also that whatever they have seen they have comprehended with more reasons and with more ardent study.

The soul, therefore, which has observed more has brought hither the mental disposition of a philosopher, that born to examine all things. Such a disposition, since it is studious of truth and wisdom and since beauty is prime among these, has in justice brought with it the study of beauty. Thus wherever Plato names the wise itself, his custom is almost always to add the beautiful itself. We perceive the image of that beauty with our sight and hearing, as both Hermias in glossing this passage and Plotinus in his book on beauty testify.[78] Thus after Plato mentioned the philosopher, in justice he immediately mentioned the

Neque tamen potest anima nuper celitus descendens **in brutum** precipitari, siquidem in aliqua brutorum commertia *tanquam ad purgatorium anime transmittuntur postquam a celesti proprietate longius iam digresse humanos etiam** mores exuerunt, et induere ferinos.

Quandiu vero anime in patria solo intellectu utentes una cum mundanis supermundanisque diis mundum intelligibilem sedulo contemplantur, illic cuncte pariter omnia vident, etsi aliter et aliter omnia. Postquam vero intellectu simul et ratione una cum diis mundanis circa celestia corpora eorumque animas considerandas [366] uti coeperunt, iam non omnes omnia contuentur, sed he quidem plura, ille vero pauciora. Hic iam ex novem differentiis visionum novem vite future auspicantur initia. Quinetiam cum novem sint precipue celestes anime (scilicet anima mundi simul et octo spherarum celestium anime) quibus anime nostre aliis alie potissimum illic habitantes accommodate sunt, merito, dum dimissis superioribus ad celestia potius se convertunt, differentias novem subire videntur ad ingenia novem huc afferenda circa facultates novem expediendas novem communiter gradibus distributas. Ubi vero dicitur hanc animam **plura** vidisse quam illam, intelligendum est non solum numero plura, sed quodcunque viderint pluribus rationibus et ardentiori studio comprehendisse.[1]

Que igitur ita plura perspexit ingenium attulit philosophicum ad omnia perscrutanda natum. Ingenium eiusmodi, cum sit veritatis et sapientie studiosum, in his[2] autem prima sit pulchritudo, merito studium pulchritudinis secum attulit. Ideo Plato ubicunque nominat ipsum sapiens, ferme semper adiungere solet ipsum pulchrum. Pulchritudinis illius imaginem visu percipimus et auditu, quemadmodum et hic Hermias et Plotinus in libro de pulchro testatur.[3] Merito igitur postquam nominavit philosophum, statim nominavit pulchri cupidum; cui subdit

---

[1]*no* ¶ P   [2]*for* in his P *reads* id   [3]*tractatur* P   *-**om.* P

man desirous of the beautiful; to him he subordinates the lover and the man of music and poetry, the former because he desires visible beauty, the latter, audible. But the soul that has gazed at somewhat fewer things or gazed more negligently descends into the mental disposition of a king; for the king wields the universal providence among men, whereas the philosopher contemplates larger matters besides. The military general and the magistrate-for-life accompany the king.

The soul, again, which sees even fewer things descends into the local politician, the businessman, and the merchant; for the prudence exercised by such men is narrower than the king's providence.

In fourth place follows the mental disposition of the physical trainer and doctor, whose providence is constrained within even more narrow limits.

But what mental disposition does he have in mind when he puts that of the priest and prophet in fifth place? Understand by this, not the divine priest, but the common feed priest, who busies himself with auguries, entrails, and public ceremonies and who depends, not on the knowledge, art, and skills the higher priests depend on, but on a sort of custom and on chance.

In sixth place and descending from the bounty of contemplation comes the imitative faculty, a servant, as it were; and this accords, not with the divine poet, but with the human poet, even the least of them.

In seventh place is any craftsman and farmer, men who are subject to external matter and have a province narrower than the imitator has.

Still further away in eighth place are the pretenders, those who proceed under a false guise of reason: the Sophist who apes the philosopher, the demagogue who pretends to be a genuine politician.

Finally and furthest away of all is the mental disposition of the tyrant, not because he apes the king, but because he introduces the arbitrary will instead of the reason. However, we can make use of any kind of mental disposition to do something

amatorem atque musicum, illum quidem propter visibilem, hunc vero propter audibilem pulchritudinem. Anima vero que aliquanto pauciora negligentiusve conspexit cum regio descendit ingenio. Rex enim universalem quidem apud homines providentiam gerit, sed philosophus ampliora etiam contemplatur. Regem co[367]mitatur belli dux atque perpetuus magistratus.[1]

Sed que anima[2] rursus pauciora vidit in virum civilem et economicum mercatoremque descendit. Horum enim prudentia angustior est quam providentia regia.[3]

Sequitur gradu quarto gymnasticum ingenium atque medicum, quorum providentia insuper angustioribus limitibus coercetur.[4]

Sed quidnam quidnam sibi vult quinto[5] gradu ingenium sacerdotis atque fatidici? Non divinum hic sacerdotem sed mercenarium plebeumque intellige, auguriis extisque et vulgaribus cerimoniis occupatum, qui neque scientia neque arte qua superiores illi sed consuetudine quadam nititur atque sorte.[6]

Sexto gradu a contemplationis liberalitate discedit[7] facultas imitatoria quasi servilis, que non divino poete competit sed humano similiterque minimo.[8]

Septimo quivis[9] artifex et agricola externe materie serviens et angustiorem[10] provinciam[11] habens[12] quam imitator.[13]

Octavo iam longius distant simulatores qui falso quodam pretextu rationis incedunt: sophista[14] philosophum simulans, declamator vero civilem.[15]

Longissime denique tyrannicum distat ingenium, non tam quia regem simulet quam quoniam pro ratione introducit arbitrium. Qualibet autem ingeniorum specie *ad aliquod bonum uti possumus atque malum. Ideo subdit Socrates, quicunque in aliqua vite specie** iuste se gesserit meliorem postea sortem

---

[1]*no* ¶ P   [2]*anime* E   [3]*no* ¶ P   [4]*no* ¶ P   [5]*sexto* P   [6]*no* ¶ P   [7]*discendit* P
[8]*no* ¶ P   [9]*quis* P   [10]*angustiore* P   [11]*provincia* P   [12]*habens om. but space*
provided P   [13]*no* ¶ P   [14]*quidem add.* P   [15]*no* ¶ P   *‑**om.* P

good or bad. Socrates therefore adds that whoever has behaved justly in any kind of life will afterwards win for himself a better fate, whoever unjustly, a worse one.

Chapter 25. The transmigration and restoration of souls—the times involved. Our soul does not become a brute beast's. [248E]

The numbers 3 and 10 are said to be perfect, since the former is the first complete number but the latter, in a way, is the universal number. Ten multiplied by itself is 100, 10 squared; multiplied again by itself is 1000, 10 cubed. Again when we multiply this 1000 by 3 we arrive at 3,000, by 10, at 10,000. Socrates uses such numbers because their perfection can signify the soul's purgation and restoration (since eventually it must emerge as perfect). And he uses them, not because there are strictly so many years, but for us to understand that, however many the years involved, the soul must be perfected with a perfect reason. There is another reason why 1,000 is appropriate for the time taken to transmigrate from generation to generation, that is, from one earthy body to another, or from an earthy to an airy or the reverse, for this solid or cubed number signifies the earth, which the *Timaeus* imagines as a cube.[79] It also signifies the material body, that is, earth as an element. Three thousand is appropriate for restoring the philosopher above, not so much because he eventually ought to be confirmed in the diligent study of philosophy after three lives in this earthy body, as for the following [two reasons]. First, the soul that has practiced philosophy in this earthy body must also do so when it migrates hence into the body of mixed or impure air; and it will do so if it perseveres in philosophizing from the very beginning of its life until the end. Second, having freed itself from the mixed body, it must eventually also continue its philosophical meditation to the utmost in the body of pure air. This is what it means to have practiced philosophy for 3,000 years. The soul is thence immediately restored to heaven to win back wisdom in place of phi-

reportaturum; qui autem iniuste, deteriorem.

[368] Tempora transmigrationis restitutionisque animarum. Animam nostram non fieri brutam. Cap. XXV.

In idem enim unde etce. Numerus ternarius et denarius perfecti dicuntur, quoniam ille quidem primus numerus est completus, hic autem quoniam est quodammodo numerus universus. Denarius in se quidem ductus centenarium facit planum; reductus autem millenarium facit solidum. Rursus adhibemus ternarium ad mille, hinc tria milia constituimus; denarium rursus ad mille, hinc conficimus decem milia. Eiusmodi numeris propter perfectionem suam ad purgationem restitutionemque anime, quoniam perfecta tandem evadere debet, Socrates utitur non quia tot proprie anni sint, sed ut intelligamus, quotcunque anni contigerint, eam perfecta ratione consummari debere. Convenit et alia ratione millenarius transmigrationi a generatione in generationem facte, a corpore scilicet terreno in terrenum, vel hinc in aerium vel vicissim. Numerus enim solidus significat terram que in Timeo figuratur cubo. Significat etiam materiale corpus scilicet elementum. Convenit termillenarius philosopho sursum[1] restituendo, non tam quia per tres in hoc terreno[2] corpore vitas deinceps sit sedulo philosophie studio confirmandus, quam quoniam oporteat animum in hoc corpore philosophatum quando hinc migraverit etiam in aerio corpore mixto philosophari (quod quidem efficiet [369] si in vita priore ad finem usque philosophando perseveraverit); et quoniam oporteat insuper exutum corpore mixto deinceps in aerio puro meditationem philosophicam ad summum continuare.[3] Hoc est igitur ter mille annis philosophatum esse. Unde mox celo redditur sapientiam pro philosophia tandem reportaturus. Oportet

---

[1]rursuꝰ P [2]terno P [3]continuamur P

losophy. But we must practice philosophy **without guile**, that is, for the sake of divine, not human, wisdom. The soul will return more quickly and effectively if it not only esteems the divine goodness as it studies the divine wisdom, but also acknowledges from the beginning its marvelous beauty and loves it ardently.

Ten thousand is appropriate for the mental dispositions of other men, those who either did not take up the study of philosophy in their first life immediately after their descent or, having begun it then, did not hold to it in a subsequent life. For they return to their native land most slowly; and this slowness is signified by the number 10,000. Nine kinds of life have been posited. If you suppose someone has already completed these nine lives (having once started on the study of philosophy, that is, but not continued in it), you will recognize that he is afterwards compelled to turn back to philosophy again, as if to the tenth life, if he is to return to his native land. Such is meant then by the number 10,000. By these steps souls are brought back, therefore, **to the same**, but to the same what? First, to the same sphere and star with which they were accommodated from the beginning—this occurs perhaps more immediately; second, to the same idea again and entirely to the same degree of contemplation and blessedness which they once enjoyed—this occurs perhaps somewhat later.

Consequently, souls who have had no part in contemplative philosophy but whose bodies have now been laid aside, if they have lived justly, are dispatched by the divine judgment **to one of heaven's places**, that is, to the air with an airy body (for the air for us is the first heaven). If they have lived unjustly, they are dispatched **under the earth**. We can interpret the earth to mean the earthy body of man. The soul can pass over, as it were, from the earthy man into the earth again, even to places under the earth set aside for punishment. But the divine judgment leads the various souls, who have already been restricted through their own inclinations, to places appropriate for them. The vegetative nature similarly leads some things upwards through [their] levity, but others downwards through [their] heaviness.

autem philosophari **sine dolo** id est non humane sapientie gratia sed divine. Celerius autem redibit et melius, si una cum sapientie divine studio non modo divinam dilexerit bonitatem, sed etiam pulchritudinem eius mirabilem agnoverit ab initio et ardenter amaverit.

Preterea numerus decem milia aliorum accommodatur ingeniis, qui non statim in prima post discessum vita philosophie studium capesserunt, vel in hac inceptum in sequente minus retinuerunt. Hi enim in patriam tardissime revertuntur; que sane tarditas per hunc numerum designatur. Iam vero cum novem vite genera disposita fuerint, si finxeris aliquem iam novem peregisse eiusmodi vitas (cum inceptum quondam philosophie studium nequaquam continuaverit), cognosces eum post vitas omnes novem cogi rursus ad philosophiam reverti quasi iam decimam modo sit in patriam reversurus. Id igitur per numerum decem milia significatum fuerit. His itaque gradibus **ad idem** animi revertuntur, sed ad quidnam idem? Primo quidem ad eandem spheram atque stellam cui ab initio accommodati fuerint, et hoc forte citius; secundo rursus[1] ad eandem ideam ad eundemque omnino contemplationis beatitudinisque gradum quo aliquando fruebantur, atque id forte serius.

Proinde contemplative philosophie expertes anime hoc [370] deposito corpore, si iuste vixerint, iudicio divino mittuntur[2] **in quendam celi locum** id est in aerem cum aerio corpore (aer enim celum nobis est primum); si iniuste, **sub terram.** Terram exponere possumus terrenum corpus hominis, quasi de homine terreno rursus transeat in terrenum, loca etiam subterranea suppliciis[3] deputata. Iudicium vero divinum sic varias animas per ipsas[4] animarum inclinationes iam contractas ad convenientia loca perducit, sicut vegetalis[5] natura[6] alia quidem sursum per levitatem, alia vero deorsum per gravitatem.

---

[1]reversus P   [2]mittantur P (*in* E *too, but corrected in corrigenda*)   [3]suplici P

[4]ipsarum P   [5]virilis P   [6]nostra P

The rational soul does not cross over into a beast in order to become the soul of the beast's body. When it has exchanged its desire and disposition for those of a beast, however, it falls into the companionship of beasts, as Proclus and Hermias maintain.[80] Perhaps it even attaches itself to their souls from above, in accordance similarly with the decrees of the divine judgment.

Some suppose that we should reckon the rational and irrational soul in the same species, as if irrational souls were nothing other than souls that had been rational but were now fallen.[81] Socrates clearly refutes such people when he says that the soul does not come out of a beast into a man, unless that very same soul had once been a man's soul, a soul, that is, which had formerly gazed on the truth itself. It is as if a man's soul were in a species other than the beast's soul; and whenever it comes into the companionship of beasts, it does not do so as a substitute for the life of a beast's body. For the shape of a beast's body is not appropriate for the rational soul, just as the shape of a man's body does not accord with the irrational soul.

In describing our soul's proper office, Socrates shows that the irrational soul proper for a beast, since it has never gazed on the truth, does not come into the shape of our soul. For our soul's proper office is its ability **to assemble one universal concept from the [many] particulars it has perceived**. This concept is commonly called the species. Through it the soul can arrive some day at the universal formula naturally implanted in it; and through this formula, at the idea, the idea that not only is called a species but in actuality is the species. The beast's soul cannot do this since it has none of the formulas of the ideas implanted in it. But thus to arrive through the formulas at the ideas (which is the office of the rational soul) is nothing other than to recall those intelligibles that the soul once saw in heaven when it followed there its mundane god. Since the philosopher, even here on earth, devotes himself to the same things as does the mundane, that is, the celestial, god, it is just he should receive wings to fly back to heaven. There he becomes divine by contemplating intelligibles rather than celestials. Similarly, his celestial god exists as a divine being principally because he gazes upon the intelligibles, along, that is, with a supercelestial divinity.

Non transit in bestiam anima rationalis ut fiat anima bruti corporis. Sed cum in ferinum se affectum et habitum commutaverit posthac in bestiarum commertia, ut Proclus Hermiasque volunt, cadit. Forte etiam bestiarum animabus se desuper applicat divino similiter iudicio decernente.

Nonnulli sunt qui putent rationalem animam atque irrationalem in eadem specie computandam, quasi irrationales anime nihil aliud sint quam ipsemet que rationales fuerant sed iam prolapse. Hos Socrates manifeste confutat, dicens animam ex bestia in hominem non venire nisi illammet animam que quondam fuerat hominis; illam inquam que ipsam prius inspexerat veritatem (quasi anima hominis in alia specie sit quam anima bruti; et siquando in brutorum[1] commertium[2] venerit, non fuerit corpori ferino pro vita, quoniam neque figura ferini corporis anime rationali conveniat, sicut neque irrationali competit hec corporis humani figura).[3]

Quod autem irrationalis anima illa bruti propria, quippe que nunquam inspexerit veritatem, non veniat in hanc corporis nostri figuram [371] ostendit Socrates, dum proprium anime nostre describit officium: id est ut **conspectis particularibus colligere conceptum unum de illis** possit **universalem**. Qui conceptus communiter species dicitur, per quem ad universalem formulam anime naturaliter[4] insitam quandoque perveniat, perque hanc ad ideam que non solum dicitur species sed existit. Id vero nequit anima bruti, quippe cum nullas idearum formulas *insitas habeat. Pervenire autem hoc pacto per formulas** ad ideas (quod est anime rationalis officium) nihil est aliud quam reminisci intelligibilium illorum, que quondam viderat in celis animus, suum[5] ibi mundanum deum sequutus. Et quia philosophus etiam in terris eisdem incumbit quibus et mundanus deus scilicet ille celestis, merito recipit alas quibus in celum revolet; ubi divinus evadat non tam celestium quam intelligibilium contemplatione, quemadmodum et celestis ille deus suus intelligibilium intuitu summopere divinus existit, divinitate scilicet quadam supercelesti.

---

[1]brutum P [2]commertitum E [3]*no* ¶ P [4]rationali P [5]sicut P *–**om. P

Chapter 26. How the contemplator may become divine and emerge as the lover of divine beauty. [249C]

In examining the reasons of all things, the legitimate philosopher repeatedly conceives common notions in himself from the common natures he perceives in individual things. Through these common notions he arrives at the formulas implanted in himself, and through them he finally attains the ideas. Through the ideas he intellectually discovers the divine wisdom and goodness. He makes correct use of these meditations, if he wholly venerates and worships the divine wisdom and goodness as soon as he discovers them. Hence he is filled full with divinity. Like a priest (for he is a theologian) he is said to have been purified to the utmost and carried off by the hieratic, by the Dionysian, frenzy.

He alone, therefore, is disposed to the amatory frenzy. Since he is accustomed to remembering intelligibles through sensibles and to worshiping the divine wisdom and goodness through them, then if ever he gazes upon visible beauty more attentively, he will in justice through it recall the divine beauty with great ease and will love it more ardently. For the divine beauty exists as the splendor of divine goodness and wisdom. This amatory frenzy is more outstanding than the other three both because **it comes from the best things**—it is excited, that is, from beauty itself and wisdom and goodness, and is filled with our unity—and also because it unites us more effectively and more firmly with God [or with a or the god].

Chapter 27. The mental disposition that is more apt for remembering. How beauty shines most. [249E]

Because of their own and their leaders' differences, some of our souls in heaven saw **more briefly** than others—more briefly meaning either fewer things, or for less time, or more negligently. The souls who thus contemplated more briefly do not bring hither the mental disposition of a philosopher or that

Quomodo contemplator fiat divinus, divineque pulchritudinis evadat amator. Cap. XXVI.

Talibus autem commentationibus[1] etce. Legitimus philosophus, dum rationes rerum omnium perscrutatur, frequenter ex communibus [372] naturis quas deprehendit in singulis communes in se concipit notiones; per quas ad formulas sibi insitas pervenit, per has tandem attingit ideas, per ideas excogitat sapientiam bonitatemque divinam. His meditationibus recte utitur, si sapientiam bonitatemque divinam cum primum invenerit summopere veneratur et colit; hinc divinitate prorsus[2] impletur, et quasi sacerdos (est enim theologus) ad summum dicitur expiatus mysterialique et dionysiaco furore correptus.[3]

Hic itaque solus ad furorem amatorium est propensus. Cum enim per sensibilia consueverit intelligibilium reminisci, sapientiamque per hec et bonitatem divinam colere, merito, siquando visibilem pulchritudinem intueatur attentius, facile admodum per hanc divine pulchritudinis recordabitur[4] (que divine bonitatis et sapientie splendor existit) eamque ardenter amabit. Furor hic amatorius tribus aliis prestantior est: tum quia **fit ex optimis** id est excitatur ipsa pulchritudine, sapientia, bonitate, et impletur unitate[5] nostra; tum quia nos cum deo efficacius firmiusque coniungit.

[373] Quod ingenium sit ad reminiscentiam aptius; et quomodo pulchritudo maxime luceat. Cap. XXVII.

Ut enim dictum est etce. Anime nostre in celo pro differentiis earum ducumque suorum alie **brevius** viderunt quam alie— brevius id est[6] pauciora, vel breviori tempore, vel negligentius. Anime igitur ita brevius contemplate ingenium huc afferunt neque philosophicum[7] neque reminiscentie divinorum aptum,[8] presertim si educationem consuetudinemque hic alienam a phi-

[1]commentanti P   [2]prorsus *om.* P   [3]*no* ¶ P   [4]recordatur P   [5]bonitate P
[6]*for* id est P *reads* enim   [7]philosophicium E   [8]aptu E

adapted for remembering divine things. This is especially true if they were allotted here an education and upbringing alien to philosophy. But the souls who there contemplated greater things and contemplated them more have brought hither the mental disposition of a philosopher. If these souls, moreover, are educated in a philosophical way, they easily recall divine things through images, and particularly those things that might have revealed their likenesses even to the senses. Now the ideas of wisdom, justice, and temperance have imparted their likenesses to souls, but not to bodies at all. Wherefore we scarcely remember them and only tardily so by way of certain hidden instruments, namely, syllogisms. But divine beauty, in that it is the splendor of the good sparkling in the series of the ideas, clearly propagates its images not only to souls but even to sensible forms. Hence it summons us back to itself through both internal and external things; and, to the degree that it has more light than the ideas, it moves and inflames souls the more. It has more light, however, because it is more accessible to us, especially through the sight, the most acute of our senses, and also because it is not a part there but the whole splendor in all the ideas, and this the most perfect. Similarly, the body's beauty is not a part of it, but precisely the pattern or ornament of the whole; and just as this beauty appears to us first in the body, so too does that splendor. It is the first to meet those ascending thither and seizes and totally delights them on every side, like the pleasure of physical intercourse. For intercourse is the delight of the whole body, and, as the most obvious of all the pleasures, excites us the most.

Chapter 28. How philosophers derive from Jupiter. Saturn and Jupiter. Contemplation in one's native land; its kind. The light there and how beauty reveals most. [250B]

Only the souls of philosophers are said to contemplate **with Jupiter** in heaven; for the souls who there gaze about with Jupiter, inasmuch as they have seen more, descend into philosophers

losophia sortite fuerint. Anime vero ampliora illic et amplius contemplate philosophicum huc ingenium attulerunt; que si philosophice insuper educantur facile per imagines divinorum reminiscuntur, eorum precipue divinorum que similitudines suas ad sensus usque protulerint. Idee quidem sapientie, iustitie, temperantie similitudines suas animis indidere, corporibus vero nequaquam; propterea vix recordamur illarum et sero quidem per instrumenta[1] quedam occulta scilicet syllogismos. Pulchritudo vero divina, quoniam est splendor ipsius boni in ipsa idearum serie micans, imagines suas non solum ad animas sed etiam usque ad formas sensibiles manifeste propagat. Hinc nos per interna et per externa revocat ad se ipsam, et quanto plus habet luminis quam idee, tanto magis movet animos et inflammat. Plus autem luminis habet non solum quoniam circa nos magis pateat, presertim per visum sensuum acutissimum, sed quoniam illic est non pars quedam sed universus in cunctis splendor et is quidem consummatissimus, sicut et pulchritudo corporis non pars quedam est sed universale specimen et exactum; et sicut hec nobis apparet prior in corpore, sic splendor ille. Primus ascendentibus illuc occurrit, ma[374]ximeque hic et ibi rapit atque delectat, sicut venerea voluptas, quia totius corporis delectatio est atque[2] manifestissima pre ceteris voluptatibus maxime concitat.

Quomodo philosophi sunt a Iove. Saturnus. Iupiter. Qualis contemplatio in patria. De luce illa; et quomodo pulchritudo maxime pateat. Cap. XXVIII.

At pulchritudinem tunc etce. Sole philosophorum anime in celo contemplari dicuntur **cum Iove**, quia que illic cum Iove speculantur, utpote que plurima viderint, veniunt in philosophos (cum Iove id est cum anima mundi; nam et ad illam et ad

---

[1]intima P   [2]est atque *om.* P

(with Jupiter means with the world-soul; for the most ample contemplation and providence pertain to the world-soul and to the philosopher). When the philosopher follows Jupiter, who is the world-soul, he also follows the planet Jupiter. For the planet Jupiter corresponds to the animate intellect, that is, to the world-soul, just as the planet Saturn corresponds to the higher Saturn, that is, to the pure, separated intellect. Plato proves that the philosopher is neither Saturnian nor utterly separated, but is Jovian rather in that he both contemplates and provides.

While the souls there contemplate the ideas, which are called **the blessed spectacles**, they are said to be initiated into sacred mysteries and to effect sacred works, since they look up at and grasp hold of higher things through the ideas. That contemplation is not vision alone, but a desirable appetite pertaining to [our] nature; it is love, joy, veneration, and providence. As Socrates's words make clear, however, these gifts mainly pertained to the philosopher-to-be when he existed **in the pure light**, that is, in the light of the highest good, the light that joins the intellect with the ideas. Through this light in the ideas and from the ideas beauty shines out at the same time in all things. It shines out as if it were going forth; for alone of divine things beauty manifestly goes forth through all and advances into the sight there and here likewise as eagerly as a liquid. The earthy body is called **an oyster shell**, as it were, because it is like a lock and because the body that is firstly and truly alive is the celestial or the airy body.

Chapter 29. The mental disposition that is prepared for remembering. The pouring in of beauty. Love as winged. [250E]

The soul said to have been recently initiated or dipped into the sacred mysteries is the soul that sees more in heaven and has been educated on earth as a philosopher. For this soul alone arrives at divine beauty from corporeal beauty. By degrees it accepts the influx of beauty through its eyes, not just of human

philosophum amplissima contemplatio et providentia pertinet).
Philosophus dum sequitur Iovem qui est anima mundi sequitur
etiam Iovem planetam; sic enim planeta Iupiter respondet intellectui animali scilicet anime mundi, sicut Saturnus planeta
Saturno superiori id est intellectui puro atque separato. Plato
vero philosophum probat[1] non saturnium et penitus segregatum
sed iovialem qui contempletur atque provideat.[2]

Anime dum illic contemplantur ideas, que **beata spectacula**
nominantur, dicuntur sacris imbute mysteriis sacraque operari,
quoniam et per illas superiora suspiciunt [375] atque capiunt. Et
contemplatio illa non visio sola est sed etiam affectio quedam
optabilis pertinens ad naturam, et amor, gaudium, veneratio,
providentia. Sed ut Socratis verba declarant hec munera ad
futurum philosophum summopere pertinebant **in luce pura**,
scilicet in luce summi boni que intellectum copulat cum ideis.
Emicat autem per hanc lucem in ideis atque ex ideis pulchritudo
simul cunctis; emicat inquam quasi procedens, quoniam hec
divinorum sola per omnia manifeste procedit, et ibi[3] similiter
atque hic in aspectum tam vehementer quam liquido prodit.
Terreum corpus dicitur quasi **ostree testudo**, quia quasi claus-
trum, et quoniam corpus primo vereque vivens est celeste scilicet vel[4] aerium.

Quod ingenium aptum ad reminiscentiam. Pulchritudinis in-fluxus. Amor alatus. Cap. XXVIIII.

Qui ergo non est mysteriis etce. Nuper sacris initiatus vel
imbutus mysteriis dicitur animus, qui et in celo plurima vidit,
et in terris est philosophice educatus, hic solus ex corporea pulchritudine pervenit ad divinam; sed gradatim pul[376]chritudi-
nis influxum per oculos accipit non humane solius sed divine,
hec enim resplendet in ista. **Influxus** dicitur, quia non solum

---

[1]*probat om.* P   [2]*no* ¶ P   [3]*sibi* P   [4]*vel om.* P

beauty but of divine also; for the one shines brightly in the
other. It is called beauty's **influx** because it not only moves the
sight but also completely affects our nature with heat and
motion and stimulates it to the sublime and reforms and transforms it. Plato's other points, especially as they bear on the
mental disposition of the lover, are sufficiently obvious either
here or in the *Symposium*. [82] Finally Plato concludes that love is
winged, because, either alone or principally, it raises us to the
sublime. This raising is necessary for the salvation of souls that
have thence set forth. So Plato calls love winged **by necessity** or
winged by nature. Another reason perhaps [for the term **influx**]
may be that love necessarily flows into us.

**Chapter 30. The orders of souls and demons according to the
stars. The planet Venus, or Juno, and the way in which she is
Jupiter's sister and spouse. The kind of souls who are her followers. Each man's god or demon. The recognition and worship of one's own demon and god. [252C]**

However many stars exist in the spheres is the number of the
orders of particular souls, whether demonic or human. But the
planets are here numbered among the stars. Since there is one
planet that is the manifest leader in one sphere, the planets are
called the world rulers. Thus the souls assigned to the planets
seem more prepared for ruling than those assigned to the fixed
stars, but with other souls it is otherwise in other things. Many
souls exist around the same star, namely those variously distributed to the different powers and effects of the same star.

The planet Venus is Jupiter's sister because she, like him, is
heaven's fortune. But because she is inferior to him and yet at
the same time very fit for him, she is also called his spouse. She
is therefore Juno and almost another, though minor, Jupiter,
just as the moon is another sun. [83] She is called Juno not so
much because of her own nature as because of the Jovian gift
she has received in abundance. Through her own nature she is
called Venus, and she signifies love and procreation; but she is

movet visum, sed naturam penitus afficit calore scilicet atque motu, excitat ad sublimia, et reformat atque transformat. Cetera satis vel hic vel in libro de amore patent, ingenioso presertim et amatori. Denique concludit amorem **alatum** esse, quoniam amor vel[1] solus vel maxime omnium nos elevat ad sublimia. Que quidem elevatio animis inde profectis necessaria est ad salutem. Quapropter amorem **necessitate** alatum[2] vocat vel natura volatilem. Forte etiam quia sepe necessario nobis illabitur.

Ordines animarum demonumque secundum stellas. Venus planeta sive Iuno quomodo soror Iovis atque coniunx. Quales anime huius pedisseque. Deus vel demon cuiusque. Agnitio cultusque proprii demonis atque dei. Cap. XXX.

Quotcunque igitur etce. Quot in spheris stelle tot ordines sunt particularium animarum, sive demonicarum sive etiam humanarum. Planete autem hic inter stellas connumerantur. Et quia unus est planeta[3] in una sphera dux manifestus, appellati sunt mundi rectores. Ideo anime planetis attribute magis ad principatum apte videntur quam [377] que fixis, sed alie[4] aliter aliisque in rebus. Circa eandem stellam multe sunt anime, varie videlicet variis eiusdem stelle viribus et effectibus[5] distribute.[6]

Venus planeta[7] est soror Iovis, quia et ipsa sicut ille fortuna celi est; sed quoniam est inferior eiusque simul valde capax, dicitur quoque coniunx. Hec ergo Iuno est ita ferme Iupiter alter quamvis minor, sicut luna sol alter. Dicitur autem Iuno non tam propter naturam propriam quam propter ioviale munus abunde susceptum. Per naturam quidem propriam Venus dicitur, et amorem genituramque significat; propter

---

[1]vel *om.* P   [2]necessitatem alatam E (*but see* Phaedrus 252B)   [3]planeta *om.* P
[4]alie *om.* P   [5]affectibus P   [6]*no* ¶ P   [7]planeta *om.* P

called Juno because of the Jovian gift, and she signifies kingly government—not government with philosophy, as with Jupiter, but government with clemency.

The souls who are the companions of this planet Venus are said to follow Juno and be Junonian if they pursue the first virtue, but to follow Venus and be Venerean if they pursue the second.

The god of each soul is not only the celestial planet itself but also the celestial or airy demon, the god's companion who is named with the same name. A soul never changes its god, but it can change its demon when it is itself radically changed. Perhaps it does not change its class of demons, though; for just as one soul is always Jovian, although in different ways, so it always has as its leader perhaps a demon from the Jovian class if not the same individual demon. For there are many Jovian demons for Jupiter's many properties, and many souls too. The orders of the Jovian demons proceed as far as the last, those next to us, and the orders of the other demons similarly. So in any world sphere there are many Saturns, Jupiters, Apollos, Junos, such demons, that is, as are subject to each god. While the soul lives under a Jovian demon, it can nevertheless perceive in every way, because of the diversity of actions, the influx also from the Martian demons.

The Apollonian soul is the one that everywhere has the Sun and the solar demon as its chief.

Since we naturally long as life's goal to go to our celestial homeland and to our own god, in justice what most contributes to this goal is to live on earth according to our own god and to that god's demon. Now unless our mental disposition is utterly perverted, it moves us towards this goal in a way by its own instinct. But inquiry and experience move and lead us to knowing it completely, to imitating it, and finally to attaining it. Therefore, what is naturally proposed to each soul is to know, to imitate, and to attain the study and office most kin to its own god and to unite at length by such a profession with its own god and leader. Wholly fortunate are they who embarked on such a study happily and immediately from the very beginning. Other-

ioviale munus Iuno dicitur, et regna significat, neque tamen cum philosophia sicut Iupiter sed cum clementia.[1]

Anime huius planete comites, si primam[2] virtutem sequuntur, Iunonem sequi dicuntur suntque iunonie; que secundam, potius sequi Venerem atque veneree.[3]

Deus cuiusque non modo est ipse celestis sed etiam demon celestis vel aerius illius dei comes eodem nomine nuncupatus. Anima nunquam mutat ipsum deum sed potest mutare demonem, quando ipsa nimium permutatur; forte vero neque demonum genus mutat. Sicut enim semper iovialis est hec anima, licet aliter atque aliter, ita forte semper ducem habet demonem[4] genere iovium; quamvis non eundem numero, siquidem circa multas Iovis proprietates multi sunt iovii demones, anime quoque multe. Procedunt autem ordines demonum ioviales usque ad ultimos nobis proximos, ceterique similiter. In qualibet ergo sphera mundi Saturni sunt et Ioves et Apollines et Iunones, scilicet demones eiusmodi deo subditi. Potest tamen anima dum sub iovio demone vivit propter [378] actionum diversitatem a martiis quoque demonibus influxum quoquomodo percipere.

Apollineus autem animus est qui solem solaremque demonem ubique prefectum habet.[5]

Cum vero finis vite naturaliter desideratus sit in patriam celestem ad proprium deum ire, merito ad finem hunc maxime confert in terris secundum proprium deum et demonem eiusmodi vivere. Iam vero nisi ingenium penitus pervertatur, ad hoc ipsum suo nos instinctu quodammodo movet, sed investigatio et experientia promovet atque perducit ad cognoscendum prorsus et imitandum et denique consequendum. Propositum est igitur naturaliter unicuique cognoscere, imitari, consequi studium et officium deo proprio cognatissimum; atque eiusmodi professione cum deo tandem duce proprio copulari. Fortunati admodum qui statim ab initio eiusmodi studium feliciter sunt ingressi, alioquin diligenter investigare coguntur. Sed prius

---

[1]*no* ¶ P   [2]propriam P   [3]*no* ¶ P   [4]demonum E   [5]*no* ¶ P

wise, men are forced to pursue their inquiries diligently. But
you must first learn who your god is before you may imitate
him in actions. You can investigate this in the external fortunes,
so to say, which befall us from without; but it is better to find
it out internally from our own desires and thoughts. For
whether these are Jovian, that is, of a philosophical, political,
or juridical nature, or Martian, that is, impetuous and warlike,
or Apollonian, that is, pertaining to prophecy, poetry, music,
and medicine, or Junonian, that is, of a regal and merciful but
not completely philosophical nature, customarily what completely reveals them to us is an enormous love for them. For
whatever you love beyond all else, and whatever you naturally
delight in most, such usually is your genius [i.e., demon] and
your god. You love nothing more fervently in a man, however,
than the beauty of the body and soul. So you can judge your
god mostly from this. For if you love Jovian shapes, Jovian
behavior, Jovian souls before all others, then suppose yourself
endowed with a Jovian genius, although you can hope, in that
you love these Jovian things more ardently, that you are also
made much more Jovian henceforth. For Jovian things are
what you need to study. You know, however, what studies pertain to Jupiter. Therefore cultivate them most and likewise
instruct your beloved in them. Both of you, if you have thus
turned to Jupiter, will emerge preeminently Jovian and com-
municate in turn whatever you were allowed to derive from that
turning. This is love's end: together to worship the god whom
we know to be our own and to be united jointly with him.

Chapter 31. The charioteer and the horses. How anyone may be seized by love. How the lover is affected. [253C]

Above we described the significance Plato accords the charioteer and horses in our soul when separated [from the body] and
in divine souls. In the soul joined [to the body], the soul agi-
tated by corporeal passions, he means the reason, as it participates in the understanding, to serve as the charioteer, and the
irascible and concupiscible powers to serve as the horses, the

quidem quis ille sit tuus deus cognoscendum est quam actionibus imiteris. Id autem investigatur externis quasi fortunis que nobis extra contingunt, invenitur vero melius intra nos ex affectibus cogitationibusque nostris. Utrum enim hec iovialia sint scilicet philosophica, civilia, iusta, an martialia scilicet vehementia, an apollinea scilicet ad presagium et poesim et musicam medicinamque pertinentia, an iunonia scilicet regia clementia quidem sed non admodum philosophica, amor ingens talia summopere declarare solet. Qualia enim pre ceteris amas, et qualibus natura potissimum delectaris, talis ferme est genius deusque tuus. Nihil autem ardentius amas quam in homine pulchritudinem corporis [379] scilicet atque animi. Ex hoc ergo maxime deum tuum perpendere potes. Si enim pre ceteris ioviales formas, mores, animos amas, ioviali genio te commendatum existimato, etsi sperare potes, hoc ipso quod iovia hec ardenter amas, te insuper multo magis hinc effici iovium. Sunt enim hec tibi studia perquirenda. Scis autem que ad Iovem studia pertinent, talia deinde summopere cole similiterque amatum instrue. Ambo, sic ad Iovem conversi, ioviales potissimum evadetis communicantes invicem quicquid per conversionem illam haurire licuerit. Hic est finis amoris: proprium deum simul cognitum colere, cumque illo communiter copulari.

Auriga et equi. Quomodo quis capiatur amore. Quomodo afficiatur amator. Cap. XXXI.

Comprehenditur autem quisquis etce. Qua significatione aurigam et equos in anima nostra etiam separata in animabusque divinis Plato ponit supra narravimus. In anima vero coniuncta, passionibus corporeis agitata pro auriga[1] rationem intelligentie participem esse vult, pro[2] equis[3] irascibilem concupisci-[380]bilemque potentiam; illa quidem est equus melior, hec vero

---

[1] *for* pro auriga P *reads* per aurigam   [2] et P   [3] equos P

former being the better horse, the latter, the worse. Since their earlier significance has now in a way been changed, he does not simply say, as previously, "the charioteer and horses," but rather, **the charioteerlike species and the forms of the horses.**

Through the qualities of the good horse as animal [i.e., as part of the soul joined to the body], he describes the qualities of the irascible power, the power of bravery. Through the qualities of the bad horse as animal, he describes the conditions of the concupiscible nature, the nature of the more idle or cowardly man. In all this, Plato rejoices and plays like a youth with poetical figures and with a rhetorically studied description of horses and of loves.

Plato locates the reason in the head, like the prince in his citadel, the power of wrath in the heart, like a military order, there to fight on behalf of reason, and the power of desire in the liver, like the mob of craftsmen and peasants. He holds that the irascible power is more eminent than the concupiscible and more nearly related to the reason and that often it rises up for reason's sake against concupiscence. So Plato describes it as holding its head high, as brave and venturesome, as aquiline [of countenance], that is, regal, as sensitive to honor and shame, as more obedient to reason. The power of desire, however, he depicts from an opposite viewpoint as crooked, that is, as deviating far from reason, as swerving aside toward the meanest things, as multiple (because desire concerns itself with many things), as contemptible, idle, cowardly, shameless, and totally disobedient to the reason.

In thinking over within itself the beauty it has just examined, the reason is often drawn to loving it. For beauty's nature is lovable, just as goodness is simply desirable. The irascible power, besides, which is attended by indignation with daring, by a sense of honor, shame, and fear, and by the desire for glory, follows after the instinct of reason (now that it has been roused for the beautiful) as if it were something worthy and glorious; nor does it deflect the reason towards more worthless things. The nature of desire, on the other hand, in the meanwhile drags the reason down towards sexual intercourse and procreation. The irascible power, roused to anger on behalf of reason, often fights against

deterior. Et quoniam significatum[1] illud prius hic iam quodammodo mutat, non dicit simpliciter, ut illic, aurigam atque equos sed **aurigalem speciem et formas equorum.**[2]

Describit vero per qualitates equi boni animalis qualitates irascibilis magnanimeque virtutis, per qualitates autem equi mali animalis conditiones concupiscibilis[3] ignaviorisque nature. Inter hec Plato tanquam iuvenis figuris poeticis et affectata[4] quadam equorum amorumque descriptione gaudet atque ludit.

Plato rationem in capite collocat ut principem in arce, iracundie vim in corde tanquam ordinem militarem pro ratione propugnaturum, concupiscendi potentiam in iecore tanquam opificum agricultorumque turbam. Irascibilem concupiscibili prestantiorem putat et rationi propinquiorem, ac sepe pro ratione insurgentem contra concupiscentiam. Ideo illam elata cervice describit magnanimam et audentem, aquilinam, id est regiam, participem pudoris, rationi magis obtemperantem. Concupiscendi vero vim opposita ratione designat, obliquam scilicet, a ratione longe deviam, ad infima declinantem; multiplicem, quia libido se circa plurima versat; abiectam et ignavam impudentemque et rationi minus obedientem.[5]

Ratio sepe pulchritudinem nuper inspectam secum reputans allicitur ad amandum. Natura enim pulchritudinis est amabilis, sicut bonitas simpliciter appetibilis. Interea vis irascibilis, circa quam est cum audacia indignatio, pudor atque timor glorieque cupiditas, iam exortum ra[381]tionis instinctum prosequitur circa pulchrum, quasi quiddam gloria dignum, neque rationem ad viliora deflectit; sed concupiscendi natura trahit interim ad coitum atque genituram. Huic sepe irascibilis[6] indignata pro ratione repugnat, quoniam appetit gloriam, timet infamiam, odit mollia. In hac pugna concupiscibilis sepe impetrat, ut ad

[1]signum P   [2]*no* ¶ P   [3]cupiscibilis E   [4]effecta P   [5]*no* ¶ P   [6]irascibili P

desire, because it longs for glory, fears disgrace, and hates voluptuous, unmanly things. In this conflict, the concupiscible power frequently obtains its request to be brought closer to sensible beauty, to enjoy at least a certain familiarity with it. In this very proximity, however, the reason, in the power of the mental disposition for philosophy that is, and having in a way recalled intelligible beauty from sensible, hastens itself towards that beauty and reins back the horses with all its strength from the tent companionship that has been established with sensible beauty. It reins back the irascible power with ease, but the concupiscible with difficulty; for the latter objects that it has been forced to abstain because of a clownish peasant's sense of shame. The reason restrains it again, forcing it at least to postpone intercourse. This once more incites the concupiscible power to tent companionship. At length reason, reason in a philosopher that is, tames desire. Such is the conflict for a temperate man, and afterwards he emerges duly calmed and eventually divine; in other words, he has proceeded from sensible beauty to divine beauty and been inspired by heaven.

Chapter 32. How the beloved loves the lover in return. [255A]

When the beloved notices he is being cultivated by a man of this caliber, he cultivates him in turn and loves and reveres him. As a result of this familiarity, he is drawn at length to loving his lover almost as much as he is ardently loved himself. So the hidden influx of divine beauty, which had flowed via sensible beauty into the philosophical lover, for this reason flows back in turn into the beloved and makes the friendship divine.

Chapter 33. How by loving and by returning love we effect our return to the heights, and the reverse. [256A]

If the lover and the beloved have been educated both morally and philosophically and have thus persevered in love and friend-

pulchritudinem sensibilem saltem consuetudine quadam propius[1] accedatur. Sed in hac propinquatione, ratio, scilicet penes ingenium philosophicum[2] ex sensibili pulchritudine intelligibilis quodammodo recordata, et ipsa ad illam properat et equos retrahit pro viribus ab instituto circa sensibilem contubernio. Facile quidem retrahit irascibilem, concupiscibilem vero difficile; hec enim rursus increpat quod propter subrusticum pudorem abstineatur. Cohibet hanc ratio rursus saltem differre commertium cogens. Hec iterum ad contubernium incitat. Ratio tandem scilicet in philosopho domat concupiscentiam. Eiusmodi pugna continentis est, qui postea temperatus evadit tandemque divinus, scilicet a pulchritudine sensibili ad intelligibilem profectus, divinitusque[3] afflatus.

[382] Quomodo amatus redamet amantem. Cap. XXXII.

Utpote igitur omni cultu etce. Amatus autem animadvertens se a tanto viro coli vicissim colit et amat et veneratur. Eius consuetudine tandem adducitur ut ferme tam vehementer amet[4] quam ardenter amatur. Hac igitur ratione divine pulchritudinis occultus influxus, qui per sensibilem pulchritudinem in philosophicum influxerat amatorem, vicissim refluit in amatum divinamque conficit amicitiam.

Quomodo amando et redamando fiat reditus ad sublimia vel contra. Cap. XXXIII.

Quare si secundum etce. Si amator et amatus moraliter et philosophice fuerint educati, atque ita semper in amore amicitiaque perseveraverint, alas denique recuperant ad astrum suum revolaturas, postquam scilicet tria certamina expediverint cum

---

[1]proprius E   [2]physicum P   [3]-que *om.* P   [4]amat P

ship always, they finally recover wings to fly back to their star, that is, after they have emerged from the three contests with victory, one of which, the last, is the soul's greatest good. The contests are called **truly Olympian** because they come, not from Olympus the mountain, but from Olympus the sky. But he who conquers in the three contests is the man who has thrice been a philosopher, as we explained above; or who has, first, entirely subdued the lower powers of the soul to his understanding, then, second, attained wisdom with the divine frenzy, then, third, flown back to celestials, having reacquired his wings; or, again, who has, first, turned himself away from corporeal beauty to the soul's moral beauty, then, second, turned himself thence to the same soul's intellectual beauty, and, third, turned himself thence to the intelligible beauty that shines in the prime intellect, as is revealed in the *Symposium.*[84]

If someone is naturally more inclined to loving because of his own nobility and generosity but has not been educated philosophically or morally from the beginning, sometimes he succumbs by chance to sexual intercourse after he has been ensnared by love. Although he is forbidden on account of this lapse to recover his wings whole, he is prepared for the wings, nevertheless, on account of the marvelous power of love (which naturally raises). Socrates touched on the following in order to portray love's sublimity. Love, even when mixed with an inferior appetite, does not cease meanwhile to raise the soul as far as it is able. If, as is probable, therefore, with the process of time, the soul honorably cuts off desire but retains love's sublimity, it can establish friendship. Having departed from this life, it is not precipitated into the depths but purged in the air for sufficient time until it philosophizes to the utmost degree.

But the soul that has not been lifted to the sublime through either philosophy or the instinct of love (in that it has never philosophized nor loved) is said to need 9,000 years to be purged and to resume its wings. For were it to proceed through the nine grades of lives, it would still not be worthy of heaven unless it arrived at the disposition of a philosopher.

victoria, quorum[1] unum scilicet ultimum est maximum anime bonum. Nominantur certamina **vere olympica,** quia non ab Olympo monte sed ab Olympo celo. Tribus vero certaminibus vincit, qui ter philosophatus fuerit quemadmodum in superioribus est expositum; vel qui primo quidem inferiores anime vires omnino intelligentie subdidit, secundo sapientiam cum furore divino fuerit consequutus, tertio resumptis alis ad celestia revolaverit; rursus qui [383] primo quidem a corporea pulchritudine ad moralem anime pulchritudinem se converterit, secundo ab hac ad intellectualem eiusdem anime pulchritudinem, tertio ab hac ad intelligibilem in intellectu primo lucentem, quemadmodum in Convivio declaratur.[2]

Siquis autem natura quidem propter generositatem sit propensior ad amandum, sed neque philosophice ab initio neque moraliter institutus, postquam illaqueatus est amore, nonnunquam ad venereum coitum forte delabitur. Etsi propter eiusmodi lapsum integras alas recipere prohibetur, tamen propter mirificam vim amoris naturaliter attollentis preparatur ad alas. Id quidem Socrates tetigit ut sublimitatem amoris exprimeret, qui etiam affectui cuidam deteriori permixtus animum interim quantum in se est elevare non desinat, itaque si quemadmodum probabile est, tempore procedente, tanquam generosus libidinem quidem amputet, amoris autem sublimitatem retinens, efficiat amicitiam. Hac vita defunctus[3] non precipitatur ad imum sed in aere quantum sat est purgatur donec ad summum philosophetur.[4]

Qui autem neque per philosophiam neque per amoris instinctum (utpote qui nunquam philosophatus fuerit, vel amaverit) ad sublimia est erectus, novem annorum[5] milibus indigere dicitur ut purgetur alasque resumat. Si enim per novem vitarum gradus processerit, nondum celo dignus erit, nisi ad habitum pervenerit philosophicum.

---

[1]quoniam P   [2]*space provided but no* ¶ E   [3]defuncturus P   [4]*space provided but no* ¶ E   [5]amorum E

Chapter 34. Whether it is permissible to write down rhetorical exercises. [257A]

Socrates looks to the god Love for the art of love and for philosophy. But should an outstanding man write down speeches in the manner of the Sophists? Socrates shows that all choose to do so in order that posterity might celebrate them for their writings. He concludes that to write is not shameful in itself, only to write badly. The proverb refers antiphrastically to Egypt's harshest place, the great bend of the Nile, as pleasant.[85] Similarly, those who verbally condemn the writing down of speeches as something frivolous or ostentatious are voicing the opposite of what they think; for they themselves in the meantime are wonderfully delighted as with something excellent.

Chapter 35. The allegory of the fable concerning the cicadas, the Muses, and the demons. [258D]

The fable of the cicadas demands we treat it as an allegory, since higher things too, like poetic ones, are almost all allegorical. Is it really strange that demons are signified by cicadas when things more divine than demons were signified by horses? Thus it seemed to the Platonists, not only to Hermias but to Iamblichus too.[86] In part I follow in their footsteps, but in part I deviate from them on the grounds of probability and reason. Socrates himself, moreover, also obviously feels the need for allegory here when he says that it does not behoove a man who is studious of the Muses to be ignorant of such things. Whoever has heard, finally, of the office that Plato attributes to the cicadas here and that he often undoubtedly attributes to demons elsewhere and especially in the *Symposium*[87] cannot deny that demonic offices are introduced by way of the cicadas. They stand by us overhead; they dispute together; meanwhile, they survey our deeds, condemning the bad and approving the good, as observers of human affairs. This is the office that Hesiod too attributes to the demons.[88] They receive gifts from the gods and

[384] Utrum liceat declamationes conscribere. Cap. XXXIIII.

Hanc tibi o dilecte amor etce. Socrates ab amore deo ama-
toriam artem philosophiamque petit. Queritur utrum prestan-
tem virum deceat orationes sophistarum more conscribere. Pro-
batur omnes id optare ut ex scriptis apud posteros celebrentur.
Concluditur non esse turpe scribere sed male scribere. Ancon
Egypti locus asperrimus per antifrasin proverbio dictus est dul-
cis. Similiter qui orationum conscriptionem verbis damnant[1]
tanquam rem levem aut ambitiosam contraria loquuntur atque
sentiunt; ipsi enim interim tanquam re preclara mirifice delec-
tantur.

Allegoria fabule de cicadis, Musis, demonibus. Cap. XXXV.

(Socrates) Quenam igitur etce. Fabula cicadarum poscit allegoriam, siquidem superiora quoque tanquam poetica ferme
omnia sunt allego[385]rica. Quid mirum demones per cicadas
significari, cum diviniora demonibus per equos fuerint desig-
nata? Ita Platonicis visum, non Hermie solum sed etiam Iamblico. Horum ego vestigia partim quidem sequor, partim vero
probabili ratione prevaricor. Ipse quinetiam Socrates allegoriam
hic quoque manifeste desiderat, ubi ait non decere Musarum
studiosum virum rerum eiusmodi ignarum esse. Denique cicadis
introduci demonia negare non poterit, quisquis earum officium
hic audiverit, quod Plato sepe alibi presertim in Convivio
demonibus proculdubio tribuit. Astant nobis supra caput; dis-
putant invicem; nostra interim[2] contuentur, improbant male-
facta, benefacta probant, tanquam humanarum rerum observa-
tores, quod demonibus Hesiodus[3] quoque dedit. Suscipiunt
divina munera; ad nos traducunt; diis officia nostra renuntiant;

---

[1]damnat P   [2]invicem P   [3]Exiodus E

pass them on to us; they make the offices that we perform known to the gods; they approach the Muses. By these and like statements Socrates obviously means us to take the cicadas here as airy demons. For these animals live **by song,** that is, by a certain sound, and via the sound by the drinking in of air; and after they appear to be dead, they are at last inwardly reformed. In the same way, the good airy demons live by song, that is, by contemplation and by the praise of divine things. They are satisfied with [or contained by] the air; and as easily as they seem to dissolve so are they recreated inwardly by the perpetual drinking in of it. Here men seem at times to be born again into demons, not into natural demons, but into demons who come from away, visiting demons, and this happens when the sublime souls of men are brought into communication with these demons. But what do we imagine men were like before the Muses? Before the influence of the Muses we suppose they were wild and ignorant. In like manner, under the good demons are bad demons by whose traps and lures, as by the Sirens' song, souls are detained in bodily delights and do not turn back, therefore, to the port of their celestial home. Souls seem to be detained in a way in the body by an influence from the good demons also. Yet this is not unjust, for the good demons also recall us meanwhile to the divine. The Muses bring us harmonious contemplations. Whoever listens to them attentively, and pursues the studies they patronize, and is oblivious of human affairs seems to die to the world, as the *Phaedo* writes of the philosopher.[89] But since they seem to have lived on the mind's nourishment alone, on the convictions instilled in them by the Muses, these men who are thus dead to the world are surely transformed by the Muses into the demons signified by the cicadas. These demons are said to arrive at length at the Muses themselves, since souls that have philosophized for a long time are recalled to celestials. The Muses, however, are thought to pertain to the celestial spheres, if it is possible at all for Calliope to be the world-soul and Urania the first heaven (since Socrates means this here when he declares that Calliope is the oldest of the Muses and Urania the second). But I have said enough

ad Musas accedunt. Hec et similia hic verba Socratis demones aerios per cicadas accipi volunt. Sicut enim hec animalia **cantu** id est sono quodam perque sonum eiusmodi aeris haustu vivunt, denique postquam videntur mortua intrinsecus reformantur, sic aerei demones boni inquam cantu id est contemplatione divinorumque laude vivunt contenti aere; et quam facile dissolvendi videntur tam facile perpetuo aeris haustu intrinsecus recreantur. Videntur autem hic homines in demones quandoque renasci, non in demones naturales sed adventitios, quando sublimes hominum anime ad horum demonum commertia transferuntur. Sed quonam pacto finguntur homines ante Musas? Quia videlicet ante Musarum influxum rudes habentur. Proinde sub [386] bonis demonibus sunt et mali, quorum insidiis et illecebris anime quasi cantu Sirenum in oblectamentis corporeis detinentur, quominus ad portum celestis patrie revertantur. Videntur anime bonorum quoque demonum influxu quodam in corpore quodammodo detineri, seorsum tamen ab iniustitia, nam boni demones interea revocant etiam ad divina. Muse contemplationes harmonicas nobis afferunt: quicunque has attentius auscultant atque hec studia prosequuntur humanorum obliti, mundo mori videntur, quemadmodum de philosopho scribitur in Phedone. Quoniam vero sola mentis alimonia vixisse videntur, Musis videlicet persuadentibus, nimirum hos ita mundo mortuos Muse in demones illos transferunt, qui per cicadas significati fuere; qui sane demones ad Musas tandem ipsas pervenire dicuntur, siquidem anime iam diu philosophate ad celestia revocantur. Muse vero ad celestes spheras pertinere putantur, si modo Calliope quidem sit anima mundi, Urania vero celum primum (quod Socrates ibi significat ubi Calliopem Musarum antiquissimam iudicat, Uraniam vero secundam). Sed de his in quarto Theologie satis. Calliope et Urania pulcherrimam vocem dicuntur emittere, siquidem concentus ipsi celestes,

about this in the fourth book of my *Theology*.⁹⁰ Calliope and
Urania are held to emit the most beautiful sound; for the celestial concords themselves, those that Pythagoras was said to
have heard also, derive principally from them. Philosophy uses
two things most: listening to [instructions in] the mental disciplines and looking at celestials. Listening and philosophical dis-
putation pertain to Calliope, but looking concerns Urania. Listening seems older than looking in that it eventually teaches us
older things and more things, although we seem to see more
than we hear in one act. Socrates concludes that we should not
become drowsy in the heat at noon, under the sun at its zenith:
we must not abuse the divine sun's light and heat, as it assists
our intelligences.

Chapter 36. The orator's office. [259E]

To say anything correct about a topic, an orator must in the
first place have knowledge of it. If he is going to argue persuasively with the people about things that are just and good, but
he and the people alike know nothing about these things even
though he thinks he does know, eventually he will harm the people and himself. For instance, suppose each heard that a horse
was the [animal] most suitable for battles, but each thought an
ass a horse. The loss resulting from not knowing this might perhaps be trivial and ridiculous, but the harm resulting from not
knowing what is good and just is wholly ruinous. For, as the
proverb says, the question here does not concern the ass's
shadow, that is, something totally trivial;⁹¹ rather, we are delib-
erating life's end itself and the life that is whole.

Chapter 37. The orator's office. [260D]

That common ability that is called oratory is not a true art
since it looks, not to the true, but only to the apparent good;
nor does it rely upon certain reason so much as it does on usage

quos Pythagoras etiam audivisse fertur, potissimum sunt ab illis. Philosophia duobus maxime utitur, auditu scilicet disciplinarum et aspectu celestium. Auditus quidem et disputatio philosophica pertinet ad Calliopem; aspectus autem[1] attinet[2] ad Uraniam. Antiquior autem videtur auditus quam aspectus, quippe cum antiquiora doceat et denique plura, [387] tametsi uno quodam actu plura videre quam audire videmur. Concluditur in meridie sub estu sub alto sole non dormitandum: non abutendum divini solis lumine et calore nostris mentibus aspirante.

Officium oratoris. Cap. XXXVI.

(So.) Igitur quodmodo etce. Orator recte de re aliqua dicturus in primis rei scientiam habere debet. Si enim populo de bonis iustisve persuasurus sit, hec vero ignoret ipse pariter atque populus sed nosse putet, tandem populo sibique nocebit. Veluti si audiverit uterque equum esse bellis aptissimum, opinetur autem asinum esse equum. Sed iactura ex hac ignorantia proficiscens forte levior futura est atque ridicula, damnum vero ex ignorantia bonorum atque iustorum pernitiosissimum. Non enim hic ut proverbio fertur de asini umbra id est de levissima re tractatur, sed de ipso vite fine vitaque tota deliberatur.

[388] Officium oratoris. Cap. XXXVII.

(So.) Num o bone vir rusticus etce. Communis illa facultas que dicitur oratoria non est ars vera, quoniam non ad verum bonum spectat sed apparens, neque tam certa ratione quam usu nititur. Preterea neque perfecte persuadere dissuadereque

---

[1]vero P   [2]attinet *om.* P

and skill. Moreover, it cannot persuade and dissuade perfectly unless it is allied with philosophy. Certainly, oratory not only concerns itself with public addresses, but also exercises its power in private disputations. Nor can it ever attain what is like the truth unless it possesses the truth itself. So you will not be able to deceive someone easily by way of what is like the truth unless you know the truth, nor lead someone from one opposite to another unless you secretly lead him by way of many intermediate steps that finally become less and less alike. You cannot achieve this, however, without philosophy.

Chapter 38. The local gods. The difference of mental dispositions according to the difference of places [262C]

Socrates often makes mention here and elsewhere of the local gods. He calls them local gods not only because the higher providence has put various of them in charge of various regions and things but also because some regions and things more than others can be partakers of this or that mundane god insofar as they are more prepared to receive the divine effect. Similarly, some of these regions and things are also called solar, others lunar, although Socrates mainly refers to the sublunar gods as the local gods; for they are thought to be allotted a less universal providence than the celestial gods. Under the local gods are also local demons, many of them under every single god, having received an even more particular charge. A little earlier he portrayed them under the name of cicadas and here under the rubric of singers and interpreters. From the differences of the local gods and demons befall the many differences, both secret and important, among various places and things, especially the differences that have a bearing on [our] mental dispositions, behavior and morals, laws, fortunes, and authorities. Conscious of his human weakness, Socrates therefore acknowledges, as a grateful and dutiful man, that he has thence received the gift not only of invention but also of precise delivery; namely, that disposing these gifts is a higher providence, to which we must principally give thanks for all good things.

potest, nisi coniunctam philosophiam habeat. Oratoria profecto non solum circa contiones publicas versatur, sed etiam in privatis disputationibus suam vim exercet; nec usquam poterit assequi similia vero, nisi teneat ipsum verum. Non ergo[1] valebit per verisimilia facile quemquam fallere, nisi noverit veritatem; neque deducere aliquem a contrario in contrarium, nisi per media multa minus deinceps minusve similia clam subducat. Id vero consequi sine philosophia nequit.

[389] Locales dii. Ingeniorum differentia pro differentia locorum. Cap. XXXVIII.

(So.) An vis in oratione Lysie etce. Localium deorum hic et sepe alibi mentionem facit. Locales autem nominat, non solum quia superior providentia alios aliis prefecerit regionibus atque rebus, sed etiam quia regiones resque alie magis quam alie huius vel illius mundani dei participes esse possunt, quatenus ad divinum effectum suscipiendum paratiores existunt. Sicut etiam alie solares dicuntur, alie vero lunares, tametsi deos sub luna locales precipue nominat; hi[2] enim minus universalem[3] quam celestes providentiam sortiti putantur. Sub diis localibus locales quoque sunt demones, sub unoquoque plures, magis etiam particularem nacti curam. Quos paulo ante sub nomine cicadarum, et hic sub appellatione cantorum interpretumque expressit. Ex differentiis localium deorum atque demonum differentie multe occulteque et maxime locis variis rebusque contingunt, presertim ad ingenia, mores, leges, fortunas, imperia pertinentes. Socrates igitur infirmitatis humane conscius non solum inventionis sed etiam elocutionis exacte munus tanquam gratus atque pius se illinc accepisse fatetur; ita videlicet superiori providentia disponente, cui bonorum omnium gratie in primis sunt habende.

---

[1]enim P   [2]hic P   [3]universales P

Chapter 39. The writer's office. Dionysus, the Muses, Pan, the Nymphs. [262D]

Socrates censures Lysias on the grounds that he has not divided the genus of love into its parts (one of which is worthy of blame, the other of praise), but has simply blamed love without making any distinctions. Socrates had [already] enjoined [him] that love must first be defined. But now, he says, he cannot recall whether he had himself defined love; and justly, for he had defined it when he was inspired with the divine frenzy. Now, as if he were someone different, he cannot remember doing so. That he had defined it correctly and thereby defeated Lysias, he attributes to the wonderful favor of the local divinities. Here he mentions mercurial Pan, the leader of clever and mercurial Nymphs. Dionysus, the Muses, Pan, and the Nymphs have all inspired Socrates: Dionysus gave him the gift of escaping from his intelligence, the Muses gave him poetry, Pan, eloquence, and the Nymphs, variety.

Chapter 40. The correct conception of a speech. [263E]

The most important thing in a speech is the order. To begin with what comes first, it should have a head that differs from what follows but be naturally suited to it. It must also have intermediate members that are joined in a certain necessary order to the head, the feet, and each other, like an animal that is well made. But Lysias's speech had none of these.

Chapter 41. The correct conception of writing. Desire or Cupid. [264E]

Having dismissed Lysias's speech, he again introduces his own two speeches on love, the one censuring, the other praising it. Using them as examples, he teaches the art of oratory so that, as he, when he was about to treat of love, had defined and

[390] Officium scriptoris. Dionysus, Muse, Pan, Nymphe. Cap. XXXVIIII.

(So.) Age itaque proemium etce. Reprehendit Lysiam cum genus amoris in suas partes non diviserit (quarum altera quidem vituperabilis sit, altera vero laudabilis) sed amorem simpliciter ipsum absque distinctione vituperaverit. Preceperat amorem primo definiendum. Ait vero nunc non recordari an definierit; et merito, nam divino furore concitus definivit, nunc vero tanquam alter quidam non recordatur. Quod autem recte definierit atque in hoc Lysiam superaverit, attribuit mirifico localium numinum beneficio; ubi Pana mercurialem commemorat, Nymphis ingeniosis mercurialibusque prefectum. Dionysus, Muse, Pan, Nymphe Socratem afflaverunt. Dionysus prestitit mentis excessum, Muse poesim, Pan facundiam, Nymphe varietatem.

[391] Recta orationis ratio. Cap. XXXX.

(Pausanias aliter Phedrus) Mearum[1] quidem rerum status etce. Precipuum in oratione est ordo: ut a prioribus ordiatur, caput habeat[2] a sequentibus differens quidem sed natura[3] conveniens; habeat et media membra, capiti et pedibus et invicem necessario quodam ordine copulata, tanquam animal bene compositum. Hec non habuit oratio Lysie.

Recta scribendi ratio. Cupido. Cap. XXXXI.

(So.) Hanc ergo ne nobis etce. Dimissa nunc oratione Lysie, duas de amore orationes suas iterum adducit in medium, unam quidem vituperantem, alteram vero laudantem. Earumque exemplis artem dicendi docet, ut, quemadmodum ipse tractaturus de amore definivit atque divisit, ita ceteri faciant. Dictum

---

[1]Merum P   [2]habet P   [3] non P

divided it, so the rest may do accordingly. The question raised was, What is frenzy? Frenzy had been divided into human and divine, and the divine into four species. Note that here when he says the amatory frenzy is Venus's, Venus, according to Hermias,[92] is beauty. So love follows Venus when it follows beauty. What other Platonists feel about this, I will deal with elsewhere.[93] He refers to love as the guardian of fair youths, for love leads souls that are **pure** [punning on *puros* and *pueros*] and delicate, and especially those that have just set out from heaven. Socrates proves, moreover, that experience with dividing and defining is necessary for every oratorical skill. Division proceeds from some one thing held in common into many particulars, but it must proceed step by step. But the skill that strives to go from the many particulars back to the one thing is the skill that excels either in definition (that which puts together one species from the genus and the differences) or in resolution (whether it rises from the particulars to the universal or turns from composite to simple things).

Chapter 42. The office of the dialectician and how necessary it is. [266B]

Socrates treasures as a divine gift the art that proceeds correctly from the one to the many or from the many to the one (in the way we have just described). He does so not only here but also in the *Philebus,* the *Republic,* the *Parmenides,* the *Sophist,* and the *Statesman.*[94] By this art he does not mean logic, which deals with words and extraneous concepts. Rather, he means metaphysics, which contemplates the ideal species, systematically divides the most common species into the less common, and with the necessary steps gathers the particular species in turn into the universal. Those who are commonly held to be orators, he adds, do not use the skill of dividing and compounding correctly; but without this skill their ability is not an art. He then describes the parts of a speech and orators and those who seem to excel in composing various of those parts.

est quid furor. Divisus furor in humanum atque divinum. Divinus in quatuor species. Inter hec nota, ubi dicit amatorium furorem esse Veneris, exponi ab Hermia Venerem esse pulchritu[392]dinem, ideo amorem sequi Venerem dum sequitur pulchritudinem. Quid alii Platonici sentiant, alibi. Amorem vocat pulchrorum presidem puerorum, nam **puros**[1] tenerosque ducit animos, precipue nuper e celo profectos. Preterea necessariam omni arti dicendi probat dividendi definiendique peritiam. Divisio quidem ex uno communi in particularia multa procedit, sed pedetentim procedere debet. Peritia vero que ex multis contendit ad unum vel definitiva est que ex genere differentiisque speciem unam conficit, vel resolutiva,[2] sive a particularibus ad universale consurgens, sive a compositis ad simplicia sese conferens.

Quod et quam necessarium officium dialectici. Cap. XXXXII.

(So.) Harum ego divisionum etce. Artem ab uno ad multa vel a multis ad unum (eo ferme modo quo diximus) rite procedentem tanquam munus divinum colit, non hic solum sed etiam in Philebo, Republica, Parmenide, Sophista, Politico. Eamque non logicam esse vult verba tractantem adventitiosque con-[393]ceptus; sed metaphysicam ideales species contemplantem, communissimas in minus communes ordine dividentem, vicissimque particulares in universales debitis gradibus colligentem. Subiungit eos qui communiter oratores habentur artificio dividendi et componendi non recte uti, eorumque facultatem absque hoc artificio non esse artem. Narrat orationis partes et oratores et qui in quavis orationis parte precellere videantur.

---

[1]pueros P   [2]solutiva P

Chapter 43. [268A]

To possess an art, one must have not only the necessary rudiments, the parts and materials, as it were, but also the form itself which is appropriate for them all, and the rational usage that contributes most to the art's goal.

Chapter 44. Three things are necessary for all arts. [269C]

Three things are necessary for all arts: a mental disposition, instruction, and practice. For the perfection of each great art philosophy is necessary. For the perfection of the great arts two things are mainly needed: sublimity of mind and power effective enough for action. And these philosophy gives. Just as a doctor must know the nature of the body and of the things to treat it with, so the orator must know the natures of souls and of the various kinds of discourse. Or, rather, he must know the nature of the world, for if he is ignorant of the world's nature he cannot know the nature of either the body or the soul perfectly.

Chapter 45. Things necessary for an orator. [270C]

The perfect orator must know that any human soul is intrinsically and naturally multiple (for it has reason, imagination, sense, and the powers of wrath and desire); and, likewise, that various souls use their various powers as much as possible and differently among themselves and are differently affected; and, again, that some of their differences are derived from the differences of their bodies. Moreover, he ought to know what kind of mental disposition is moved by what kind of discourse and accommodate his discourse to each one, just as a musician must bring various harmonies to various things.

Cap. XXXXIII.

(So.) Mittamus exigua etce. Possidere artem non est solum habere necessaria rudimenta, que quasi partes et materie sunt, sed ipsam quoque convenientem cunctorum formam, usumque rationalem ad finem artis precipue conducentem.

[394] Tria omnibus artibus necessaria. Cap. XXXXIIII.

(Phe.)[1] Talis profecto o Socrates etce. Tria omnibus artibus necessaria; ingenium, doctrina, exercitatio. Philosophia necessaria est ad maxime cuiusque artis perfectionem. Ad perfectionem artium maximarum duo potissimum requiruntur: mentis sublimitas et vis ad agendum efficax. Hec duo philosophia prestat. Ut medico necessarium est cognoscere naturam et corporis et rerum adhibendarum, sic oratori naturas animorum atque sermonum; immo et universi, ignorata enim universi natura, non potest natura vel corporis vel animi perfecte cognosci.

Necessaria oratori. Cap. XXXXV.

(So.) De nature igitur etce. Perfectus orator scire debet animam quamlibet humanam intrinsecus esse suapte natura multiplicem (habere enim rationem, imaginationem, sensum, irascendi atque concupiscendi vires), item alias animas aliis suis[2] viribus [395] uti quam plurimum et aliter inter se aliterque affectas esse; rursus ex corporum differentiis nonnullas differentias reportare. Nosse preterea debet qualibus sermonibus qualia moveantur ingenia, et suos cuique sermones accommodare, quemadmodum musicus alios aliis adhibere concentus.

---

[1]Pau. aliter Phe. P   [2]sui E

Chapter 46. The things an orator needs. [271C]

Having acquired the common rules I have outlined, the orator who is about to speak must shrewdly look for and sense the mental dispositions of most of his audience when he enters the forum, if he is going to address his words to each of them. Besides, he must observe the advantage offered by particular occasions in order to know when to speak according to place, time, and character, when to be silent, and how to use each part of a speech with propriety.

Chapter 47. Oratory is said to be satisfied with what is only like the truth. [272B]

The story goes that, when he saw the sheep being eaten now by the shepherds and now by the dogs, the wolf exclaimed, "Oh, what an uproar there would be had I done this."[95] Similarly, the popular orator, when he hears that Socrates has praised oratory to such a degree and with so many words on the grounds that, along with philosophy, it possesses the truth itself of things, will strenuously object: "If we were to extol Oratory to this degree and so profusely, oh, what an outburst against us would come from the philosophers. Since Oratory is not so proud among us that she claims the truth for herself, she is satisfied with what is like the truth, because the crowd, if not the wise man, will accept this as probable."

Chapter 48. The orator needs truth. [273C]

Socrates again affirms that one cannot know what is like the truth unless one knows the truth itself; and that one cannot have this knowledge without the skill of dialectic, which proceeds correctly from the one to the many and from the many to the one. He also affirms that oratory's end is persuasively to say those things that not only move its listeners in a particular way

Necessaria oratori. Cap. XXXXVI.

(So.) Verba quidem ipsa etce. Orator communes quas dixi regulas consequutus, cum prodit in forum, mox oraturus, sagaciter explorare et persentire debet, quo plurimum ingenio sint auditores, si modo suos cuique sit sermones adhibiturus; preterea opportunitatem in singulis observare, ut pro loco, tempore, persona loqui sciat, atque silere, et qualibet orationis parte decenter uti.

[396] Oratoria dicitur verisimili contenta. Cap. XXXXVII.

Ceterum scriptor ita etce. Fabula fingit lupum, cum videret oves tum a pastoribus tum a canibus devorari, exclamavisse: O, si ego id fecissem, quantus rumor. Similiter popularis orator, ubi audiverit oratoriam a Socrate adeo extolli idque multis verbis ut ipsam cum philosophia veritatem rerum teneat, prorsus obiciet: Si nos oratoriam tantum extulissemus tamque[1] prolixe, o quantus inter philosophos rumor contra nos esset exortus. Oratoria, siquidem apud nos non adeo superba est ut verum sibi arroget, verisimili contenta est, quod non sapienti quidem probabile sit sed vulgo.

Necessarium oratori verum. Cap. XXXXVIII.

(So.) O, quam callide abstrusam etce. Affirmatur iterum verisimile cognosci non posse, nisi cognoscatur ipsum verum, idque ha[397]beri non posse absque dialectico artificio recte procedente ab uno ad multa et a multis ad unum. Oratorie finem esse ea ad persuasionem dicere, que non solum quomodolibet moveant auditores, sed etiam que sapientiores et meliores effici-

---

[1]tanquam E

but also make them wiser and better, especially when it comes to divine worship. Moreover, we should celebrate the gods with praises that are well composed. The Pythagoreans and Orphics did this and taught this.[96] For we are the servants not of men but of the gods.

Chapter 49. The allegory concerning Mercury and Jupiter and the use of letters. [274B]

The class of disciplines which pertains primarily to Mercury includes arithmetic, geometry, astronomy, the skill of speaking and of writing, and every game involving the highest degree of skill. The divinity of Mercury we think of as pertaining most to these and such like qualities firstly in Jupiter, the world's artificer; secondly, in an intellectual god above the world; thirdly, in such a faculty in the world-soul; fourthly, in the planet Mercury; fifthly, in the Mercurial order of demons; and sixthly, in human souls that follow Mercury and the Mercurial demons. In seventh place we put the animals and other things endowed with certain Mercurial properties, such as the ibis, apes, and keen-scented dogs.

Socrates's account is both allegorical and anagogical, that is, Naucratis is a place in Egypt wholly subject to Mercury, even though the whole of Egypt is also subject to Mercury. A certain man flourished in this city who was full of the Mercurial divinity inasmuch as his soul had once upon a time existed in heaven as a Mercurial soul. First he is called Theuth, that is, Mercury, and a god, since he was filled with this god.[97] Then he is called a demon in order to make it obvious that such gifts are handed down from Mercury himself via a Mercurial demon to a Mercurial soul. The Mercurial soul and the demon brought their inventions to the king, Thamus. Although an actual man, Thamus, reigned in Egypt, nevertheless anagogically Thamus is the Mercurial divinity in heaven or above heaven. Ammon, however, is that higher Jupiter who comprehends the Mercurial gift. Inferior beings are said to depend on their superiors in the judging of inventions; and this is just.

ant, presertim circa divinum cultum; preterea compositis laudibus celebrare deos. Id Pythagorici Orphicique fecerunt atque docuerunt. Non enim hominum servi sumus sed deorum.

Allegoria de Mercurio et Iove et usu litterarum.
Cap. XXXXVIIII.

(So.) De arte hactenus et inscitia[1] etce. Genus disciplinarum in primis pertinens ad Mercurium continet arithmeticam, geometriam, astronomiam, loquendi scribendique artificium, artificiosissimos quosque ludos. Mercurii vero numen primo quidem cogitamus in Iove mundi opifice ad hec potissimum et talia pertinens; secundo in quodam intellectuali supra mundum deo; tertio in facultate quadam anime mundane tali; quarto in planeta Mercurio; quinto in mercuriali demonum ordine; sexto in animabus humanis Mercurii mercurialiumque pedissequis. Septi[398]mo tandem gradu locamus animalia ceteraque mercurialibus quibusdam proprietatibus insignita, ut ibim et simias canesque sagaces.

Narratio Socratis allegorica et anagogica est. Naucratim Egypti locum esse summopere Mercurio subditum, tametsi Mercurio Egyptus quoque tota subigitur. Item in hac urbe quondam hominem floruisse, mercuriali numine plenum, utpote cuius animus olim mercurialis extitisset[2] in celo. Hic primo Theuth id est Mercurius deusque nominatur, hoc videlicet deo plenus, deinde demon, ut declaretur ab ipso Mercurio deo per mercurialem demonem ad animum mercurialem eiusmodi dona traduci. Mercurialis animus simulque demon inventa sua in regem Thamum referunt. Etsi regnavit homo Thamus in Egypto, anagogice tamen Thamus est numen in celo vel supra celum mercuriale, Ammon autem superior ille Iupiter munus mercuriale comprehendens. Non iniuria inferiores in iudicio inventorum a superioribus dependere dicuntur.

---

[1]inscitiam P   [2]exitisset E

Finally, Socrates concludes that we can either use the discipline of writing and any other discipline correctly or, likewise, misuse them; and thus that the practical knowledge of writing, which can help to serve memory and wisdom, sometimes also declines to the opposite because of human negligence or overconfidence in it.

While invention pertains to instinct and to natural conception, judgment and discretion pertain to reason and to perfect understanding. Therefore judgment is more preeminent. Both together are referred to Jupiter Ammon. Separately, however, while invention and, as it were, the material form of an art are referred to the demonic or human Mercury, judgment and the usage leading to the end are referred to Thamus, who is higher than either the human or demonic Mercury. Although Socrates's account seems to include Thamus and Ammon under the same person, reason in its precision distinguishes between them. The ibis, the Egyptian bird, is said to resemble a sort of stork that has the shape of a heart;[98] it advances with uniform steps and gives birth to eggs from its throat, just as Mercury produces his offspring from the mouth. These and other, as it were, Mercurial symbols signify wisdom, geometry, eloquence, and interpretation.

Chapter 50. The honored and true use of writing. [275B]

While Phaedrus objects to Socrates that he frequently attributes his inventions to the Egyptians and the rest, he does not dare object that Socrates attributes them to the gods. Socrates replies that we should not attend to who is speaking but to what is being said, that we should accept what is true and good even from an oak if it speaks to us. Living discourse impressed by the teacher in the soul of his pupil Socrates puts before written works, and he has many reasons for doing so. Socrates does not forbid us to write, but he does condemn overconfidence in writings; he condemns it, I say, in the words of the oracle of Jupiter Ammon, which was expounded above on the advice of King Thamus.

Concluditur denique nos disciplina scribendi et qualibet alia recte uti posse pariter et abuti; atque ita scribendi peritiam recordationi sapientieque servituram nonnunquam etiam posse propter humanam negligentiam vel confidentiam ad opposita labi.

Inventio quidem ad instinctum[1] conceptumque naturalem pertinet, iudicium autem atque discretio ad rationem intelligentiamque perfectam; hoc ergo prestantius est. Utrumque simul refertur in Iovem Ammonem; seorsum vero inventio quidem et quasi materialis quedam artis forma in mercurium demonicum vel humanum, iudicium vero [399] et usus ad finem ducens ad Thamum Mercurio humano vel demonico superiorem. Etsi narratio videtur sub eadem persona Thamum Ammonemque comprehendere, ratio tamen exacta distinguit. Ibim avem egyptiam ferunt quasi ciconie similem, que figuram cordis habet; passibus incedit equalibus, ova parit gutture, sicut suos fetus ore Mercurius. Hec et alia quasi mercurialia symbola sapientiam geometriamque et eloquium interpretationemque significant.

Venerabile verum usum scribendi. Cap. L.

(Phe.)[2] Facile tu o Socrates etce. Phedrus obicit Socrati quod inventa sua frequenter attribuat Egyptiis atque ceteris; quod autem diis attribuat, non audet obicere. Respondet Socrates, non attendendum quis dicat, sed quid[3] dicatur; atque verum bonumque etiam ex quercu, si loquatur, suscipiendum. Sermonem vivum a docente discentis animo impressum multis rationibus anteponit scriptis. Scribere quidem non vetat, sed confidentiam [400] damnat in scriptis. Damnat inquam ipso Iovis Ammonis oraculo, quod in superioribus Thami regis consilio est expositum.

---

[1]institutum P   [2]Pau. aliter Phe. P   [3]quis P

Chapter 51. The use of writing. [276B]

Gardens of Adonis are those cultivated for the sake of flowers, not fruits or produce. Whoever entrusts doctrines to letters
may think he is cultivating such gardens as if he were playing a
game, the game that is the most beautiful of all games. But he
who introduces the various disciplines into intelligences worthy
of them is practicing a better agriculture, one that is serious and
worthy of the highest study. Plato confirms the same in his *Letters.*[99] Again the conclusion follows on the correct conception
of speaking.

Chapter 52. The use of writing. [277D]

Of little account are the mentalities of those writers who suppose the job of writing worthy of the highest study, and who
trust that instruction will stay both clear and safe in writings,
and who never contemplate anything that is higher or more
secret than what is within the grasp of a pen and writings. On
the other hand, we should honor those who ponder on matters
higher than they speak of and whose hope is to commend the
lawful offspring of understanding, not to sheets of paper, but
to souls, and to souls worthy of the mystery. These men suppose the use of writing a game. Rightly, they can be called philosophers [i.e., lovers of wisdom]. Only a god, though, is meet
to be judged wise.

Chapter 53. The speech or prayer to Pan and the local gods. What should be chosen. [278E]

In that it was truly philosophical, he puts the mental disposition of Isocrates before that of any of the orators. As a man
notable for his piety, Socrates, just as he had from the beginning and elsewhere throughout the dialogue, so here at the end
likewise again attributes all the power of invention and elo-

Usus scribendi. Cap. LI.

(So.) Omnino sed hoc quoque etce. Adonis horti sunt qui non fructuum[1] frugumve sed florum gratia coluntur. Quicunque litteris doctrinas mandat hortos eiusmodi se colere putet quasi ludentem; qui sane ludus ludorum omnium est pulcherrimus. Meliorem vero agriculturam seriamque et summo studio dignam exercet, qui disciplinas dignis mentibus inserit. Confirmantur eadem in Epistolis. Sequitur conclusio rursus de recta ratione dicendi.

[401] Usus scribendi. Cap. LII.

(So.) Quod[2] autem de illa etce. Parvifacienda sunt eorum scriptorum ingenia, qui scribendi ministerium summo studio dignum estimant, confiduntque disciplinam in scriptis perspicuam tutamque fore, neque quicquam altius secretiusque contemplantur quam quod calamo scriptisque comprehenditur. Contra vero venerandi sunt qui altiora cogitant quam loquantur, legitimosque intelligentie fetus non cartis sperant commendare sed animis, et his quidem mysterio dignis. Scribendi vero usum existimant quasi ludum. Hi sane cognominari recte philosophi possunt; sapiens autem solus deus est iudicandus.

Oratio ad Pana localesque deos. Quod optandum. Cap. LIII.

(Phe.)[3] Tu vero quid facis? etce. Isocratis ingenium, quoniam valde philosophicum esset, omnibus oratorum ingeniis anteponit. Socrates iterum insignis pietate vir, quemadmodum ab initio passimque per dialogum, similiter et in fine omnem inventionis elocutionisque virtutem deorum beneficio tribuit. Et

---

[1]fructum E   [2]Quid P   [3]Pau. aliter Phe. P

quence to the kindness of the gods. Since the highest god often acts through intermediary gods and through those gods close to us, Socrates often mentions the local gods. Now he finally addresses his speech or prayer to them, just as previously he had paid attention to them repeatedly. He is searching for that which is principally good, the main object of debate in this dialogue, namely the inward beauty that he declares to exist in wisdom. I have dealt with the rest of the things pertaining to this speech or prayer in [my introduction to] the *Alcibiades Minor*.[100] What Pan and the rest of the gods in this place are, however, give ear to briefly.

It is certain that both he and they are local sublunar gods. He is called Pan (as if he were all), because he occupies the greatest rank in the order of local gods. For just as the supercelestial gods are brought back to the prime intellect and the celestial gods to the world-soul, so all the sublunar gods and demons, the local ones, are finally brought back to Pan, who reigns everywhere under the moon. Wherever I have called the highest god Pan, however, then I have spoken, not with a Platonic reason, but with some other.[101]

THE END

quoniam deus [402] ille supernus sepe per medios agit nobisque propinquos, locales sepe deos commemorat, ad quos et orationem nunc suam postremo convertit, sicut in superioribus iterum iterumque servavit. Petit autem id precipue bonum de quo plurimum est in hoc dialogo disputatum, pulchritudinem scilicet intimam quam in sapientia declarat existere. Cetera quidem ad orationem hanc attinentia in Alcibiade minore tractavi: quid vero sit Pan ceterique hoc in loco dii breviter audi.[1]

Certum est et hunc et illos esse locales sub luna deos. Sed Pan nominatur velut omne, quoniam in ordine localium gradum tenet amplissimum. Sicut enim supercelestes dii ad intellectum primum, celestes autem ad mundi animam, sic ad Pana passim sub luna regnantem sublunares dii demonesque omnes locales inquam denique referuntur. Sicubi vero summum deum Pana vocaverim, non platonica ratione tunc sed alia sum loquutus.

FINIS[2]

[1] *no* ¶ P   [2] Finis *om.* E

Texts IV Seven Earlier Ficinian Accounts of the Phaedran Charioteer Texts and Translations

Headnote

The situation with these extracts is quite different from that with the *Phaedrus* commentary and summae, since critical editions exist for all but the *De Voluptate*. For the *De Amore* I have used the autograph edited by Raymond Marcel (*Marsile Ficin: Commentaire sur le Banquet de Platon* [Paris, 1956], pp. 258-260); for the *Platonic Theology,* Marcel's critical edition (*Marsile Ficin: Théologie Platonicienne de l'immortalité des âmes,* 3 vols. [Paris, vols. 1 and 2, 1964; vol. 3, 1970], 3:156-157, 159, 193-196, and 204); for the *Philebus* commentary, my own critical edition (Berkeley and Los Angeles, 1975, pp. 353-355); and for the *De Voluptate,* the editio princeps in Ficino's *Jamblichi de mysteriis et alia* (Venice, 1497). All the translations are my own. Superscript numbers 102-121 in the translations are keyed to references that appear on pages 249-252 below.

I   De Voluptate (1457), Chapter 1

Let me make a beginning with the prince of philosophers,
Plato. Having divided the soul into two parts, the intelligence
and the senses, he attributes gladness and joy to the intelligence,
pleasure to the senses. But he thinks gladness and joy differ
among themselves in that all joy is laudable, but gladness is partially laudable, and partially blamable. For he holds that gladness in the possession of some good is an elation of the intelligence, an elation, nevertheless, that is equally capable of
observing or exceeding moderation. But joy is that jocundity
that one derives from contemplation or from some other use of
the virtues. Plato maintains the same in the *Phaedrus* when he
would speak of the first, true life enjoyed by the soul in its heavenly home; he says, "The soul is nourished by and rejoices in
truth's contemplation."[102] Hence Plato frequently calls joy the
intelligence's nourishment: for he intends truth to resemble a
field, the contemplation of that truth, its fruits, and the joy
fully enjoyed by the intelligence in truth's contemplation, the
nourishment derived from the two. Plato says this in the same
Phaedrus when he would treat of the shadows in which the soul
was sunk and submerged when it came from the true light on
high: "There is a great struggle to see the Plain of Truth, where
it may be; for the food proper to the soul grows tall from this
meadow, and the nature of the wings, by which the soul may be
raised, is nourished by that food."[103] Plato calls wings those
[powers] by which the soul flies back to the heights from
whence it had descended, its thoughts set on earthly things. But
the soul can fly back with two powers, the contemplative and
the moral. As I interpret him, Plato means these two powers to
be the soul's wings. The soul may recover them by the contemplation of truth and divine objects, just as it lost them by the
desire for earthly things. When the soul, having recovered its
wings, has flown back to the heights through the exercise of
both natural [i.e., contemplative] and moral philosophy
equally, then two rewards are returned, Plato supposes, to the
returning soul: one is the contemplation of divinity, the other is

I **De voluptate I** (Complete)

Plato igitur (ut ab eorum principe initium faciam), cum animum in duas partes distribuisset, mentem scilicet ac sensum, menti laetitiam et gaudium attribuit, sensibus voluptatem. Verum prima duo haec inter se differre putat, quod omne gaudium laude sit dignum, laetitia vero partim laudanda, partim vituperanda sit. Esse enim laetitiam in boni alicuius possessione quandam mentis elationem, quae tamen modestiam excedere pariter atque servare queat; gaudium vero illam ipsam, quae ex contemplatione aut alio quopiam virtutum usu suscipitur, iucunditatem. Itaque et ipse idem in Phaedro, cum de prima illa ac vera vita qua in caelorum sedibus animus fruitur loqueretur, ait, "Veritatis contemplatione nutritur et gaudet." Unde saepenumero gaudium mentis alimoniam vocitat: nam ipsam agro similem vult esse veritatem, frugibus vero veritatis ipsius contemplationem, alimoniae deinde quae ex iis duobus capitur gaudium quo mens veritatis contemplatione perfruitur. Quapropter et idem in eodem Phaedro cum de iis tenebris in quas animus e summa ac vera luce depressus ac demersus est disputaret, ubi inquit, "Multus inest conatus veritatis campus quonam sit intueri; nam conveniens animae cibus ex illo extitit et alarum natura, qua anima elevatur ac alitur." Alas Plato vocat quibus animus ad supera unde ob terrenarum rerum cogitationem descenderat revolat; id autem cum duabus virtutibus, contemplativa videlicet atque morali, consequi possit. Easdem Plato, ut ego interpretor, virtutes animae ipsius alas intelligit, quas veritatis divinarumque rerum contemplatione recuperet, quemadmodum horum appetitione terrenorum amiserat. Cum vero per utriusque philosophiae naturalis pariter et moralis exercitationem recuperatis alis ad superos revolaverit, tum redeunti animo duo putat praemia reddi: et unum quidem esse divinitatis contemplationem, alterum perfectum quoddam atque absolutum

a perfect, absolute joy that the soul enjoys fully in the very knowledge of God. In the *Phaedrus* Plato calls the contemplation "ambrosia" and the joy "nectar" when he writes, "Having seen the things that truly are [= the Ideas] and been nourished by them, the soul descends [through] the interior of heaven again and returns home. On his arrival, the charioteer stops the horses at the stable and offers them ambrosia and nectar also to drink."[104] In the manner of Pythagoras, Plato calls reason "the charioteer," but the soul's remaining parts and natures "the horses," since the reason may lead, but the others may be completely led and overruled. I believe that this is what a number of eminent seers mean for the most part when, in talking of the soul, they mention either ambrosia or nectar or a charioteer. So much [we may learn] from our Plato's divine opinion about the nature of this joy. Hermes Trismegistus seems to have had the same in mind when he said of the highest God, "You have granted us reason, sensation, and understanding: reason that we may search for you with our notions, sensation that we might know you, and knowledge that knowing you we may rejoice that you have revealed yourself to us totally."[105] But this must suffice on joy.

II De Amore (1468-1469), Speech 7, Chapter 14

Since the soul descends by four degrees, it must ascend by four. But the divine madness is what raises us to the heights, as its definition indicates. There are four kinds of divine madness, therefore: first the poetic, then the hieratic, third the prophetic, and fourth the amatory. Poetry comes from the Muses, the hieratic mysteries from Dionysus, prophecy from Apollo, and love from Venus. The soul cannot return to the One unless made one itself. But it has become many, since it has fallen into the body, has been distributed among different operations, and regards the infinitude multitude of corporeals. Thus its higher parts are virtually asleep, and the lower rule the rest, the former being afflicted with torpor, the latter with perturbation. But the whole

gaudium, quo in ea ipsa Dei cognitione animus perfruatur. Illud quidem ambrosiam, hoc nectar Plato in Phaedro appellat his verbis, "Quae vere sunt speculata anima atque iis enutrita subiens rursus intra caelum domum revertitur. Cum autem redierit, auriga ad praesepe sistens equos obiicit ambrosiam et super ipsam nectar potandum." Aurigam more Pythagorae rationem vocat, equos vero caeteras animi partes atque naturas, quod illa ducat, reliqua vero ducantur omnino atque regantur. Atque idem arbitror a nonnullis praestantioribus vatibus, cum aut ambrosiam aut nectar aut aurigam circa animum nominant, plerunque significari. Haec igitur ex divina Platonis nostri de ipsius gaudii natura sententia, quod idem videtur intellexisse Mercurius Trismegistus, cum de summo Deo haec diceret, "Condonas nos ratione, sensu, intelligentia: ratione ut te suspicionibus indagemus; sensu ut te cognoverimus; cognitione ut te cognoscentes gaudeamus quod te ostenderis nobis totum." Sed de gaudio haec hactenus.

II De Amore VII. 14 (ed. Marcel, pp. 258-260) (Complete)

Quapropter sicut per quatuor descendit gradus, per quatuor ascendat necesse est. Furor autem divinus est qui ad supera tollit, ut in eius definitione consistit. Quatuor ergo divini furoris sunt speties. Primus quidem poeticus furor, alter mysterialis, tertius vaticinium, amatorius affectus est quartus. Est autem poesis a Musis, mysterium a Dionysio, vaticinium ab Apolline, amor a Venere. Redire quippe ad unum animus nequit nisi ipse unum efficiatur. Multa vero effectus est, quia est lapsus in corpus, in operationes varias distributus et ad corporalium rerum multitudinem respicit infinitam. Ex quo partes eius superiores pene obdormiunt, inferiores aliis dominantur. Ille torpore, iste perturbatione afficiuntur. Totus autem animus discordia et

soul is full of discord and dissonance. So first the soul requires the poetic madness: it can arouse the torpid parts by way of musical sounds (*tonos*), soothe those that are perturbed by its harmonious sweetness, banish dissonant discord by bringing diversities into concord at last, and temper the soul's various parts. But this is not enough, for multiplicity still remains in the soul. So next comes the hieratic madness, which pertains to Dionysus. By way of atonements, sacred rites, and every divine observance, this madness directs the intention of every part towards the intelligence, which worships God. Hence, since the soul's single parts are returned to one intelligence, the soul from many [parts] is now made into one whole. But we still need a third madness to lead the intelligence back to the unity itself, the head of the soul. Apollo achieves this through prophecy; for when the soul rises above the intelligence to the unity, it presages future events. Finally, when the soul has been made into the one—the one that dwells in the soul's nature and essence—it remains only for it to recall itself immediately to the One above essence, namely God. Celestial Venus achieves this through love, that is, through desire for divine beauty and ardor for the good.

Thus the first madness tempers discords and dissonances; the second makes one whole from the tempered parts; the third raises the one whole above the parts; and the fourth leads the whole to the One above both it and essence. In the *Phaedrus* Plato calls the intelligence dedicated to the divine in man's soul "a charioteer"; the soul's unity, "the head of the charioteer"; the reason and opinion that range over natural objects, "the good horse"; and the confused fantasy and the senses' appetite, "the bad horse." The nature of the whole soul he calls "a chariot" because the soul's motion is circular, as it were: beginning from itself, it eventually returns to itself as it attends to its own nature; having set out from the soul, that is, its consideration returns to the soul. Plato attributes "wings" to the soul: through them it may be borne towards the sublime. We suppose one wing is that searching out by which the intelligence continually strives for the truth, the other wing, that desire for the good

inconcinnitate repletur. Poetico ergo furore primum opus est, qui per musicos tonos que torpent suscitet, per harmonicam suavitatem que turbantur mulceat, per diversorum denique consonantiam dissonantem pellat discordiam et varias partes animi temperet. Neque satis hoc est. Multitudo enim adhuc restat in animo. Accedit ergo mysterium ad Dionysium pertinens, quod expiationibus sacrisque et omni cultu divino, partium omnium intentionem in mentem, qua deus colitur, dirigit. Unde cum singule animi partes ad unam mentem redacte sint, iam totum quoddam unum ex pluribus factus est animus. Tertio vero adhuc opus est furore; qui mentem ad unitatem ipsam, anime caput, reducat. Hoc Apollo per vaticinium efficit. Nam cum anima supra mentem in unitatem surgit, futura presagit. Demum cum anima facta est unum, unum, inquam, quod in ipsa natura et essentia anime est, restat ut illico in unum, quod est super essentiam, id est, deum se revocet. Hoc celestis illa Venus per amorem, id est, divine pulchritudinis desiderium bonique ardorem explet.

Primus itaque furor inconcinna et dissonantia temperat. Secundus temperata unum totum ex partibus efficit. Tertius unum totum supra partes. Quartus in unum, quod super essentiam et super totum est, ducit. Plato in *Phedro* mentem divinis deditam in anima hominis aurigam vocat; unitatem anime, aurige caput; rationem opinionemque per naturalia discurrentem, equum bonum; phantasiam confusam appetitumque sensuum, malum equum. Anime totius naturam, currum, quia motus suus tamquam orbicularis a se incipiens in se denique redit dum sui ipsius naturam animadvertit. Ubi consideratio eius ab anima profecta in eamdem revertitur. Alas animo tribuit, per quas in sublime feratur, quarum alteram putamus esse indagationem illam qua mens assidue ad veritatem adnititur, alteram boni desiderium, quo nostra voluntas semper affi-

with which our will is always affected. These parts of the soul lose their order when confounded by the body and its perturbations. So the first madness distinguishes the good horse, namely, reason and opinion, from the bad horse, the confused fantasy and the senses' appetite. The second madness subjects the bad horse to the good and the good to the charioteer, namely, the intelligence. The third directs the charioteer towards his head, namely, the unity, the intelligence's crown. The last madness turns the charioteer's head to the universal head. There the charioteer is blessed; and "at the stable," that is, at divine beauty, "he stops the horses," that is, assembles and prepares all the parts of the soul subjected to himself. "He offers them ambrosia, and also nectar to drink," namely, the vision of beauty and the gladness proceeding from it. Such are the results of the four divine madnesses. In the *Phaedrus* Plato discusses them in general; in the *Ion* he treats specifically of the poetic madness,[106] and in the *Symposium* of the amatory. Orpheus was concerned with all these madnesses: his books bear witness to this. We have also learned that Sappho, Anacreon, and Socrates were enraptured principally by the amatory madness.

III Commentarium in Philebum (1469), from Book 1, Chapter 34

The highest part is a certain unity, the crown of the soul, and this, the soul's head, is lifted by two wings and flies to the one good itself. For it explores and looks around with the intellect and searches out with the will; it seizes hold with the intellect and retains with the will. When the intellect seizes hold, it is wisdom, that is, understanding; when the will clings on, it is pleasure. The ultimate end always corresponds to the first mover, because what moves moves for its own sake. For victory corresponds to the general; the intermediary steps between the general and victory correspond to his subordinates. For the end for every single thing subsequent to the general is some limited

citur. He partes anime suum amictunt ordinem, quando pertur-
bante corpore confunduntur. Primus itaque furor, bonum
equum, id est, rationem opinionemque, a malo equo, id est, a
phantasia confusa et sensuum appetitu distinguit. Secundus
malum equo bono, bonum aurige, id est, menti subicit. Tertius
aurigam in caput suum, id est, in unitatem, mentis apicem, dirigit. Postremus caput aurige in caput rerum omnium vertit. Ubi
auriga beatus est, et ad presepe, id est, ad divinam pulchritudinem sistens equos, id est, accomodans omnes sibi subiectas
anime partes. Obicit illis ambrosiam et super ipsam nectar
potandum, id est, visionem pulchritudinis et ex visione letitiam.
Hec quatuor furorum opera sunt. De quibus generatim in
Phedro disputat. Proprie vero de poetico furore in *Ione,* de
amatorio in *Convivio.* Omnibus iis furoribus occupatum fuisse
Orpheum libri eius testimonio esse possunt. Amatorio maxime
Saphon, Anacreontem, et Socratem fuisse correptos accepimus.

III   Commentarium in Philebum I. 34 (ed. Allen, pp. 353-355) (Extract)

Suprema pars est unitas quaedam, apex animae, quod animae
caput duabus alis ad unum ipsum bonum instigatur et advolat.
Nam intellectu explorat atque circumspicit, voluntate petit;
intellectu rapit, retinet voluntate. Raptus intellectus sapientia,
id est, intelligentia est; adhaesio voluntatis est voluptas. Semper
primo moventi ultimus respondet finis, quia quod movet sui
gratia movet. Duci enim respondet victoria; aliis agentibus
media quae inter ducem et victoriam sunt. Unicuique enim
sequentium certum opus finis est, principi ultimum quod per

objective; for the general the end is the ultimate end perfected through the limited objectives. However, the first thing is what moves the soul towards the one good. That unity is the soul's "head." For in the *Phaedrus* it is written: "The souls which were about to be blessed raised their heads above heaven."[107] Plato also refers to the head as the "charioteer" when he says: "The charioteer, when he's stopped the horses at the stable, throws them ambrosia and also potable nectar."[108] For the soul's crown, which at first spurred the intellect and the will towards the good, having attained it, arrests the intellect's pursuit and the will's ardor; that is, it no longer moves them. It stops them so they do not depart thence (for lightness has drawn fire upwards and detains it in the upper regions) and throws "ambrosia," that is, vision, to the intellect and "nectar," that is, joy, to the will. It is not because the soul's unity is the first to see or to rejoice, for it is above the understanding and the will, but because it is the first to move them, and the mover is the one that secures and restrains the moved. What is the good of the soul's unity? It is to be formed by the first one, like air by light, iron by fire. But the unity is formed by the one when it has formed the intellect and the will and converted them from their diversion towards lower things to higher things and united them to itself. When this conversion has been completed insofar as it is humanly possible, the intellect is formed by vision and the will by pleasure. After they have been formed, at last the unity, since it is no longer impeded, will plunge itself into the first one absolutely. The unity's good will be to become the one itself. But the intellect's and the will's good will be to become one act for the one's sake.

Three ends or happinesses become apparent here. The first is when, through the impulse of the charioteer, the soul enjoys wisdom and pleasure, having been converted by the intelligence and will towards higher things (insofar as it can attain them while it is still busy ruling the body). The second is when, having relinquished the body, the soul directs every intention towards the intelligence. Here the understanding is entire, and its entirety is inner pleasure. The third instantly follows it. It is the

opera illa perficitur. Primum autem quod ad bonum unum movet animam. Unitas illa eius caput est. Nam in Phaedro dicitur:

"Animae quae beatae futurae sunt supra coelum extulerunt caput." Quem etiam aurigam vocat cum dicit:

"Auriga ad praesepe sistens equos obicit illis ambrosiam et super ipsam nectar potandum." Nam apex animae, qui primo ad bonum intellectum instigavit calcaribus et voluntatem, eo accepto, intellectus indaginem sistit et voluntatis ardorem, id est, non movet amplius, sed retinet, ne inde discedant. Levitas enim ignem sursum traxit, et ignem in superioribus detinet et obicit intellectui ambrosiam, id est, visionem, voluntati nectar, id est, gaudium. Non quia unitas illa primo videat aut gaudeat, est enim super intelligentiam et voluntatem, sed quia primo movit et quae movit firmat et cohibet. Quid huius unitatis bonum? Ut primo uno formetur, ut aer lumine, igne ferrum. Formatur autem uno, cum ipsa intellectum voluntatemque formaverit, haecque ad inferiora diversa ad superna converterit et ea secum univerit. Qua quidem conversione, quoad homini possibile est, peracta, intellectus visione formatur, voluptate voluntas. Quibus formatis tandem unitas, utpote non amplius impedita, in unum primum se prorsus immerget; eritque huius unitatis bonum unum ipsum fieri. Intellectus autem et voluntatis bonum unus actus ad unum.

Hic tres fines beatitudinesque elucent. Primus est quando anima aurigae ipsius instinctu, mente et voluntate conversa ad supera, quatenus dum regendo corpori occupatur assequi potest, sapientia et voluptate fruitur. Secundus cum relicto corpore omnem intentionem in mentem direxerit, ubi intelligentia illa integra est, cuius integritas interior est voluptas. Tertius post hanc e vestigio sequitur: unitatis ipsius ab uno formatio.

fashioning of the unity itself by the one. The first sort of happiness is human and pertains to the soul as soul. The second sort is divine and pertains to the intelligence and to the soul when it has been transformed into the intelligence. The third sort is [to be] a god, for where God's form is, there God dwells. Plato talks about the last two sorts of happiness in the *Phaedrus*.[109] In this dialogue he enlarges on the first sort, the human happiness, which, by virtue of the fact that it is human, consists in a compound made from understanding and pleasure in the intellect and the will.[110] But this does not happen until the elements have first been joined together in the best possible way. For the good does not dwell in a mass of things badly put together.

IV   Theologia Platonica (1474), from Book 17, Chapter 2

With good reason I leave aside a number of problems on this subject of the fictitious powers of numbers and figures, problems that many people have treated with curiosity and fecklessness alike. The sum of the Pythagorean and Platonic mystery is this, and I will omit the details. They customarily call the understanding "unity" because it is accomplished through simple intuition; knowledge, "duality" because it starts from a beginning to prove a conclusion; opinion, "trinity" because, additionally, it inserts between the two by way of an ambiguity the conclusion's opposite; and sensation, finally, "quaternity" because it seems to concern itself mainly with composites from the four elements.[111] Again—without going into details—they call the soul a "chariot" because it produces circular movements, and they postulate its path is a straight line insofar as it moves and regards bodies, a lower circle (like a planetary orbit) when it returns to itself, and a higher circle (like the orbit of the fixed stars) insofar as it is converted to higher things. They also attribute to this chariot "two wings," the impulse of the intellect towards the truth and of the will towards the good; a "charioteer," the intelligence; a "head" for the charioteer, the divine unity higher than the intelligence; "superior horses," identity

Prima humana est et animae quantum anima est; secunda divina et mentis est et animae, cum mens erit effecta; tertia deus quidam est, ubi enim Dei forma, ibi est Deus. Has duas in Phaedro exponit Plato. Hoc in libro primam illam atque humanam, quae, quoniam humana est, in composito quodam ex intelligentia et voluptate in intellectu et voluntate consistit. Neque in hoc est prius quam optime iuncta fuerint. Neque enim bonum est in congerie male disposita.

IV Theologia Platonica XVII. 2 (ed. Marcel, 3:156-157) (Extract)

Missa non absque ratione facio multa, quae multi hac in parte de fictis numerorum figurarumque virtutibus tam leviter quam curiose pertractant. Haec est pythagorei mysterii et platonici summa. Mitto quod solent intelligentiam, quoniam per simplicem fit intuitum, saepe "unitatem" cognominare, scientiam vero "dualitatem," quoniam ex principio probat conclusionem, sed opinionem "trinitatem," quia insuper conclusionis oppositum ambiguitate quadam affert in medium, sensum postremo "quatrinitatem," propterea quod circa composita ex quatuor elementis plurimum versari videtur. Mitto rursus, quod animam ideo "currum" vocant, quia motus efficit circulares, quodve in ea lineam ponunt quodammodo rectam, quantum corpora movet et respicit, deinde circulum quemdam inferiorem, quasi planetarum orbem, quando redit in semetipsam, circulum quoque superiorem, quasi stellarum orbem fixarum, quatenus ad superiora convertitur. "Alas duas," scilicet instinctum intellectus ad ipsum verum atque voluntatis ad ipsum bonum, "aurigam" mentem, "caput" aurigae divinam unitatem mente superiorem, "equos superiores," scilicet idem et sta-

and rest; "inferior horses," difference and motion; and "a good and a bad horse," the irascible nature and the concupiscible, for wrath seems closer to reason than desire.

To sum up briefly. In this manner Pythagoreans and Platonists suppose all rational souls, ours and those higher than ours [the heroic, demonic, and angelic], are composed in virtually the same way.

V Theologia Platonica (1474), from Book 17, Chapter 3

Particularly and most clearly in the *Phaedrus* Plato . . . says that various souls accompany various gods in heaven. In contemplating the Ideas, the souls summon all their strength and enact with their intelligence a like circuit as their god. In succession they consider the divine objects above heaven, the celestial within heaven, and the natural below heaven. Insofar as they can imitate gods, they remain with those who dwell above. Again, while they repeat the many circuits from causes to effects and the reverse, Plato says, the soul that has intuited the Idea at the circuit's head does not fall in the circuit (which is continuous, thanks exclusively to the Idea); but it falls when the bad horse, the concupiscible power—excited by the generative power, which has been waxing stronger now its time has come— turns away from contemplating to generating. Plato next enumerates nine lives—not because only nine exist, but because they descend down through the seven planets, the fire, and the air.[112] Finally, he describes the many transmigrations through lower things and the return to those above. Undoubtedly, many of his comments here are poetical rather than philosophical.

VI Theologia Platonica (1474), from Book 18, Chapter 4

Let us return to the body closest to the soul. The Magi call it "the soul's vehicle,"[113] that is, the little aethereal body received from the aether as the soul's immortal garment. Naturally cir-

tum, "equos inferiores," scilicet alterum atque motum. Item "equum bonum atque malum" scilicet irascendi et concupiscendi naturam. Ira enim propinquior rationi quam libido esse videtur.

Denique, ut summatim dicam, hac ratione Pythagorici et Platonici omnes rationales animas tum nostras tum nostra superiores pene similiter esse compositas arbitrantur.

V Theologia Platonica XVII. 3 (ed. Marcel, 3:159) (Extract)

Quas quidem vicissitudines Plato tum saepe alibi, tum in Phaedro praecipue describit, atque ibi manifestius, ubi animas, inquit, alias aliorum deorum in caelo comites esse atque in contemplandis ideis similem pro viribus cum deo suo discursionem mente peragere, tum super caelum circa divina, tum in caelo circa caelestia, tum sub caelo circa naturalia gradatim consideranda. Et quatenus deos imitari possunt, eatenus apud superos permanere. Item cum multiplices a causis ad effectus atque vicissim circuitus repetant, ait animum, qui intuitus est ideam, quae caput circuitus est, in circuitu illo, qui per ipsam proprie ideam continuatur, non cadere, sed tunc labi cum malus equus, id est concupiscendi vis incitata per vim generandi iam suo quodam tempore invalescentem, a contemplando divertit ad generandum. Deinde vitas dinumerat novem, non quod tot solum sint, sed quia per septem planetas ignemque et aerem delabuntur. Demum transmigrationes multas per inferiora reditumque ad superiora describit, ubi multa proculdubio poetica sunt potius quam philosophica.

VI Theologia Platonica XVIII. 4 (ed. Marcel, 3:193-196) (Extracts)

Sed iam ad corpus animae proximum redeamus. Hoc vocant Magi "vehiculum animae," aethereum scilicet corpusculum acceptum ab aethere, immortale animae indumentum, naturali

cular in shape because it is from the region of the aether, it transforms itself into the likeness of man when it enters the human body, but reverts to its former shape when it departs. This the Magi consider necessary because angels are such that they are potentially separable from and have actually been separated from bodies, whereas irrational souls are neither potentially nor actually separable. Thence it follows that rational souls, as the mean between the two, must be such that they are always potentially separable—since they will not perish if bodies are taken from them—but always actually joined—since the familiar body, which they preserve as immortal through their own immortality, they derive from the aether. In the *Phaedrus* Plato calls this body the "chariot" alike of the gods and souls,[114] and in the *Timaeus,* the "vehicle."[115] The souls of spheres and celestial souls use it in its purest form; demons' souls, in a less pure; and our souls, because it is mixed with the earthy body, in the least pure. Hence Zoroaster's injunction:

Μὴ πνεῦμα μολύνῃς, μηδὲ βαθύνῃς τὸ ἐπίπεδον,

that is, "Don't soil the spirit, nor add depth to what is plane."[116]

He calls the vehicle itself "spirit" and "plane," not because it is not a body and does not have depth, but because in its extreme tenuity and brilliant purity it's as if it were not a body at all. He warns us, therefore, given our excessive yearning for the elemental body, not to force the vehicle, even after this life, to be squalid and heavy through union with the elemental murk, which the ancient theologians called the soul's "shadow." Yet they do not suppose that the soul's rational part adheres closely to the vehicle; but rather that the rational soul itself, insofar as it is both rational and a companion of celestial souls, imparts a vivifying act to the vehicle, an act that we have already often called the soul's "idol." In the book on the generation of the world Plato names it the soul's mortal "form" (*species*),[117] not because it must die someday, but because it would collapse were

quidem figura rotundum propter aetheris regionem, sed in humanam effigiem sese transferens, quando corpus humanum ingreditur, atque in priorem se restituens, cum egreditur. Quod ob eam causam Magi necessarium arbitrantur, quoniam angeli tales sunt ut et virtute separabiles et actu separati sint a corporibus, irrationales animae neque virtute separabiles neque actu. Ex quo sequitur rationales animas tamquam medias tales esse debere, ut virtute quidem semper separabiles sint, quia si illis subtrahantur corpora, non peribunt, actu autem sint semper coniunctae, quia familiare corpus nanciscuntur ex aethere, quod servent per immortalitatem propriam immortale, quod Plato "currum" tum deorum tum animarum vocat in Phaedro, "vehiculum" in Timaeo, quo utantur animae sphaerarum caelestesque purissimo, daemonum animae minus puro, nostrae quoque minus propter terreni corporis mixtionem. Quam ob causam ita praecipit Zoroaster:

Μὴ πνεῦμα μολύνῃς, μηδὲ βαθύνῃς τὸ ἐπίπεδον,

Id est: "Ne foedes spiritum, neque in profundum exaugeas quod est planum."

"Spiritum planumque" appellat ipsum vehiculum, non quia corpus non sit atque profundum, sed quia propter tenuissimam et splendidam puritatem sit quasi non corpus. Praecipit ergo, ne propter nimium corporis elementalis affectum cogas ipsum etiam post hanc vitam sordidum atque grave superfore caliginis elementalis adiunctione, quam animae "umbram" prisci theologi nuncuparunt. Neque tamen volunt rationalem animae partem proxime haerere vehiculo, sed rationalem ipsam animam, quantum et rationalis est et comes caelestium animarum, {a}edere actum vivificum in vehiculum, quod animae "idolum" saepe iam appellavimus, quam "speciem" animae mortalem in libro de Mundi generatione Plato nuncupat, non quia moriatur aliquando, sed quia subtracto vehiculo rueret, ut quidam putant. Sicut enim lunae splendor in nube promit ex seipso pal-

the vehicle withdrawn—or so some think. For just as the
moon's splendor projects its paleness from itself onto a cloud,
so the soul sends forth the idol onto its celestial body, as a
comet its tail. This idol would vanish were the celestial body to
vanish, just as the moon-blanching is destroyed when the clouds
disperse. Yet since the vehicle will never be withdrawn, Zoroaster says:

Ἔστι καὶ εἰδώλῳ μερὶς εἰς τόπον ἀμφιφάοντα,

that is, "There is a place for the idol too in the transparent
region."[118] For the idol will return to heaven at the same time as
the vehicle and the rational soul. . . .

They opine, however, that dwelling in this idol is a certain
irrational and confused fantasy, and such senses too that you
can see and hear equally through the entire vehicle (though very
few men use the senses properly—and rarely at that). Through
them you can often perceive the heavens' wonderful harmonies
and also the voices and bodies of demons; and this occurs whenever someone, having abandoned his earthy body, betakes himself for a while to his celestial body [the Phaedran chariot]. . . . I
shall not discuss the opinion of many Platonists that the soul
uses three vehicles: the first being immaterial and simple, the
celestial vehicle; the second, material and simple, the aereal
vehicle;[119] and the third, material and compound, the vehicle
constituted from the four elements. To the first the soul gives an
irrational but immortal life; to the second, an irrational but
long-lasting life—one that can endure for a certain time in the
simple body after the compound one has been dissolved; to the
third, finally, an irrational life that must dissolve when the body
dissolves. Moreover, in the first life communicated to the
vehicle the sense is common and not susceptible to change; in
the second life, the sense is susceptible to change through still
common (that is, is equally whole through the whole vehicle); in
the third life, finally, the sense is both divided up and susceptible to change.

lorem, sic anima in corpore caelesti emittit idolum, quasi [stella]
crinita comam. Quod evanesceret, si evanesceret corpus illud,
sicut pallor exstinguitur, nubibus dissipatis. Quia tamen numquam vehiculum subtrahetur, Zoroaster inquit:

Ἔστι καὶ εἰδώλῳ μερὶς εἰς τόπον ἀμφιφάοντα,

Id est: "Est idolo quoque locus in regione perspicua." Quia
scilicet cum vehiculo simul et anima rationali recurret in caelum....
    Inesse autem idolo huic opinantur phantasiam quamdam
irrationalem atque confusam; sensus praeterea tales, ut per
totum vehiculum videatur pariter atque audiatur, quibus sensibus proprie homines quam paucissimi utantur et raro. Sentiri
vero per illos saepe concentus caelorum mirabiles vocesque et
corpora daemonum, quotiens aliquis ad tempus, terreno corpore derelicto, sese in corpus suum caeleste receperit....
    Mitto quod Platonici multi putant animam tribus uti vehicu-
lis: primo quidem immateriali et simplici, id est caelesti,
secundo materiali et simplici, id est aereo, tertio materiali atque
composito, id est ex elementis quatuor constituto; et primo quidem dare vitam irrationalem, sed immortalem, secundo vero
vitam irrationalem, sed longaevam, quae videlicet composito
corpore aliquando dissoluto ad certum tempus supersit in simplici corpore; tertio denique vitam et irrationalem et una cum
dissoluto corpore dissolvendam. Praeterea in prima vita com-
municata vehiculo sensum esse communem atque impatibilem,
in secunda patibilem et communem, id est per vehiculum universum sensum pariter universum, denique in tertia sensum
divisum pariter atque patibilem.

VII   Theologia Platonica (1474), from Book 18, Chapter 8

In the *Phaedrus* [Plato says that] the souls that emerge from Lethe's waters fly upward.[120] First they take part in the celestial circuit with the celestial gods, and then in the supercelestial circuit with the supercelestial gods. The order they follow is such that various souls circle round with various heavenly beings and repeat these same circuits by turns. But Plato means nothing other than the following. When souls have been liberated from elemental bodies, they occupy celestial vehicles (restored now to their proper circular shape), and dwell in the celestial region.[121] Various souls along with various stars and heavenly beings (those to whom they are especially related either by nature or by disposition) then work together in governing the world to a certain degree and also discourse through the species of things similarly with the reason. Finally, with the supercelestial gods, that is, the angels, they join together in gazing at the Ideas and in instantaneously completing that supercelestial circuit. They accomplish both circuits happily with both sets of divine beings.

Plato adds that the souls are nourished there with the same foods as the gods, that is, with ambrosia and nectar. He supposes that ambrosia is the sweet, clear gazing at the truth, but nectar the excellent and effortless providing [for inferiors].

VII Theologia Platonica XVIII. 8 (ed. Marcel, 3:204)
(Extract)

Huc tendit platonicum illud in Phedro, animas quae ex
Lethea emerserint aqua altius evolare, ibique primo caelestem
una cum diis caelestibus, deinde supercaelestem cum supercaelestibus circuitum agere, eo scilicet ordine ut aliae cum aliis ibi
numinibus circumvagentur circuitusque huiusmodi alternis vicibus repetant. Hoc autem nihil aliud sibi vult, quam solutas ab
elementalibus corporibus animas, in caelestibus iam vehiculis in
figuram propriam circularem scilicet restitutis, caelestem colere
regionem, atque alias una cum stellis caelicolisque aliis, quibus
vel natura vel habitu magis familiares sunt, tum in certa quadam mundi gubernatione congruere, tum per rerum species
similiter ratione discurrere. Rursus cum diis supercaelestibus, id
est angelis, in ipso idearum intuitu et quasi quodam circuitu
subito consentire et una cum utrisque foeliciter utrumque
peragere.

Addit eisdem una cum superis illic alimentis, scilicet ambrosia et nectare vesci. Ambrosiam quidem esse censet perspicuum
suavemque veritatis intuitum, nectar vero excellentem facilli-
mamque providentiam.

References in the Texts

¹As his authorities, Ficino refers in his own life of Plato (*Op.*, p. 763) to Diogenes Laertius (*Lives of the Philosophers* 3. 2) and to Policrates (i.e., to the *Policraticus* 7. 5 of John of Salisbury); see Kristeller, *Studies*, p. 40, n. 36. Other ancient sources might include Plutarch, *Symposium* 8, q. 1, [Pseudo-?] Apuleius, *De Dogmate Platonis* 1. 1, and Olympiodorus, *Life of Plato* 1. Origen, *Contra Celsum* 1. 37; 6. 8, and Jerome, *Adversus Jovinianum* 1. 42, both discuss Plato's Apollonian generation in the context of Christ's birth. For Ficino it would also have had allegorical dimensions, A-POLLO being the NOT-MANY (an etymology he derived from Plotinus, *Enneads* 5. 5. 6, repeated several times, *Op.*, pp. 126, 1313, and considered Pythagorean in origin; cf. Cicero, *De Natura Deorum* 2. 27).

Ancient tradition also held that Plato was born on Apollo's birthday and was dedicated to him. For Ficino this was not the seventh of Thargelion but November 7 (*De Amore* 1, opening). This may puzzle those "who fail to realize," as J. H. Randall, Jr., notes, "that the birthday of an Italian saint—as Plato had become—is the day he enters eternal life—the day of his death" (*Plato: Dramatist of the Life of Reason* [New York, 1970], p. 18). Plato's parents also took care to dedicate him to Pan (the ALL) and to the nine Muses; and hence he lived, according to Ficino (*Op.*, p. 770) following Seneca (*Epist.* 58), nine times nine years. Apollo, Pan, and the Muses are therefore the deities presiding over the youthful *Phaedrus* and the occasion it describes.

²Ficino derived the notion that the *Phaedrus* was Plato's very first dialogue from Diogenes, *Lives* 3. 38: "there is also a report that the first dialogue Plato wrote was the *Phaedrus;* for its subject [*problēma*] is one which a young man would naturally choose. But Dicaearchus censures the style of the entire dialogue, which he thinks in bad taste [*phortikon*]"—the reference is to fragment 42 (ed. Wehrli). Olympiodorus repeats the story in his *Life of Plato* 3 but notes that the style was youthfully "dithyrambic." Cicero's *Orator* 13. 41-42 might have given Ficino pause, however, if he had read it carefully.

³This is a general reference to the *De Amore,* but for the *Theologia Platonica* Ficino has the last three books especially in mind.

⁴Thrasyllus (d. A.D. 36) had divided Plato's works into tetralogies—upon what authority Diogenes does not mention (*Lives* 3. 56-61)—and had put the *Phaedrus* last in the third tetralogy, following the *Parmenides,* the *Philebus,* and the *Symposium.* Others established their themes, or skopoi, as the one, the good, love, and beauty, respectively. Within the tetralogy, the *Parmenides* and the *Philebus* formed an obvious pair, as did the *Symposium* and the *Phae-*

drus. From the beginning of his career as a commentator, Ficino was sensitive to the links between the *Symposium* and the *Phaedrus* and to the absurdity of treating their themes in isolation.

⁵*Theologia Platonica* 17. 2, 3; 18. 4, 8 (ed. Marcel, 3:156 ff., 193-196, 204). In this volume see Texts IV, extracts IV, V, VI, and VII.

⁶*Theologia Platonica* 17. 2, 3 (ed. Marcel, 3:154-159). The nine degrees, according to summa 24, constitute those of the world-soul and of the eight ruling celestial souls (that is, of the fixed stars and of the seven planetary spheres). Elsewhere Ficino includes among the ruling souls those of the four elemental spheres, Vulcan, Juno, Neptune, and Vesta/Pluto, and thus arrives at the Phaedran cavalcade of twelve soul-gods. See refs. 36, 83, and 112 below.

⁷Note that Ficino is using the adjectival form *Ophioneus* (itself a transliteration of the Greek) nominatively. He refers to Pherecydes again as a cosmogonist in the middle of his *Apology* epitome (*Op.,* p. 1388): "[Plato] a Pherecyde Syro multos ab Iove daemones rebellasse, quorum exercitus Ophioneus duxerit serpentinus"; cf. *Orphicorum Fragmenta* (ed. Kern, p. 98, no. 29); Apollonius Rhodius, *Argonautica* 1. 496-505; and Claudian, *Rapt. Pros.* 3. 348.

Not only was Pherecydes reputed to be Pythagoras's instructor and the first man to pronounce the soul eternal (Cicero, *Tusc.* 1. 16. 38; *Div.* 1. 50. 112), he was also, Pliny says, the inventor of prose (*Hist. Nat.* 7. 205). As the latter Ficino seems to condemn him as a popularizer and thus profaner of mysteries: "Neque . . . tanquam Pherecides Syrus abdita coelestium animorum terreno cuilibet patefeci" (*Op.,* p. 756. 1); yet he believes him a seer—"Pherecides quoque philosophus multa prenuntiasse memoratur" (*Sup. Fic.* 2:101)—and a prophet (*Op.,* p. 203).

Cf. Diels, *Vorsokr.* 1:43-51; Diogenes, *Lives* 1. 116-122; Plotinus, *Enneads* 5. 1. 9; Porphyry, *Vita Pythag.* 55; Augustine, *Contra Academicos* 3. 17; Lactantius, *Div. Inst.* 7. 7-8; Origen, *Contra Celsum* 6. 42.

⁸*Timaeus* 41D (Ficino's only hint at the astrological possibilities for the myth).

⁹Cf. Ficino's letter to Cosimo, "Excusatio Prolixitatis" (*Op.,* p. 615. 2). *Canticis* may also refer to other works attributed to Solomon: the pseudepigraphical *Odes* and *Psalms, Ecclesiastes,* or the *Wisdom of Solomon.*

¹⁰*Philebus* 16B-17A, 58A; cf. Ficino's *Philebus* commentary 1.23 plus unattached chapter 4 (ed. Allen, pp. 214-225, 432-437). See ref. 94 below.

¹¹*Gorgias* 464B-465E, 500B-501A, 518A-D.

¹²Diogenes, *Lives* 8.85, claims that until Philolaus (Plato's reputed teacher) there were no writings at all on the Pythagorean philosophy; the Pythagoreans relied on oral transmission of the words of their master, the formula *autos epha* ("he declared") being sufficient testimony to something's truth. Cf. Iamblichus, *Life of Pythagoras* 31. 188 ff.

¹³*Letter* 2. 312D-313C; *Letter* 7. 341B-345C. Cf. Ficino's epitomes, *Op.* pp. 1530-1532 and 1534-1535.

¹⁴*De Amore* 7. 14, 15 (ed. Marcel, pp. 258-260); and the argumentum (epitome) to the *Ion* (*Op.*, pp. 1281-1284). See Texts IV, extract II and ref. 106 below.

André Chastel has a brief chapter on the *furores* (*Marsile Ficin et L'Art* [Geneva and Lille, 1954], pp. 129-135).

Note that the Phaedran sequence reverses that proposed in Ficino's epistolary tract, *De Divino Furore* (*Op.*, pp. 612-615), written December 1, 1457, and addressed to Peregrino Agli.

¹⁵*Timaeus* 47CD. Cf. Ficino's commentary on the *Timaeus,* chaps. 33 and 34 (*Op.*, pp. 1458-1460); also his *De Divino Furore* (*Op.*, p. 614), Porphyry's *Life of Pythagoras* 31, and Macrobius's *In Somnium Scipionis* 2. 3 (ed. Stahl).

¹⁶1 Cor. 13:1-13.

¹⁷*Theologia Platonica* 1. 4; 5. 1 (ed. Marcel, 1:56-58, 174-175).

In his epitome to the *Phaedo* (*Op.*, p. 1390), Ficino observes that Socrates reserved one argument in support of the soul's immortality for the *Phaedrus* alone, namely that the soul is the principle of motion and thus is perpetually moved by itself and lives forever. Socrates omitted this in the *Phaedo,* Ficino continues, because "this reason is common not only to our souls but to those of the celestial [gods] and demons too," whereas the *Phaedo* is concerned specifically with proofs appropriate for human souls. In actual fact, Plato also discussed the self-motion argument at some length in the *Laws* (891-899)—see ref. 18 below.

Note that Ficino would have known Cicero's translation of this entire syllogistic passage (245C-246A) in the *Tusculanae* 1. 23.

¹⁸See ref. 17 above. Ficino's introduction to *Laws* 10 (*Op.*, pp. 1515-1520) is especially concerned with the self-motion argumentation at 893B-899D; cf. Proclus, *Theologia Platonica* 1. 14.

¹⁹*Theologia Platonica* 1. 3 (ed. Marcel, 1:44-55).

²⁰*Op.*, pp. 1136-1206; see especially chaps. 38, 41, and 48. This was a working formula derived from the negative argumentation of the *Parmenides's* first hypothesis (137C-142A). Cf. Plotinus, *Enneads* 5. 1. 8, 11; 5. 3. 11; and Proclus, both *Theologia Platonica* 1. 12; 2. 10-12, and *In Parm.* 6 and 7.

For an introduction to the Neoplatonic interpretation of the first hypothesis of the *Parmenides* and to its history, see Saffrey and Westerink 1:lx-lxxxix; 2: ix-xx; and 3:xvii-xxxvi.

²¹See ref. 20 above.

²²*Phaedrus* 246B, "Pasa hē psychē pantos epimeleitai tou apsychou," which Ficino translates, "Omnis animus totius inanimati curam habet." Cf. Plotinus, *Enneads* 4. 3. 1 and 7.

²³*In Platonis Phaedrum Scholia,* p. 130 (ed. Couvreur); in Ficino's own Latin translation (MS. Vat. Lat. 5953), fol. 222v.

²⁴This is probably a reference to *Timaeus* 31B-32B.

²⁵*De Oraculis Chaldaicis* (ed. Kroll, p. 64)—included in Des Places's edi-

tion (Paris, 1971) as Fr. 104. Cf. *Theologia Platonica* 18. 4 (ed. Marcel, 3: 194), i.e., Texts IV, extract VI above, and also ref. 116 below.

For Psellus's adoption of the Proclan explanation that the terms signify the soul's two garments (*indumenta*) over and above the material body, Kroll refers us to Psellus's own exegesis of the *Oracles* at 1137C (ed. Migne) and cross-refers us to Synesius, *De Insomniis* 151D; to Proclus, *In Remp.* 36. 25, 43. 24, 171. 20, and *In Tim.* 45B; and to Olympiodorus, *In Phaedone* 136. 10 (p. 64; cf. p. 4).

A manuscript in the Laurentian Library (Plut. 36. 35, fol. 26r-v) contains a Latin translation of sayings entitled *Magica* (superscribed *id est philosophica*) *dicta magorum ex Zoroastre*. Nearly halfway through, as verse 26, our dictum occurs as, "Ne spiritum infeceris neque profundum reddas epipedon id est superficiem" (fol. 26r). This version of the *Magica dicta*, like the versions of the Orphic *Hymns*, and of Proclus's hymns to the Sun, to Venus, and to the Muses, preceding it, has been tentatively attributed in the past to Ficino (see Kristeller, *Sup. Fic.* 1:cxlv; 2:97-98). That Ficino's rendering in the *Phaedrus* commentary does not correspond to it does not in itself disprove his authorship, since his rendering in the *Platonic Theology* is different again. Marcel had no justification, however, for attributing the Laurentian Library's version without comment to Ficino (in his edition of the *Platonic Theology* 1: 64n), and Ilana Klutstein of Hebrew University, Jerusalem, is currently working on a dissertation that argues against Ficino's authorship of it.

[26]*Enneads* 1. 1. 4, 5; 3. 3. 4; 3. 4. 1, 5; 4. 3. 9, 10, 20; 4. 7. 1; 6. 4. 12-16; etc.

[27]*Philebus* 20CD, 22B, 67A; cf. Ficino's commentary 1. 30 (ed. Allen, pp. 290-297). Hermias also refers here to the *Philebus*, p. 134 (ed. Couvreur), fols. 223v ff. (trans. Ficino), but it would be an inevitable association for any Neoplatonist.

[28]*Republic* 6. 507B-509B; 7. 517BC. Cf. Plotinus, *Enneads* 5. 1. 8; also Proclus, *Theol. Plat.* 2. 7, and *In Remp.* 11 (ed. Kroll, 1:276. 23-281. 7).

[29]*Philebus* 65A; cf. Ficino's commentary 1. 31 (ed. Allen, pp. 298-315).

[30]*Phaedrus* 250B-D; *Symposium* 195A-196B. Cf. *De Amore* 5. 2, 7 (ed. Marcel, pp. 179 ff., 190 ff.). Strictly speaking, the *Symposium*'s three epithets apply not to Beauty but to Love's beauty.

[31]*Phaedrus* 250D; *Symposium* 180DE, 195A-196B, and passim.

[32]*Republic* 6. 507B-509B; 7. 517BC; *Cratylus* 396B. Cf. Cicero, *De Natura Deorum* 2. 25; Ficino, epitome of the *Cratylus, Op.*, p. 1311; and Pico della Mirandola, letter to Ficino in Ficino's eighth book of letters, *Op.*, p. 889. 4, where the pun on *satur/Saturnus* is repeated.

[33]In fact, it was not until Proclus that "the Platonists" postulated three orders of supramundane gods. See Proclus, *Theol. Plat.* 1. 4-5 and 3. 7-28 (on the intelligible gods), 4 (on the mixed gods), 5 (on the intellectual gods), and 6. 2 (a summary account).

In par. 5 of chap. 11 Ficino will assign these three orders to the convex, the

height (*profundum*), and the concave of the intellectual heaven. Proclus had argued that the *Phaedrus* was one of the best sources for an understanding of the three "Platonic" orders; see Saffrey and Westerink 1:lxv-lxvi.

³⁴This is a vague reference to the *Theologia Platonica* 4. 1, more precisely probably to pp. 153 ff. (ed. Marcel, 1). Here Ficino had named the twelve Olympians as the Pythagoreans had linked them to the brightest star in each of the zodiacal signs, like souls to hearts, the signs of course occupying the outermost of the world spheres, that of the fixed stars; cf. the *De Amore* 5. 13 (ed. Marcel, p. 198). He went on to observe that the Olympians were only represented in their full dodecade in the first and last spheres, those of the fixed stars and of earth (*cuius [duodenarii] numeri signum in sphaera prima habemus et ultima*).

Less probably, Ficino might also be referring to his account at pp. 164-165, where he had used the Orphic pantheon to assign a male and female deity to each of the four sublunary spheres, and a Muse along with Bacchus under one of his cognomens to the seven planetary spheres, to the sphere of the fixed stars, and to the world-soul; cf. ref. 90 below.

Note that Ficino seems to depart from his Neoplatonic predecessors in assigning the same set of names to the leaders of both the mundane and the supermundane dodecades.

³⁵*Philebus* 30D; cf. Ficino's commentary 1. 11 (ed. Allen, pp. 136-137), and Plotinus, *Enneads* 3. 5. 8; 4. 4. 9.

³⁶*Metaphysics* 12. 8. 1073a ff. Cf. Plato, *Timaeus* 41D; *Laws* 10. 898C-899B; 12. 967A-E; *Epinomis* passim; and Plotinus, *Enneads* 5. 1. 9.

The dodecade is led and ruled by the soul who also rules over the planet Jupiter; that is, in the animate realm Jupiter is primarily the world-soul and secondarily the soul of the planet and its sphere. This duplication of role is critical for Ficino's analysis—however curious it may first seem to us—and is the consequence of his assumption that the *Phaedrus* myth could be reconciled with astronomy (i.e., with the Ptolemaic system, which was also Plato's, he believed, and Aristotle's).

³⁷Boccaccio, *Genealogie Deorum Gentilium Liber* 1, proem 11B-12B (ed. Romano, pp. 12-15). Boccaccio follows the authority of the mysterious Theodontius in making Demogorgon the first and highest of the pagan gods, coeternal with eternity and chaos, and the father of Pan, the Fates, and so forth: "Sonat igitur, ut reor, Demogorgon grece, terre deus latine. Nam demon deus ut ait Leontius, Gorgon autem terra interpretatur. Seu potius sapientia terre, cum sepe demon sciens vel sapientia exponatur. Seu, ut magis placet aliis, deus terribilis, quod de vero Deo qui in celis habitat legitur: Sanctum et terribile nomen eius" (p. 15).

³⁸*Cratylus* 396BC; cf. Ficino's epitome, *Op.*, p. 1311.

³⁹Ficino makes it clear at *Op.*, p. 1547, that the *third* book of Plotinus's queries concerning the soul was for him, as it is for us, *Enneads* 4. 5; this ref-

erence, however, is to the *second* book, that is, 4. 4, and specifically to 4. 4. 9-10 (cf. *Philebus* 30D and also *Enneads* 3. 5. 8). The references to the book on the three principles is to *Enneads* 5. 1. 4 and 7 (cf. *Cratylus* 396 BC and also *Enneads* 5. 5. 3 and 5. 8. 13).

⁴⁰*Enneads* 4. 4. 10.

⁴¹*Letter* 6, 323D. Cf. Ficino's argumentum, *Op.*, pp. 1533-1534.

⁴²*Enneads* 3. 5. 2, 3, 4, 5, 8. See ref. 93 below.

⁴³Cicero, *De Natura Deorum* 2. 27. See ref. 92 below.

⁴⁴Notably in the *De Amore* 2. 3 (ed. Marcel, p. 149) and passim.

⁴⁵*Symposium* 180DE. Cf. *De Amore* 2. 7 (ed. Marcel, pp. 153-155). Summa 30 further complicates the status of Venus by equating her (at times?) with Juno, following Plotinus; see ref. 83 below.

⁴⁶Ficino probably has the *Hymn to Jove* (15) specifically in mind, but the principle that any one god "contains" all the others is fundamental to his conception of Orphic theology; see D. P. Walker, "Orpheus the Theologian and the Renaissance Platonists," *Journal of the Warburg and Courtauld Institutes* 16 (1953): 100-120.

⁴⁷*Op.*, pp. 965-975, particularly chap. 9 (pp. 970-971): "In Sole prisci Gentium Theologi omnia Gentilium numina collocarunt. Quod quidem Iamblichus et Iulianus Macrobiusque testantur."

⁴⁸Epitome, *Op.*, p. 1311 (glossing *Cratylus* 396A-C): "Coelius in quolibet numine aspectum ad superiora designat, Saturnus respectum ad semetipsum, Iupiter prospectum inferioribus providentem." Cf. Plotinus, *Enneads* 5. 8. 13, and Ficino's *Philebus* commentary 1. 26 (ed. Allen, pp. 246-247). This triple formula had become a commonplace in later Neoplatonism.

⁴⁹Probably a reference to the *Parmenides* 137C-142A. See n. 20 above.

⁵⁰For Iamblichus's views Ficino probably turned directly to the *De Mysteriis:* to 1. 3, 4, and 5 (ed. Des Places, pp. 42 ff.), and specifically to 2. 3 ff. (ed. Des Places, p. 79; trans. Ficino, *Op.*, pp. 1879. 3 ff.) where the full list of superior beings is first enumerated. He could also have turned, as for the views of Syrianus and of Proclus himself, to Proclus's commentaries on the *Timaeus* and on the first and second books of the *Republic.*

The multiplication of demonic orders is found throughout post-Plotinian Neoplatonism, as is the practice of naming them and their individual members after their presiding gods; see Proclus, *Theol. Plat.* 1. 26 (ed. Saffrey and Westerink, 1:115. 7-12); *In Tim.* 3:204. 23-32 (ed. Diehl); and *In Alc.* 72. 12-74. 10; 78. 10-79. 14; 158. 3-159. 5 (ed. Westerink).

⁵¹*Timaeus* 28B, 30C-32B.

⁵²See ref. 20 above.

⁵³*Timaeus* 33B ff. and passim.

⁵⁴*Republic* 6. 508A-509B; 7. 517BC.

⁵⁵*Laws* 5. 745B-E, 746D; 6. 771BC (and there are, of course, twelve books to the *Laws*); cf. Ficino's epitomes of bks. 5 and 6, *Op.*, pp. 1502, 1504-1505.

There is no obvious reference for the *Republic;* but in the third chapter of his *Expositio circa numerum nuptialem in octavo de Republica* (= his minor commentary on *Republic* 8. 546B-547A), *Op.,* p. 1415. 2, Ficino says, apropos of a reference to the *Timaeus* 35B ff., that twelve and eighteen are the means between eight and twenty-seven and that hence "Plato colit magnopere duodenarium ceu primum inter solida medium." Twelve, he continues, is *openly* venerated in the *Laws,* the *Phaedo,* the *Timaeus,* the *Phaedrus,* and the *Critias,* but only *secretly* so in the *Republic,* "Quapropter Plato numerum hunc universalis formae mundanae vel humanae atque civilibus gubernatorem esse iudicat." Cf. *Theologia Platonica* 4. 1 (ed. Marcel, 1:153).

For twelve as the symbol of "perfect procession," see Proclus, *Theol. Plat.* 6. 18, 19 (ed. Portus, pp. 394-400). For the "dodecahedron" by means of which the Demiurge "fashioned heaven" with the constellations at *Timaeus* 55C, see Proclus, *In Remp.,* diss. 13 (ed. Kroll, 2:45. 6-46. 18).

⁵⁶Ficino is almost certainly recalling Hermias's anonymous doxography of presumably Middle- and Neoplatonic opinions about the meaning of the twelve gods in the *Phaedrus* 246E ff. (pp. 135-136 [ed. Couvreur], fols. 226r-v [trans. Ficino]. To synopsize Hermias's account: Some held them to be the twelve cosmic spheres (those of the fixed stars, the seven planets, and the four sublunary elements); others, the spheres' souls; others, the intellects presiding over the souls; others, that Zeus was the Sun, and the other ruler gods were the zodiacal signs; and finally Iamblichus (and therefore Syrianus and Hermias himself) held them, or at least Zeus, to be beyond the heavens, that is, supramundane. See John M. Dillon, *Iamblichi Chalcidensis: In Platonis Dialogos Commentariorum Fragmenta* (Leiden, 1973), p. 251, also ref. 58 below.

⁵⁷*Theologia Platonica* 4. 1 (ed. Marcel, 1:153-155, 164-165).

⁵⁸The supramundanists are Iamblichus, Syrianus, Proclus, and Hermias. See, for example, Hermias, p. 136 (ed. Couvreur), fol. 226v (trans. Ficino): "The divine Iamblichus, however, drawing on the name 'Zeus,' refers the subject of the present passage [246E] to the single Demiurge of the cosmos, who is described also in the Timaeus" (trans. Dillon, p. 95). All of these later Neoplatonists seem to have been drawn to the connection between the Zeus of the *Phaedrus* and the Demiurge of the *Timaeus* 28A, a connection that Ficino refused, in this instance at least, to grant.

Both Dillon (p. 251) and Bent Dalsgaard Larsen (*Jamblique de Chalcis: Exégète et philosophe* [Aarhus, 1972], p. 371) argue that Iamblichus was the first to expound the supramundanist view; cf. ref. 59 below.

The Plotinus reference is to the *Enneads* 5. 8. 10, 12, and 13: "Zeus, sovereign over the visible universe... the manifested god" (12); cf. 4. 3. 7. In glossing the *Symposium* 203BC at 3. 5. 8, and with the reference to "great Zeus" at *Phaedrus* 246E specifically in mind, Plotinus seems to adopt, however, the alternative view. On the grounds that Soul is represented by Aphrodite, he argues that Zeus cannot be Soul but is, rather, Mind. As Saffrey and

Westerink note in their edition of Proclus's *Platonic Theology,* 2:xlvii, however, Plotinus is in fact thinking of Zeus as the world-soul, for he and Aphrodite are a pair: she "dwells with him" as the "royal soul" united with his
"royal intellect." The passage is sufficiently ambiguous, nevertheless, to
authorize a supramundanist explanation, particularly if it is taken in isolation.
Ficino made brilliant use of it in his own analysis of the *Symposium* 203BC in
the *De Amore* 6. 7 (ed. Marcel, pp. 208-210), though he unequivocally equates
the Jupiter here with the world-soul, as we might expect.

⁵⁹The arguments in this paragraph resemble those in Proclus's *Platonic
Theology* 4. 5 (ed. Portus, pp. 187-188); see Introduction, nn. 25 and 26
above. Proclus specifically mentions Iamblichus's interpretation of the *Phaedrus* 246E-247B: "If one declares that the 'heaven' towards which Zeus leads
the way, and all the Gods follow, and along with them the daemons, is of the
intelligible order, he will be giving an inspired interpretation of Plato in accordance with the facts, and he will be in agreement with the most renowned of
the commentators. For Plotinus [5. 8. 10] and Iamblichus consider this
'heaven' to be an intelligible entity" (ed. Portus, p. 188. 15 ff.). Similarly, in
4. 23, Proclus observes: "For great Iamblichus, having declared the great
heaven to be an order of intelligible gods, which he has in some places identified with the Demiurge, takes the 'inner vault of heaven' [247AB] as the order
of creation situated immediately beneath it and as it were the membrane cov-
ering the heaven. This is what he said in his [lost] *Commentaries on the Phaedrus*" (ed. Portus, p. 215. 21 ff.).

The translations are Dillon's, pp. 95 and 97—see his analyses, pp. 251-253,
and those of Larsen, p. 371. Hermias does not mention Iamblichus on these
particular lemmas, and Proclus is our sole source.

Note that Ficino can accept Iamblichus's view that "heaven" must be intelligible while rejecting his supramundane interpretation of Zeus, and thus
adopt in effect Plotinus's view (despite his reservations about Plotinus's over-
literal reading of the mythical hymn, or at least of parts of it; see Introduction, n. 47 above).

⁶⁰*Cratylus* 396BC; cf. Plotinus, *Enneads* 5. 8. 13.

⁶¹The myth of Oreithyia (in Latin *Orithyia*)—the commentary's variant
Herethrie is inexplicable, given the name's appearance at *Phaedrus* 229B—
would be familiar to Ficino from Ovid, *Metamorphoses* 6. 683; Vergil, *Geor-
gic* 4. 463 and *Aeneid* 12. 83; Propertius, *Elegies* 2. 26. 51 and 3. 7. 13; and
Cicero, *De Legibus* 1. 1. 3. Cf. Hermias, p. 29 (ed. Couvreur), fol. 150r-v
(trans. Ficino), where Oreithyia is glossed as the soul of Phaedrus and Boreas
as Socrates!

⁶²Cf. Vergil, *Aeneid* 6. 136 ff. The equation of *sylva* there with *hyle,* meaning both "forest" and "elemental matter," was a medieval and Renaissance
commonplace, deriving from Servius's gloss on the episode and incorporated
into Chalcidius's and later commentaries on the *Timaeus*. See Ficino's

excerpt, "On the triple life and the triple end," at one time attached to his *Philebus* commentary (ed. Allen, pp. 448-449).

The Nymphs's presidency over the act of generation is also glossed by Hermias, pp. 53-56 (ed. Couvreur), fols. 168r-170r (trans. Ficino).

[63]*Republic* 10. 617E, 620DE (in the tale of Er—the guardian genii); cf. Ficino's epitome, *Op.*, pp. 1436-1437; *Phaedo* 107D-108B; and Plotinus, *Enneads* 3. 4. 3-6.

[64]Iamblichus, *De Mysteriis*—see Ficino's own translation/adaptation, *Op.*, pp. 1876. 2; 1878. 4; and especially 1904. 2-1906. 2.

[65]*Hymn to Eros* 58. 4; cf. *De Amore* dedication and 3. 3 (ed. Marcel, pp. 134, 135, 164).

[66]*Symposium* 203A-E; *De Amore* 6. 7 (ed. Marcel, pp. 208-210). Cf. Plotinus, *Enneads* 3. 5. 2, 5, 7-9.

[67]*Enneads* 1. 3. 1; 1. 6. 6, 7; 3. 5. 2; 5. 8. 9, 10; 6. 8. 15, 16.

[68]Since ancient Greek philosophy had no word for or conception of the will in the Augustinian sense, Ficino is reinterpreting Plotinus, and the reference is proably to *Enneads* 4. 4. 35 and 6. 8. 6, 13, 21.

[69]See Texts IV, extract II, and ref. 106 below; also ref. 14 above.

[70]*De Mysteriis,* in Ficino's *Op.*, pp. 1873-1908, passim, but especially pp. 1884. 2-1887 and 1894. 2-1900. 3; *Theologia Platonica* 13. 2 (ed. Marcel 2: 205-214).

Cf. Porphyry, *De Abst. Animal* 2, in Ficino's *Op.*, pp. 1934-1937, and Proclus, *De Sacrificio et Magia,* in Ficino's *Op.*, pp. 1928-1929.

[71]See *Theologia Platonica* 13. 4, 5 (ed. Marcel, 2:229-245) for further references.

[72]2 Cor. 12:1-5; Ficino's tract, *De Raptu Pauli, Op.*, pp. 697. 2-706. For Ficino's view of the oracular workings of Dodona, see Allen, "The Sibyl in Ficino's Oaktree," *Modern Language Notes* 95, 1 (January 1980): 205-210.

[73]*Republic* 3. 398AB; 8. 568BC; 10. 595A-C, 605A, 607A, 608B; *Laws* 7. 801CD, 817A-E; 8. 829C-E; 11. 935E-936A.

[74]*Timaeus* 40AB; cf. Plotinus, *Enneads* 2. 2. 2.

[75]*Republic* 6. 508A-509B; 7, 517BC.

[76]*Philebus* 61B-E, the general conclusion; cf. Ficino's commentary 1. 34, 36 (ed. Allen, pp. 354-355, 368-369 ff.).

[77]This is a particular aspect of the problem of evil and its origins.

For Plato, see *Charmides* 156E; *Protagoras* 345A ff.; *Sophist* 228A ff.; *Republic* 2, 379A-308A; 3, 391C; 10, 609C ff.; *Statesman* 273B ff.; *Timaeus* 41D ff., 86B ff.; *Theaetetus* 176A ff.; and so forth.

Plotinus concentrates upon the problem in *Enneads* 1. 8 (actually, chronologically, one of the last treatises), though raising it elsewhere—for example, in 2. 9; 4. 3. 9-23; 4. 8; and so forth. See Ficino's Plotinus commentary, *Op.*, pp. 1581-1591, especially pp. 1585. 2, 1587. 2, and 1589. 4 to the end.

Proclus vigorously opposed the theory that there was an Idea of evil, a

theory espoused apparently only by Amelius among the Neoplatonists; see *In Remp.* diss. 4 (ed. Kroll, 1:32. 13-33.7); *In Parm.* 3 (ed. Cousin, 3: cols. 829-831); *Theol. Plat.* 1. 18 (Saffrey and Westerink 1:82-88). On Proclus's singular theory that evil first appears at the level of particular souls, that is, of human rather than divine souls, see Saffrey and Westerink 3:22n, with further references.

Intensio and *remissio* became a standard antithetical pair for Scholasticism. See Anneliese Maier, *Zwei Grundprobleme der scholastischen Naturphilosophie: das Problem der intensiven Grösse, die Impetustheorie* (Rome, 1951), pp. 3-109 ("De intensione et remissione formarum").

Cf. Hermias, p. 163 (ed. Couvreur), fol. 242r-v (trans. Ficino).

[77]Hermias, p. 166 (ed. Couvreur), fol. 245r (trans. Ficino); Plotinus, *Enneads* 1. 6. 1-3.

[79]*Timaeus* 32B, 55B-E. For the Proclan significance of these multiples of ten in the *Phaedrus,* see *In Remp.*, diss. 13 (ed. Kroll, 2:21, 52-54, 66-70).

[80]Hermias, pp. 167-171 (ed. Couvreur), fols. 246r-249r (trans. Ficino); Proclus, *In Tim.* (ed. Diehl, 3:294. 18-295. 25); *In Remp.*, diss. 16 (ed. Kroll, 3: 309. 3-341. 8).

Cf. Plato, *Timaeus* 42C ff.; Augustine, *Civ. Dei* 10. 30; and Ficino, *Theologia Platonica* 17. 3, 4 (ed. Marcel, 3:164-174). Ficino seems to assume that Proclus as well as Porphyry denied metempsychosis.

[81]Notably, according to Ficino, Plotinus, *Enneads* 1. 1. 11; 3. 4. 2; and 6. 7. 6, 7. See his Plotinus commentary, *Op.*, pp. 1549. 3-1554; 1709. 3-1711; 1788. 5; and also his *Theologia Platonica* 17. 3 (ed. Marcel, 3:164). Cf. ref. 80 above.

[82]*De Amore* 6. 9, 10; 7. 2, 9, 10 (ed. Marcel, pp. 212-223, 242-245, 253-255), and passim.

[83]Plotinus, *Enneads* 3. 5. 8. Ficino ignores the problem, however, of how Juno can still remain a separate member of the Olympian dodecade, presiding in her own right over the sphere of air. This has a direct bearing on the issue of the nine lives; see ref. 6 above and ref. 112 below.

[84]*Symposium* 210A-212A (the ladder of Diotima).

[85]*Phaedrus* 257DE: the proverb *glykys ankōn* was variously explained in antiquity (see the notes by Thompson, p. 84, and de Vries, pp. 184-187), but Ficino would almost certainly have turned in the first place to Hermias's gloss, pp. 210-211 (ed. Couvreur)—in Ficino's own Latin translation, fol. 275v—which clearly says that a bend in the river (which made the journey between two points much longer) had come to be called, antiphrastically, the Pleasant Bend.

[86]Hermias, pp. 213-216 (ed. Couvreur), fols. 277v-279v (trans. Ficino). See P. A. Bielmeier, *Die neuplatonische Phaidrosinterpretation* [Paderborn, 1930], p. 28; Dillon, pp. 255-256; and Larsen, p. 372, for Hermias's account of Iamblichus's views on the cicadas.

Interestingly, Diogenes (*Lives* 3. 7) quotes some verses from Timon (Fr. 30D) to the effect that Plato was "a sweet-voiced speaker, musical in prose as the cicala who, perched on the trees of Hecademus, pours forth a strain as delicate as a lily" (trans. Hicks)!

⁸⁷*Symposium* 202B-203A; see *De Amore* 6. 3, 4, 8, 10 (ed. Marcel, pp. 201-205, 211, 221). Cf. ref. 63 above. In a note concluding one of his "excerpts" from Proclus's commentary on Plato's *Alcibiades* 1, Ficino observes, "Diotima magnum daemonem appellat amorem. Et Socrates ubi de amore disputat, disputat etiam de daemonibus" (*Op.*, p. 1912. 1).

⁸⁸This reference is obscure. In his article "Astres, Anges et Génies chez Marsile Ficin," in *Umanesimo e Esoterismo: Atti del V Convegno Internazionale di Studi Umanistici*, ed. E. Castelli (Padua, 1960), pp. 85-109, Maurice de Gandillac discusses Ficino's reference to Hesiod's 30,000 demons in his letter to Cardinal Giovanni de' Medici (*Op.*, pp. 930.4 to 931): "La source de Marsile est très probablement ici le *De defectu oraculorum* de Plutarque, moins parce qu'on y trouve la référence à Hésiode (elle figure aussi dans la *République* [5, 468E-469A] et dans le *Cratyle* [397E-398C—both quoting *Works and Days*, pp. 120 ff.; cf. Ficino's *Cratylus* epitome, *Op.*, p. 1312]) que parce que l'idée même qu'il se fait des 'Génies' protecteurs se rattache très évidemment à la démonologie du moyen-platonisme" (p. 104).

Note the same reference occurs again in Ficino's letter to Giovanni Francesco Ippoliti, count of Gazzoldo, *Op.*, p. 763.

The allusion in the *Works and Days* and the mention in Plutarch are both, therefore, appropriate.

⁸⁹*Phaedo* 63E-68B.

⁹⁰*Theologia Platonica* 4. 1 (ed. Marcel 1:164-165); see refs. 15 and 34 above.

⁹¹The phrase, *peri onou skias*, occurs at *Phaedrus* 260C. Cf. Hermias, p. 220 (ed. Couvreur), fol. 282v (trans. Ficino).

⁹²Hermias, p. 233 (ed. Couvreur), fols. 291v-292r (trans. Ficino). See ref. 43 above.

⁹³*De Amore* 7. 7 (ed. Marcel, pp. 208-210); *Philebus* commentary 1. 11 (ed. Allen, pp. 134-141); Plotinus commentary, *Op.*, p. 1714. 2, 3. See ref. 42 above.

⁹⁴*Philebus* 16A-17A, 57E ff.; cf. Ficino's commentary 1. 23-28 and unattached chap. 4 (ed. Allen, pp. 214-263, 432-437); *Republic* 7. 532A-539D; *Parmenides* 135A-136C; *Sophist* 235A-C, 253D ff.; and *Statesman* 266D, 286D-287A. All five of the dialogues cited include, of course, instances of the dialectical method being deployed.

⁹⁵See Ficino's translation of Hermias's gloss on 272C (in Couvreur, p. 249), "Illud lupi proverbium est, quando lupus videns pastores ut canes vorantes pecudes, inquit, Si ego id fecisse[m], quantus rumor factus esset?" (fol. 304r).

⁹⁶In the *Theologia Platonica* 14. 10 (ed. Marcel, 2:283) Ficino notes that it is not only simple men (*rudes homines*) who adore God, but also clever men

(*ingeniosi*) and wise men (*sapientes*) such as the Persian Magi, Egyptian priests, Hebrew prophets, Orphics, Pythagoreans, Platonic philosophers, and ancient Christian theologians. Theirs, as this summa 48 notes, is the worship of "well-composed praise" (*laudibus compositis*), praise that utilizes the stratagems of oratory and dialectic.

⁹⁷In his *Philebus* commentary 1. 29 Ficino identifies Theuth here with Hermes Trismegistus (ed. Allen, pp. 270-273).

⁹⁸See Hermias's gloss on the ibis, p. 254 (ed. Couvreur), fols. 307v-308r (trans. Ficino).

⁹⁹*Letter* 7, 341-344; cf. Ficino's argumentum, *Op.,* pp. 1534-1535. See Edgar Wind, *Pagan Mysteries in the Renaissance,* rev. ed. (New York, 1968), p. 9.

¹⁰⁰At the end of his epitome of the *Alcibiades* 2—subtitled "On Prayer"— Ficino treats of this Socratic prayer to Pan (*Op.,* p. 1134).

¹⁰¹See ref. 100 above; in the epitome Ficino calls Pan *Deus, pater omnium.* Like other Medicean humanists Ficino etymologized Cosimo's name as the *cosmos* and therefore as *pan* (the ALL). As ALL things Pan corresponded to Saturn, the prime intellect and highest god (*Op.,* p. 844. 1). See André Chastel, *Arte e umanesimo a Firenze al tempo di Lorenzo il Magnifico* (trans. from the French by Renzo Federici, Turin, 1964), pp. 232-238 (on Signorelli's "Triumph of Pan" and its intellectual context).

¹⁰²*Phaedrus* 247D. For this and the following refs. 103 and 104, we should bear in mind that Ficino had not yet translated the *Phaedrus* himself and was almost certainly using—as ref. 103 in particular suggests—Bruni's 1424 translation; see Introduction, n. 15 above (I have used the version found in the Laurentian Library's MS Plut. 76. 43, fols. 38v-50r). Cross comparison should be made for this and the following references, however, to Ficino's 1484 translation as edited above in Texts I. In the case of this quotation from 247D, the versions in the *De Voluptate,* in the 1484 translation, chap. xxi, and in Bruni, fol. 47r, are absolutely identical.

¹⁰³*Phaedrus* 248BC; cf. ref. 102 above. While Bruni's version is almost identical, "Multus inest conatus veritatis campus quonam sit intueri; nam conveniens animae cibus ex illo existit et alarum natura qua anima elevatur hoc alitur" (fol. 47v), Ficino's in his 1484 translation, chap. xxiii, differs considerably.

¹⁰⁴*Phaedrus* 247E; cf. ref. 102 above. As with the earlier quotation of 247D, the versions of this quotation from 247E in the *De Voluptate,* in the 1484 translation, chap. xxii, and in Bruni, fol. 47v, are virtually identical.

¹⁰⁵This quotation is from the epilogue to the Latin *Asclepius* attributed to Apuleius (ed. A. D. Nock, *Corpus Hermeticum,* 4 vols. [Paris, 1945], 2:354-355). The passage in Nock's edition reads: "[41]...praebere dignaris condonans [condonas *given as a good variant*] nos sensu, ratione, intellegentia: sensu, ut te cognouerimus; ratione, ut te suspicionibus indagemus; cognitione, ut te cognoscentes gaudeamus, ac numine saluati tuo gaudemus, quod te nobis

ostenderis totum; gaudemus, quod nos in corporibus sitos aeternitati fueris consecrare dignatus.'' Interestingly, the same passage recurs in Ficino's *Opera Omnia* (where Apuleius's *Asclepius* was included with Ficino's translation of the *Pimander*): ''. . . cum donas sensu nos ratione, intelligentia, ut te cognitione cognoscentes gaudeamus, ac numine saluati tuo gaudeamus, quod nobis te ostenderis totum, gaudeamus'' (1871. 3). Note that the passage in the *De Voluptate* is nearer to Nock's text than the version at p. 1871. 3; which is to say, Ficino probably had access to a better text than the editors who decided to include the Latin *Asclepius* in the various editions—all posthumous—of his own *Opera Omnia*!

[106]Cf. the abbreviated but in other respects almost identical account in Ficino's epitome for the *Ion* (*Op.,* p. 1282): ''Primus itaque furor inconcinna et dissonantia temperet [= temperat]; secundus temperata unum totum ex partibus efficit; tertius unum totum supra partes; quartus in unum, quod super essentiam et totum est, ducit. Primus bonum equum, id est, rationem opinionemque, a malo equo, id est, a phantasia confusa et natura, distinguit. Secundus malum equum bono, bonum aurigae, id est, menti, subiicit. Tertius aurigam in caput suum, id est, in unitatem, mentis apicem, dirigit. Postremus caput aurigae in caput rerum omnium vertit. Ubi auriga beatus est, et ad praesepe, id est, divinam pulchritudinem, sistens equos, obiicit illam [= illis] ambrosiam et super ipsam nectar potandum, id est, visionem pulchritudinis et ex visione laetitiam. Haec quatuor furorem [= furorum] opera sunt, de quibus generatim in Phaedro Plato disputat, proprie vero de furore postremo, id est, amore, in Symposio, de primo, hoc est, furore poetico, in praesenti dialogo qui Io inscribitur.'' Cf. refs. 14 and 69 above.

Note that the *De Amore* and the *Ion* epitome both propose the following ascending sequence for the divine madnesses: poetic, hieratic, prophetic, and amatory; unlike the *De Divino Furore* (see ref. 14 above), they and the *Phaedrus* commentary agree in regarding the amatory madness as the climactic one.

[107]*Phaedrus* 248A, garbled.

[108]*Phaedrus* 247E.

[109]*Phaedrus* 247C-248A, 249B-D.

[110]*Philebus:* the general conclusion, 61C to the end.

[111]*Timaeus* 31B-32C.

[112]By the time Ficino wrote summa 24 of the *Phaedrus* commentary, he had changed his mind on this issue and interpreted the descent of the soul and its nine lives in terms of the nine celestial spheres: those of the world-soul, of the fixed stars, and of the seven planets; cf. refs. 6, 36, and 83 above.

[113]The theory of the astral, aethereal, or spiritual body (or bodies) as the soul's vehicle(s) (*ochēma*) or envelope(s) (*peribolē*) has a long and complicated history, dependent as it is in many respects on the history of the notion of spirit itself on the one hand and of the irrational soul and its functions on

the other. Among the Neoplatonists it seems to have been first fully developed by Porphyry and Iamblichus on the basis of hints in Plotinus's *Enneads* (2. 2. 2; 3. 5. 6; 4. 3. 15 and 17; etc.), but it was read back into Plato's figurative allusions to "vehicles" and "chariots" in the *Phaedo* 113D, *Timaeus* 41DE, 44DE, and 69C, *Laws* 10. 898E-899B, and, of course, the *Phaedrus* 247B and passim. See E. R. Dodds, ed., *Proclus: The Elements of Theology,* 2nd ed. (Oxford, 1963), app. II ("The Astral Body in Neoplatonism"); also his commentary on propositions 205-210 on pp. 304-309; G. Verbeke, *l'Évolution de la doctrine du pneuma du stoïcisme à saint Augustin* (Paris and Louvain, 1945); H. Lewy, *Chaldaean Oracles and Theurgy* (Cairo, 1956), p. 184n; and P. Moraux, s.v. *Quinta Essentia,* in Pauly-Wissowa-Kroll, *Realencyclopädie der classischen Altertumswissenschaft* 24, 1 (1963), cols. 1251-1256: "Das ätherische Vehikel der Seele." Of especial interest for the Renaissance is D. P. Walker's "The Astral Body in Renaissance Medicine," *Journal of the Warburg and Courtauld Institutes* 21 (1958): 119-133.

Ficino definitely knew about Iamblichus's attribution of an aethereal body or vehicle to the gods, and airy one to the demons, and an earthy one to man, since he had translated and adapted the *De Mysteriis;* see particularly 3. 6-17 (ed. Des Places, pp. 105-124; in Ficino's *Op.,* pp. 1884. 2-1887). He must also have known the discussion in Synesius's *De Insomniis* 142A ff., and passim, likewise translated and adapted by himself (*Op.,* pp. 1968-1978); and that in Hermias's *In Phaedrum,* p. 69, likewise translated (MS. Vat. lat. 5953, fols. 179v-180r).

For Proclus's views he could turn to *In Remp.* (ed. Kroll, 1:39 and 119; 2: 161, 164, 166 ff., 349, etc.); *In Tim.* (ed. Diehl, 3:234-238, 296-299, etc.); *Elements of Theol.* (ed. Dodds, props. 205-210); *Theol. Plat.* 3. 5 (Saffrey and Westerink 3:18-19 and accompanying notes on pp. 113-114). Note that Ficino does not accept Proclus's equation of the "aethereal" body with the body of purer elements adopted by the demons and its consequent subordination to the "astral" vehicle; instead, he prefers to work, as this extract makes clear, with the series: the earthy, the airy, and the aethereal body, the latter equated with the "celestial" body (in summa 25, however, he does introduce a further complication by suggesting there are two kinds of airy body!).

[114]*Phaedrus* 247B.

[115]*Timaeus* 41DE, 44DE, 69C; cf. refs. 8 and 113 above.

[116]*De Oraculis Chaldaicis* (ed. Kroll, p. 64); cf. ref. 25 above.

[117]*Timaeus* 69C.

[118]*De Oraculis Chaldaicis* (ed. Kroll, p. 61). Kroll refers us to Psellus's exegesis at 1124A (ed. Migne) and to the dictum already noted in refs. 25 and 116 above. In the Laurentian MS Plut. 36. 35, fol. 26r (see ref. 25 above) the Latin rendering is "Est etiam idolo pars in loco circumlucenti" (as v. 27).

[119]Cf. Texts II, chap. 8, par. 3, and Texts III, summae 25 and 28 above; also Ficino, *Op.* p. 1437 (on *Republic* 10) and p. 1788, chap. 7 (on *Enneads* 6. 7. 6).

[120]*Phaedrus* 248C, "the load of forgetfulness"; 249C-E; 250C; etc.; cf. Ficino, *Op.*, p. 1437 (on *Republic* 10. 621A-C).

[121]The special use of the term *heaven* in the *Phaedrus* should have stopped him from referring to the region occupied by the celestial gods as itself celestial; see Texts II, headnote.

Appendix: The Prague Manuscript

Besides the Plato editions of 1484 (F) and 1491 (V), there are, as we saw in the headnote to Texts II, three manuscripts containing the prefatory argumentum to the *Phaedrus*. Nevertheless, until recently, there has been only one authoritative text for the full commentary and summae, that of the editio princeps of 1496 (E). From this derived the progressively deteriorating texts in the *Opera Omnia* of 1561, 1576, and 1641. Kristeller, however, has discovered another version of the full commentary and summae in a fifteenth-century Italian manuscript (P) now in the Lobkowitz Collection of the University of Prague (catalogued as RVI Ef 11). Since I could get no reply from Prague, he kindly lent me his microfilm copy for collation and analysis and a review of his general entry for the manuscript in the forthcoming third volume of his *Iter Italicum*. Briefly, P contains various Ficino texts, primarily translations from Proclus, Athenagoras, Priscianus Lydus, Alcinous, Speusippus, and Pythagoras; in other words, much of the material now bringing up the rear of Ficino's own *Opera Omnia*.

My own analysis of the *Phaedrus* material is as follows. After three blank pages and beginning on page 309 (the manuscript is paginated, not foliated) comes the heading *Argumentum Marsilii Ficini in Phedrum* (cf. the argumentum's heading in all the manuscripts and editions of the *Phaedrus* translation). The chapter heading and numbering of chapter 1 follow and then the text, beginning *Plato noster poetice muse,* with subsequent chapters titled and numbered as in E. No paragraphing occurs until chapter 4 (again compare the situation in all the manuscripts and editions of the *Phaedrus* translation). Thereafter it coincides with E's except that it is less fine and represents, I think, an intermediary stage, for nowhere does P have a paragraph break not found in E (the penultimate paragraph of chapter 5 is an obvious error), but the reverse is not true. After chapter 3 is the subscript *Hec fuerit hactenus totius dialogi*

summa, as in E. And on the second, misnumbered, page 342 (it should be 344: the mistake is never rectified, so there are two pages numbered 342 and 343), that is, at the end of the eleven chapters of commentary, is the postscript and title, *Finis argumenti in Phedrum. Sequitur commentum cum summis capitulorum.* Then follow the summae, numbered as in E from 1 to 53 but wanting E's headings throughout. At the end of the text on page 402 is *Finis,* and pages 403 to 406 are blank.

Two other general characteristics deserve note. First, the copyist has left a blank space, sometimes disproportionately large, after each summa: these can only be for the revisions for F as they appear in E (P must, if this is so, postdate 1484). Second, a mysterious figure, Pausanias—one recalls Banquo's third murderer—appears twice by himself and four times as an alternative for or another name of (*aliter*?) Phedrus as the designated speaker of a summa incipit (whereas E has him appear just once, and then as an alternative):—

summa 2: Pau. P (E blank)
summa 10: Pausanias P (E blank)
summa 40: Pausanias aliter Phedrus P and E
summae 44, 50, 53: Pau. aliter Phe. P; Phe. E.

Both F and V have Pausanias for these six instances as for many others (Phedrus not being offered as an alternative), though at the beginning both list only two dramatis personae, Socrates and Phedrus. I cannot discover where Ficino derived this curiosity: Plato never says that Phedrus was also called Pausanias, though he does have him succeed Phedrus as the next panegyrist of Love in the *Symposium.* The fact that Pausanias is disappearing in P and has almost vanished in E perhaps points to Ficino's growing realization that Phedrus only had one name; and it again suggests that P's version predates E's.

Specifically, P shares the same references to the *Theologia Platonica,* the *De Sole,* the *Parmenides* commentary, and so on as E and contains no textual additions. Also, apart from omitting the odd word (and of course the revisions for F and the summa headings), it has only three notable omissions (pp. 165, 167, 173 above), all of them in the summae. For the most part P's variants are the result of scribal carelessness, though occa-

sionally they offer an acceptable, rarely a better, reading.

In short, all the evidence so far—the references, the chapter numbering and headings, the paragraphing, and the variants themselves—points unequivocally to P's version being slightly, but not radically, earlier than E's. However, since Ficino saw E through the press and it remains, pretty consistently, the better text, it must form the basis of any critical edition, given the absence of an autograph.

There is some further evidence that may, when the various stages of the *Phaedrus* translation have been fully charted, help to date P and perhaps even the drafting of E more precisely. Surprisingly, the incipits for the summae in P and E do not invariably correspond to the text in F and V! Thus, in summa 4 P and E have *Quid* where F and V have *Qui;* in summa 6 P and E have *Agite* where F has *Si agite,* and V, *Sic Agite;* and in summa 53 P and E have *quid facis* where F and V have *quid facies;* that is, P and E agree in these instances to differ from the editions. But in two others P agrees with the editions and differs from E: in summa 52, where E has *Quod,* F, V, and P have *Quid;* and, more notably, in summa 20, where E has *ad mensam,* F, V, and P have *ad convivium.* The last instance is particularly interesting, since E's incipit anticipates a revision not introduced till the end of its own summa (see p. 54 above, apparatus); none of the other F incipits mentioned above, however, are thus revised by E. Once again, the evidence points to P's embodying an intermediate stage where it shares some incipit variants with F and V, others with E.

Finally, and most conclusively, P's summae incorporate some references to the Plato text as Ficino himself had revised it in E: for instance, summa 21 in the course of its analysis quotes the lemmas *contemplatore* and *inviolabili nutrita,* not *contemplante* and *inmaculata se vertens.* Though Ficino may have jotted down revisions to his Latin translation of the *Phaedrus* over a period of years, the likelihood is that he devised most of them in the early 1490s and specifically in 1493 in preparation for the projected deluxe edition—in which case, though P represents an intermediate stage, it must predate E's by a matter of months, not years.

Select Bibliography

Allen, Michael J. B. "The Absent Angel in Ficino's Philosophy." *Journal of the History of Ideas,* XXXVI, 2 (1975), 219-240.

———. "Cosmogony and Love: The Role of Phaedrus in Ficino's *Symposium* Commentary." *Journal of Medieval and Renaissance Studies,* X, 2 (1980), 131-153.

———, and Roger A. White. "Ficino's Hermias Translation and a New Apologue." *Scriptorium,* XXXV (1981).

———. "Ficino's Lecture on the Good?" *Renaissance Quarterly,* XXX, 2 (1977), 160-171.

———. "The Sibyl in Ficino's Oaktree." *Modern Language Notes,* XCV, 1 (1980), 205-210.

———. "Two Commentaries on the 'Phaedrus': Ficino's Indebtedness to Hermias." *Journal of the Warburg and Courtauld Institutes,* XLIII (1980), 110-129.

———. See also under Ficino.

Anastos, M. V. *Pletho's Calendar and Liturgy.* Dumbarton Oaks Papers, 4 (1948), 183-305.

Anichini, Giuseppe. *L'Umanesimo e il problema della salvezza in Marsilio Ficino.* Milan, 1937.

———. "Umanesimo e salvezza in Marsilio Ficino." *Rivista di filosofia neoscolastica,* XXXIII (1941), 205-221.

Armstrong, A. H., ed. *The Cambridge History of Later Greek and Early Medieval Philosophy.* Cambridge, 1970.

Baron, Hans, ed. *Leonardo Bruni Aretino: Humanistisch-philosophische Schriften.* Leipzig-Berlin, 1928.

Bessarion, Giovanni. *In Calumniatorem Platonis.* Venice, 1469. See under Mohler.

Bielmeier, P. A. *Die Neuplatonische Phaidrosinterpretation.* Rhetorische Studien, hrsg. v. Drerup, Heft 16. Paderborn, 1930.

Boccaccio, Giovanni. *Genealogie Deorum Gentilium Libri.* Ed. Vincenzo Romano. 2 vols. Bari, 1951.

Burckhardt, Jacob. *The Civilization of the Renaissance in Italy.* Trans. S. G. C. Middlemore. Rev. and ed. Irene Gordon. New York, 1961.

Canavero, Alessandra Tarabochia. "S. Agostino nella *Teologia Platonica* di Marsilio Ficino." *Rivista di folosofia neo-scolastica,* LXX (1978), 626-646.

Cassirer, Ernst. *The Individual and the Cosmos in Renaissance Philosophy.* Trans. Mario Domandi. New York & Evanston, 1963.

Cassuto, Umberto. *Gli Ebrei a Firenze nell'età del rinascimento.* Florence, 1918.

Chastel, André. *Art et humanisme à Florence au temps de Laurent le Magnifique.* Paris, 1961. Italian version: *Arte e umanesimo a Firenze al tempo di Lorenzo il Magnifico.* Trans. Renzo Federici. Turin, 1964.

——. *Marsile Ficin et l'art.* Geneva and Lille, 1954.

Cody, Richard. *The Landscape of the Mind.* Oxford, 1969.

Collins, Ardis B. "Love and Natural Desire in Ficino's *Platonic Theology.*" *Journal of the History of Philosophy,* IX, 4 (1971), 435-442.

Comito, Terry. *The Idea of the Garden in the Renaissance.* New Brunswick, New Jersey, 1978.

Corradi, Mario. "Alle origini della lettura neoplatonica del 'Convito': Marsilio Ficino e il 'De Amore'." *Rivista di filosofia neo-scolastica,* LXIX, 3 (1977), 406-422.

Cosenza, M. E. *Biographical Dictionary of Humanism and Classical Scholarship.* 5 vols. Boston, 1962.

Curtius, E. R. *European Literature and the Latin Middle Ages.* Trans. W. R. Trask. Harper ed., New York, 1963.

De Gandillac, Maurice. "Astres, anges et génies chez Marsile Ficin." In *Umanesimo e Esoterismo: Atti del V Convegno Internazionale di Studi Umanistici.* Ed. E. Castelli. Padua, 1960. Pp. 85-109.

Della Torre, Arnaldo. *Storia dell'Accademia Platonica di Firenze.* Florence, 1902.

Des Places, Édouard, ed., and trans. *Oracles Chaldaïques.* Paris, 1971. Cf. also under Kroll, G.

Devereux, James A. "The Object of Love in Ficino's Philosophy." *Journal of the History of Ideas,* XXX, 2 (1969), 161-170.

——. "The Textual History of Ficino's *De Amore.*" *Renaissance Quarterly,* XXVIII, 2 (1975), 173-182.

De Vries, G. J. *A Commentary on the Phaedrus of Plato.* Amsterdam, 1969.

Diels, H., and W. Kranz. *Die Fragmente der Vorsokratiker.* 6th ed., 3 vols. Zurich and Berlin, 1964.

Dillon, John M. *Iamblichi Chalcidensis: In Platonis Dialogos Commentariorum Fragmenta,* Leiden, 1973.

Diogenes Laertius. *Lives of the Philosophers.* Ed. and trans. R. D. Hicks. 2 vols. Cambridge, Mass., and London, 1959.

Dress, Walter. *Die Mystik des Marsilio Ficino.* Berlin and Leipzig, 1929.

Ficino, Marsilio. *Commentaria in Platonem.* Florence, 1496.

——. *In Convivium Platonis, sive de amore.* Ed. and trans. Raymond Marcel as *Marsile Ficin: Commentaire sur le Banquet de Platon.* Paris, 1956.

——. *Marsilio Ficino: Lessico Greco-Latino: Laur. Ashb. 1439.* Ed. Rosario Pintaudi. Rome, 1977.

——. *The Letters of Marsilio Ficino.* Trans. Members of the Language Department of the School of Economic Science in London. 2 vols. London, 1975 and 1978.

————. *In Philebum.* Ed. and trans. Michael J. B. Allen as *Marsilio Ficino: The Philebus Commentary.* Berkeley and Los Angeles, 1975; repr. 1979.

————. *Opera Omnia.* Basel, 1576; repr. Turin, 1959.

————. *Platonis Opera Omnia.* Florence, 1484; 2nd ed. Venice, 1491.

————. *Supplementum Ficinianum.* Ed. P. O. Kristeller. 2 vols. Florence, 1937.

————. *Theologia Platonica de immortalitate animorum.* Ed. and trans. Raymond Marcel as *Marsile Ficin. Théologie Platonicienne de l'immortalité des âmes.* 3 vols. Paris, vols. I and II, 1964; vol. III, 1970.

Garin, Eugenio. *L'età nuova.* Naples, 1969.

————. *Giovanni Pico della Mirandola: vita e dottrina.* Florence, 1937.

————. "Images and Symbols in Marsilio Ficino," in *Portraits from the Quattrocento.* Trans. V. A. and E. Velen. New York, 1972. Pp. 142-160.

————. "Ricerche sulle traduzioni di Platone nella prima metà del sec. XV." *Medioevo e Rinascimento: Studi in onore di Bruno Nardi.* Florence, 1955. Vol. I, pp. 339-374.

————. "Ficino." *Storia della filosofia italiana.* 2nd ed., Turin, 1966. Pp. 373-436.

George of Trebizond. *Comparationes phylosophorum Aristotelis et Platonis.* Venice, 1523; repr. Frankfurt-Am-Main, 1965.

Guthrie, W. K. C. *A History of Greek Philosophy.* 5 vols. so far, Cambridge, 1962-1978—specifically vol. 4 (1975).

Heitzman, Marian. "La libertà e il fato nella filosofia di Marsilio Ficino," *Rivista di filosofia neo-scolastica,* XXVIII (1936), 350-371; XXIX (1937), 59-82.

Heninger, Jr., S. K. *Touches of Sweet Harmony: Pythagorean Cosmology and Renaissance Poetics.* San Marino, Calif., 1974.

Hermias. *Hermiae Alexandrini in Platonis Phaedrum Scholia.* Ed. P. Courveur. Paris, 1901; repr. Hildesheim, 1971.

Huizinga, Johan. *Homo Ludens.* Beacon Press Ed., Boston, 1962.

Iamblichus. *Jamblique: Les Mystères D'Égypte.* Ed. and trans. Édouard Des Places. Paris, 1966. Trans. (adapted) Marsilio Ficino. *Opera Omnia.* Basel, 1576. Pp. 1873-1908.

Keller, Alexander G. "Two Byzantine Scholars and their Reception in Italy." *Journal of the Warburg and Courtauld Institutes,* XX, 3-4 (1957), 363-370.

Kesters, H. *Plaidoyer d'un Socratique contre le Phèdre de Platon: XXVIe discours de Thémiste.* Louvain, 1959.

Klein, Robert. "L'enfer di Ficin." In *Umanesimo e Esoterismo: Atti del V Convegno Internazionale de Studi Umanistici.* Ed. E. Castelli. Padua, 1960. Pp. 47-84.

————. "L'imagination comme vêtement de l'âme chez Marsile Ficin et Giordano Bruno." *Revue de métaphysique et de morale,* LXI (1956), 18-39.

Klibansky, Raymond. *The Continuity of the Platonic Tradition during the Middle Ages.* London, 1939, 1950.

————, et alii, eds. *Corpus Platonicum Medii Aevi.* 4 vols. London, 1940-62.

———. "Plato's Parmenides in the Middle Ages and the Renaissance." *Medieval and Renaissance Studies,* I (1943), 281-335.

———, Erwin Panofsky and Fritz Saxl. *Saturn and Melancholy.* London, 1964.

Kristeller, Paul O. "L'état présent des études sur Marsile Ficin." *Platon et Aristote à la Renaissance: XVIe Colloque International de Tours.* Paris, 1976. Pp. 59-77.

———. "The First Printed Edition of Plato's Works and the Date of its Publication (1484)." *Science and History, Studies in Honor of Edward Rosen: Studia Copernicana XVI.* Ed. Erna Hilfstein, Pawel Czartoryski, Frank D. Grande. Wroclaw, Poland, 1978. Pp. 25-35.

———. *Iter Italicum.* Currently 2 vols. London and Leyden, 1963, 1967.

———. "Marsilio Ficino as a Beginning Student of Plato." *Scriptorium,* XX (1966), 41-54.

———. *The Philosophy of Marsilio Ficino.* New York, 1943. Italian version: *Il pensiero filosofico di Marsilio Ficino.* Florence, 1953.

———. *Renaissance Concepts of Man.* New York, 1972.

———. "Renaissance Platonism." In *Facets of the Renaissance.* Ed. William H. Werkmeister. Rev. ed., New York, Evanston and London, 1963. Pp. 103-123.

———. *Renaissance Thought I.* New York, 1961.

———. *Renaissance Thought II.* New York, 1965; repr. Princeton, 1980.

———. *Renaissance Thought and Its Sources.* Ed. Michael Mooney. New York, 1979.

———. *Studies in Renaissance Thought and Letters.* Rome, 1956.

———. See also under Ficino.

Kroll, G., ed. *De Oraculis Chaldaicis.* Breslau 1894; repr. Hildesheim, 1962. Cf. also under Des Places.

Kuczyńska, Alicja. *Filozofia i teoria piękna Marsilia Ficina.* Warsaw, 1970.

Larsen, Bent Dalsgaard. *Jamblique de Chalcis: Exégète et Philosophe.* Plus supplement, *Testimonia et fragmenta exegetica.* Aarhus, 1972.

Lewy, H. *Chaldaean Oracles and Theurgy.* Cairo, 1956.

Maier, Anneliese. *Zwei Grundprobleme der scholastischen Naturphilosophie: das Problem der intensiven Grösse, die Impetustheorie.* 2nd ed., Rome, 1951.

Marcel, Raymond. "L'apologétique de Marsile Ficin." *Pensée Humaniste et Tradition Chrétienne au XVe et au XVIe ss.* Paris, 1950. Pp. 159-168.

———. *Marsile Ficin.* Paris, 1958.

———. See also under Ficino.

Marchesi, C. *Bartolomeo della Fonte.* Catania, 1900.

Masai, F. *Pléthon et le Platonisme de Mistra.* Paris, 1956.

Mohler, Ludwig. *Kardinal Bessarion als Theologe, Humanist und Staatsmann.* 3 vols. Paderborn, 1923-1942.

Monfasani, John. *George of Trebizond: A Biography and a Study of his Rhetoric and Logic.* Leiden, 1976.

Moraux, P. "Quinta Essentia." In Pauly-Wissowa-Kroll, *Realencyclopädie der classischen Altertumswissenschaft,* XXIV, 1 (1963), cols. 1251-1256: Das ätherische Vehikel der Seele.

Nock, A. D., ed., and A.-J. Festugière, trans. *Corpus Hermeticum.* 4 vols. Paris, 1945.

Panofsky, Erwin. *Renaissance and Renascences in Western Art.* Harper ed., New York, 1972.

———. *Studies in Iconology.* Harper ed., New York, 1962.

Parmenides. *Poema.* Ed. Leonardo Tarán as *Parmenides: A Text with Translation, Commentary, and Critical Essays.* Princeton, 1965.

Pfeiffer, Rudolf. *A History of Classical Scholarship* 1300-1850. Oxford, 1976.

Pintaudi, Rosario. See under Ficino.

Plato. *Platonis Opera.* Ed. John Burnet. Oxford Classical Texts. Trans. Marsilio Ficino. *Platonis Opera Omnia.* Florence, 1484; Venice, 1491. Trans. Benjamin Jowett. *The Dialogues of Plato.* Rev. 4th ed. 4 vols. Oxford, 1964.

———. *Phaedrus.* Trans. and com. R. Hackforth. Cambridge, 1972.

———. *Phaedrus.* Ed. Claudio Moreschini as *Plato. Parmenides. Phaedrus.* Rome, 1966.

———. *Phaedrus.* Ed. and trans. L. Robin. Paris, 1947.

———. *Phaedrus.* Ed. W. H. Thompson. London, 1868.

———. *Phaedrus.* Trans. Paul Vicaire. Paris, 1972.

———. *Phaedrus.* See also under De Vries.

Plotinus. *Enneads.* Ed. with French trans. E. Bréhier. Paris, 1924-28. English trans. Stephen MacKenna. Rev. B. S. Page. 3rd. ed., London, 1962.

Proclus. *The Elements of Theology.* Ed. and trans. E. R. Dodds. Rev. ed., Oxford, 1963.

———. *Procli commentarium in Platonis Parmenidem.* In *Procli Opera Inedita.* Ed. V. Cousin. Paris, 1864. Cols. 617-1244.

———. *Procli in Platonis Rem publicam commentarii.* Ed. G. Kroll. 2 vols. Leipzig, 1899, 1901.

———. *Procli in Platonis Theologiam.* Ed. Aemilius Portus. Hamburg, 1618; repr. Frankfurt-am-Main, 1960.

———. *Proclus: Théologie Platonicienne.* Ed. and trans. H. D. Saffrey and L. G. Westerink. 6 vols. planned. Paris, vol. 1, 1968; vol. 2, 1974; vol. 3, 1978.

———. *Procli in Platonis Timaeum commentaria.* Ed. E. Diehl. 3 vols. Leipzig, 1903-1906.

———. *Procli Tria Opuscula:* De decem dubitationibus circa providentiam; De providentia et fato et eo quod in nobis; De malorum subsistentia. Ed. H. Boese. Berlin, 1960.

Randall, Jr., J. H. *Plato: Dramatist of the Life of Reason.* New York, 1970.

Ryle, Gilbert. *Plato's Progress.* Cambridge, 1966.

Saffrey, H. D. "Notes platoniciennes de Marsile Ficin dans un manuscrit de

Proclus, cod. Riccardianus 70." *Bibliothèque D'Humanisme et Renais-sance*, XXI, 1 (1959), 161-184.

——. See also under Proclus.

Saitta, Giuseppe. *Marsilio Ficino e la filosofia dell'Umanesimo*. Rev. 3rd. ed., Bologna, 1954.

Schiavone, Michele. *Problemi filosofici in Marsilio Ficino*. Milan, 1957.

Schmitt, Charles B. "L'Introduction de la philosophie platonicienne dans l'enseignement des universités à la Renaissance." In *Platon et Aristote à la Renaissance: XVIe Colloque International de Tours*. Paris, 1976. Pp. 93-104.

——. "*Prisca theologia e philosophia perennis:* due temi del Rinascimento italiano e la loro fortuna." In *Il Pensiero Italiano del Rinascimento e il Tempo Nostro: Atti del V Convegno Internazionale del Centro di Studi Umanistici*. Florence, 1970. Pp. 211-236.

Sheppard, Anne. "The Influence of Hermias on Marsilio Ficino's Doctrine of Inspiration." *Journal of the Warburg and Courtauld Institutes*, XLIII (1980), 97-109.

Tigerstedt, E. N. *The Decline and Fall of the Neoplatonic Interpretation of Plato: An Outline and Some Observations*. Commentationes Humanarum Litterarum: Societas Scientiarum Fennica 52. Helsinki, 1974.

——. "*Furor Poeticus:* Poetic Inspiration in Greek Literature before Democritus and Plato." *Journal of the History of Ideas*, XXXI, 2 (1970), 163-178.

——. *Plato's Idea of Poetical Inspiration*. Commentationes Humanarum Litterarum: Societas Scientiarum Fennica 44, 2. Helsinki, 1969.

——. "The Poet as Creator: Origins of a Metaphor." *Comparative Litera-ture Studies*, 5 (1968), 455-488.

Trinkaus, Charles. *Adversity's Noblemen: the Italian Humanists on Happi-ness*. New York, 1940.

——. *In Our Image and Likeness*. 2 vols. London, 1970.

Valla, Lorenzo. *De vero falsoque bono*. Ed. Maristella de Panizza Lorch. Bari, 1970.

Verbeke, G. *L'Évolution de la doctrine du pneuma du stoïcisme à saint Augustin*. Paris and Louvain, 1945.

Verdenius, W. J. "Der Begriff der Mania in Platons Phaidros." *Archiv für Geschichte der Philosophie*, XLIV (1962), 132-150.

——. "Notes on Plato's Phaedrus." *Mnemosyne*, Series IV, 9 (1955), 265-289.

Walker, D. P. *The Ancient Theology*. London, 1972.

——. "The astral body in Renaissance medicine." *Journal of the Warburg and Courtauld Institutes*, XXI (1958), 119-133.

——. "Orpheus the Theologian and the Renaissance Platonists." *Journal of the Warburg and Courtauld Institutes*, XVI (1953), 100-120.

——. "The *Prisca Theologia* in France." *Journal of the Warburg and Courtauld Institutes*, XVII (1954), 204-259.

————. *Spiritual and demonic magic from Ficino to Campanella.* London, 1958; Notre Dame, 1975.

Walzel, Oskar. "Von Plotin, Proklos und Ficinus." *Deutsche Vierteljahrsschrift für Literaturwissenschaft und Geistesgeschichte,* XIX (1941), 407-429.

Westerink, L. G. *Anonymous Prolegomena to Platonic Philosophy.* Amsterdam, 1962.

————. See also under Proclus.

Wind, Edgar. "The Christian Democritus." *Journal of the Warburg Institute,* I (1937-38), 180-182.

————. *Pagan Mysteries in the Renaissance.* Rev. ed., New York, 1968.

Yates, Frances A. *The French Academies of the Sixteenth Century.* London, 1947.

————. *Giordano Bruno and the Hermetic Tradition.* London, 1964.

Zambelli, Paola. "Platone, Ficino e la Magia." In *Studia Humanitatis: Ernesto Grassi zum 70 Geburtstag.* Ed. Eginhard Hora and Eckhard Kessler. Munich, 1973. Pp. 121-142.

Zanier, Giancarlo. *La medicina astrologica e la sua teoria: Marsilio Ficino e i suoi critici contemporanei.* Rome, 1977.

Zoroaster. See under Des Places and Kroll.

INDEXES

to Ficino's Commentary

(i.e., to Texts ii, iii, and iv)

Index of Works Specifically Cited

Note: For other authorities cited by name but not by work, see Index of Names.

Index of Names

Index of Mythological and Astrological Figures

Index of Subjects and Notable Concepts

DATE DUE

GAYLORD			PRINTED IN U.S.A.